The Famine of 1932–1933 in Ukraine: An Anatomy of the Holodomor

The Famine of 1932–1933 in Ukraine: An Anatomy of the Holodomor

Stanislav Kulchytsky

Translated from the Ukrainian
by Ali Kinsella

Canadian Institute of Ukrainian Studies Press
Edmonton • Toronto
2018

CANADIAN INSTITUTE OF UKRAINIAN STUDIES PRESS

University of Alberta
Edmonton, Alberta
Canada T6G 2H8

University of Toronto
Toronto, Ontario
Canada M5T 1W5

Copyright © 2018 Canadian Institute of Ukrainian Studies

ISBN 978-1-894865-53-1 (softcover).

Library and Archives Canada Cataloguing in Publication

Kul'chyts'kyĭ, Stanislav Vladyslavovych
[Ukraïns'kyĭ Holodomor v konteksti polityky Kremlia pochatku 1930-kh rr. English]
    The famine of 1932–1933 in Ukraine : an anatomy of the Holodomor / Stanislav Kulchytsky ; translated from the Ukrainian by Ali Kinsella.

Translation of: Ukraïns'kyĭ Holodomor v konteksti polityky Kremlia pochatku 1930-kh rr.
Includes bibliographical references and index.
ISBN 978-1-894865-53-1 (softcover)

    1. Ukraine—History—Famine, 1932–1933. 2. Famines—Ukraine—History—20th century. I. Kinsella, Ali, 1986–, translator II. Klid, Bohdan, 1951–, writer of introduction III. Title. IV. Title: Ukraïns'kyĭ Holodomor v konteksti polityky Kremlia pochatku 1930-kh rr. English.

DK508.8377.K85413 2018   947.708'41   C2018-901426-1

Book and cover design by Halyna Klid.

Photographic insert, pp. 61-88: Alexander Wienerberger's photographs in the archive of the Vienna Catholic Archdiocese are reproduced by permission of the copyright holder, Samara Pearce.
Soviet propaganda posters on front cover: "The captain of the Land of Soviets leads us from victory to victory!" (B. Efimov, 1933); Tourist poster from Stalin's Intourist agency: "The New Travel Land, USSR Soviet Russia" (M. Litvak and R. P. Feder, ca. 1930).
Photograph: "Dekulakized" (1930), signed by the peasant Marko Zhelizniak (Hordii Pshenychny Central State CinePhotoPhono Archives of Ukraine).
Photograph of Stanislav Kulchytsky supplied by the author.

All rights reserved.
No part of this publication may be reproduced, stored in a retrieval system, or transmitted in any form or by any means, electronic, mechanical, photocopying, recording, or otherwise, without the prior permission of the copyright owner.

Printed in Canada

CONTENTS

vi	Acknowledgements
vii	Note on Transliteration
viii	Direct losses from the Holodomor (excess deaths), 1932–34
ix	Map "Rural Direct Famine Losses of Population in Ukraine, 1933"
xi	Bohdan Klid, "Stanislav Kulchytsky: A Historian and His Writings in Changing Times"
xix	To the Reader
xxiii	Preface
1	Chapter 1. The Birth of the Communal State
13	Chapter 2. The First Onslaught
20	Chapter 3. The Great Break
38	Chapter 4. The Collective-Farm System under Stalin's Requisitions
61	Photographs from the album of Alexander Wienerberger
89	Chapter 5. The "Crushing Blow"
115	Chapter 6. The Holodomor
140	Afterword
149	Glossary
158	Abbreviations and Acronyms
161	Bibliography
169	Author's Selected Works
171	About the Author
172	Index

Acknowledgements

The Famine of 1932-1933 in Ukraine: An Anatomy of the Holodomor was prepared for publication by the Holodomor Research and Education Consortium (HREC) of the Canadian Institute of Ukrainian Studies, Faculty of Arts, University of Alberta. HREC undertook the translation of Stanislav Kulchytsky's monograph *Ukraïns'kyi holodomor v konteksti polityky Kremlia pochatku 1930 rr.* as part of its efforts to make available in English seminal works by Ukrainian scholars of the Holodomor.

In addition to acknowledgments found elsewhere in this volume, we would like to thank Liudmyla Hrynevych (Institute of Ukrainian History, National Academy of Sciences of Ukraine) and Bohdan Klid (Holodomor Research and Education Consortium) for their close reading of the original text and suggested amendments; Myroslav Yurkevich for editing the translated text; Liudmyla Hrynevych and Oksana Yurkova (Institute of Ukrainian History) for supplying the photographs of Communist Party officials and Soviet leaders; and Anastasia Leshchyshyn and Daria Glazkova for preparing the index. We are grateful to CIUS Press and its executive director, Marko R. Stech, for undertaking the publication of this volume.

We thank the Temerty Foundation for making this publication possible through its generous support of the Holodomor Research and Education Consortium.

 Holodomor Research and Education Consortium (HREC)
www.holodomor.ca

Note on Transliteration

In the text of this book, a modified version of Library of Congress transliteration is used to render Ukrainian and Russian personal names. This system, designed to ease reading by avoiding non-English diacritics and word endings, omits the soft sign, simplifies the spelling of masculine surnames ending in –ий (e.g., Petrovsky, not Petrovs'kyi or Petrovskii), and renders initial iotated vowels in personal names with Y rather than I (e.g., Yaroslav, Yurii).

In bibliographic references, however, the full Library of Congress system (ligatures omitted) is used to make possible the accurate reconstruction of the Cyrillic original, and the soft sign (ь) is rendered with a prime (').

Direct losses from the Holodomor (excess deaths), 1932–34

Province (Oblast)	Total numbers (thousands)	Per 1,000 of population
Northern Region		
Vinnytsia	545	126
Kyiv	1,111	200
Chernihiv	254	91
Kharkiv	1,038	191
Southern Region		
Dnipropetrovsk	368	102
Odesa	327	108
Donetsk	231	54
Moldavian ASSR	68	120

Source:
O. Wolowyna, S. Plokhii, N. Levchuk, O. Rudnytsky, A. Kovbasiuk, P. Shevchuk, "Rehional'ni vidminnosti vtrat vid holodu 1932–1934 rr. v Ukraïni" (Regional Differences of Losses Due to the Famine of 1932–34 in Ukraine), *Ukraïns'kyi istorychnyi zhurnal* (Kyiv), 2017, no. 2: 93.

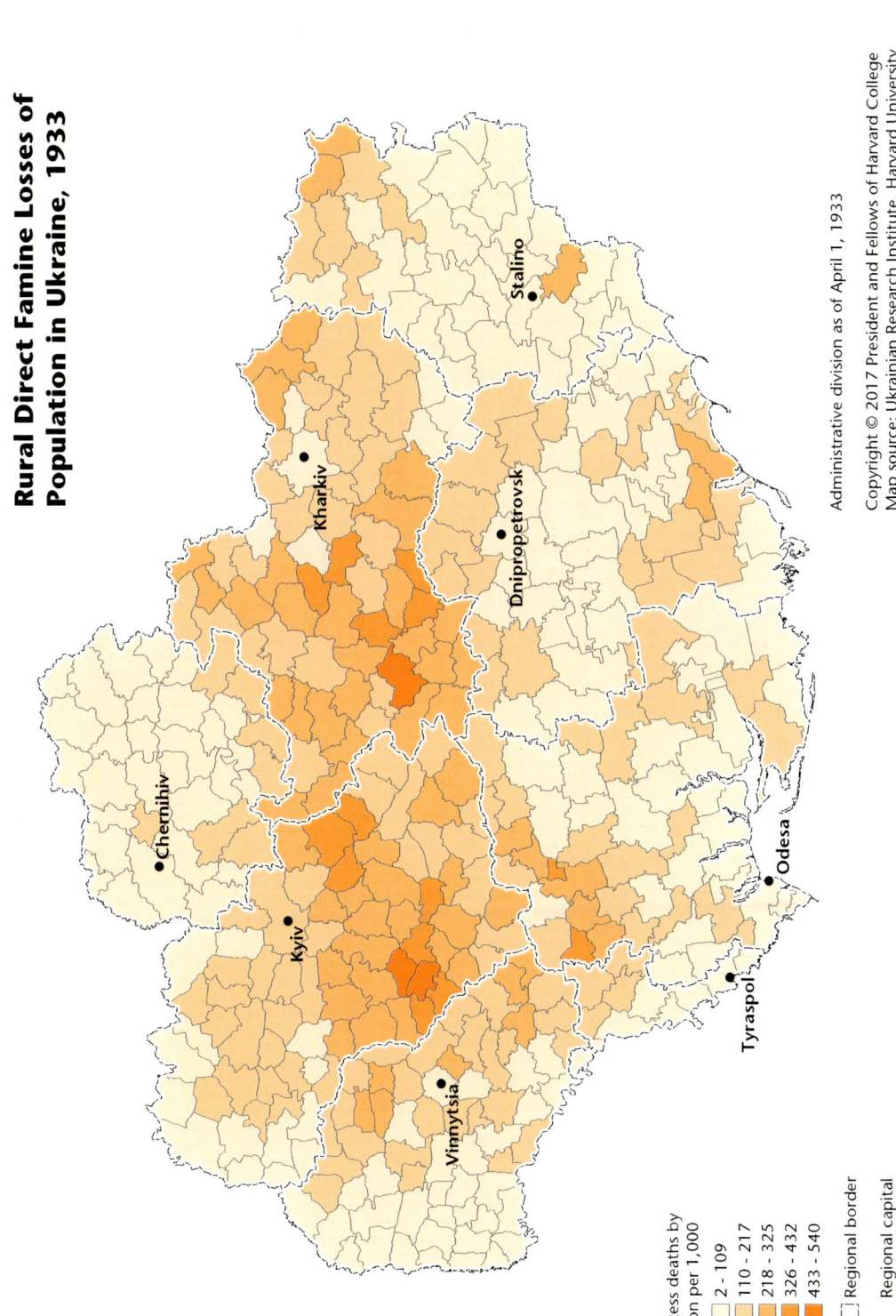

Stanislav Kulchytsky: A Historian and His Writings in Changing Times

Bohdan Klid

The publication of this monograph on the famine (Holodomor) of 1932–33 in Ukraine by Stanislav Kulchytsky, one of Ukraine's most prolific and best-known historians,[1] follows thirty years of study and many publications on this topic by the author. It appears in print more than four years after political demonstrations in Kyiv that ended with the shooting of about 100 protesters and led Ukraine's pro-Russian president, Viktor Yanukovych, to flee to Russia. He was succeeded by a pro-European Union government. As a consequence, Russia occupied and annexed part of Ukraine's territory (the Crimea) and intervened militarily in the eastern part of the country in support of a pro-Russian rebellion that it had instigated. Today Ukraine finds itself in a state of war with Russia, albeit one that is simmering and undeclared.

These latest dramatic events of the new millennium come in the wake of a century in which Ukraine and its people found themselves at or near the epicenter of several historically important and sometimes tragic events, including wars and revolutions. The author of this study has witnessed and lived through some of the more important ones.

Stanislav Kulchytsky was born in Odesa in 1937, during Stalin's Great Terror, experienced World War II and the postwar difficulties and famine of 1946–47 as a child, and was a teenager when Stalin died in 1953. He began his scholarly career in the early 1960s, a period marked by the first attempt at de-Stalinization in the USSR under Nikita Khrushchev. The policy of partial de-Stalinization was abandoned by Leonid Brezhnev but vigorously revived by Mikhail Gorbachev. The political changes fostered by Gorbachev under the slogan of *perestroika* (restructuring) led to the emergence of political protests and national movements for autonomy and independence in the non-Russian republics of the USSR. In August 1991, following the failed coup against Gorbachev, Ukraine declared independence, triggering the collapse of the Soviet Union in December of that year. In 2004, Ukraine was once again rocked by political protests known as the Orange Revolution, which led to the election of a pro-Western president.

While the education of historians, the historical literature they focus on, and their work with sources largely determine their choice of subjects and the presentation and interpretation of their findings, the historical events that they witness and the political, cultural, and intellectual environments in which they work can also be

---

[1] For an up-to-date bibliography and materials on Kulchytsky's scholarly career, including a historiographical essay, see *Istoryk na zlami epokh. Stanislav Kul'chyts'kyi: Materialy do biobibliohrafiï. Interv'iu. Spohady*, comp. I. Kuz'mina and O. Iurkova (Kyiv: Instytut istoriï Ukraïny NAN Ukraïny, 2016). Part of this foreword is based on materials in that book. See http://resource.history.org.ua/item/0012866, accessed July 30, 2017.

important factors. In the former Soviet Union, historical scholarship was subject to political and ideological constraints imposed by the Communist Party. This also influenced or determined what a historian studied and how a topic was presented and understood. Historians studying Ukraine, in addition to ensuring that their interpretations followed prescribed Marxist-Leninist ideological guidelines of the period, tried to avoid topics or interpret events in a way that might cause them to be accused of nationalism, for such an accusation could end a career or even lead to imprisonment.

Kulchytsky's early career and period of maturation as a scholar and administrator came in the late Soviet era. He worked from 1964 at the Institute of Economics, Academy of Sciences of the Ukrainian SSR, as an economic historian, then transferred in 1972 to the Institute of History, also at the Academy of Sciences (now the Institute of Ukrainian History, National Academy of Sciences of Ukraine), where he specialized as an economic historian writing on Soviet industrialization of the interwar period. Soon after moving to the Institute of History, Kulchytsky also began taking on administrative responsibilities, and from 1977 to 2015 he headed the institute's Department of Ukrainian History of the 1920s and 1930s.[2]

Dr. Kulchytsky was a well-established scholar and administrator when in the fall of 1986 he was assigned by the Communist Party of Ukraine to take part in the work of a committee struck in response to the establishment of the US Congressional Commission on the Ukraine Famine.[3] Scholars on the committee were expected to come up with studies that would "expose the falsifications of Ukrainian bourgeois nationalists."[4] Up to this point, Kulchytsky, although a specialist on the interwar era, had not conducted research on the forbidden topic of the famine of 1932–33 in Ukraine. Having studied the industrialization of the 1930s, however, he knew about

---

2 As head of the department dealing with the early Soviet period, Kulchytsky planned research that led to the publication of many monographs and articles on such subjects as Stalinist repressions, the Holodomor, and other famines in Ukraine. These sometimes appeared in collections of articles under the imprint of the Institute of Ukrainian History. Kulchytsky also mentored and advised young historians and students specializing in the period and served on many important scholarly committees. Since 1988 he has been a member of the editorial board of *Ukraïns'kyi istorychnyi zhurnal* (Ukraine's premier historical journal). He served as deputy director of the *Entsyklopediia istoriï Ukraïny* (from 1997). Kulchytsky has also had an important voice in the overall direction of the institute's scholarly work, serving from 1977 to 1979 and 1990 to 2009 as its deputy director (responsible for scholarship).

3 The commission was established in 1985 "to conduct a study of the 1932–1933 Ukraine Famine in order to expand the world's knowledge of the famine and provide the American public with a better understanding of the Soviet system by revealing the Soviet role in it." See *Investigation of the Ukrainian Famine, 1932–1933. Report to Congress* (Washington, DC: United States Government Printing Office, 1988), p. v. James Mace, who had become known as an expert on the famine and was collaborating with Robert Conquest on a study of it (subsequently published as *The Harvest of Sorrow*), was appointed the commission's staff director in February 1986.

4 Stanislav Kulchytsky, "Why did Stalin exterminate the Ukrainians?" *The Day* (Kyiv), November 8, 2005 (part two of a two-part article), Internet edition, https://day.kyiv.ua/en/article/history-and-i/why-did-stalin-exterminate-ukrainians-2, accessed July 10, 2017.

the famine and had made notes in the 1960s on estimates of population loss based on available statistics.[5]

At that time, serious research on the famine required working in restricted-access archival and other special collections. According to Kulchytsky's account, after several months of work with these hitherto unstudied sources, some of his views on the history of the Soviet period began to change, although he still had not freed himself from the stereotypes embedded in official concepts of Soviet history that he had long taken for granted. His work resulted in a report to the Communist Party authorities recommending that the famine be officially recognized. As Kulchytsky later recalled, his report was couched in terms palatable to those who had hitherto maintained silence about the famine.[6] The taboo on discussing the famine was finally broken on December 25, 1987, when the first secretary of the Communist Party of Ukraine, Volodymyr Shcherbytsky, mentioned it in a speech commemorating the establishment of the Ukrainian SSR. Soon afterward, Kulchytsky submitted his reworked report for publication as a scholarly article.[7] Popular versions also appeared in two newspapers aimed at the Ukrainian diaspora.[8]

The appearance of Kulchytsky's first articles on the famine drew the attention of Dr. James Mace, who wrote a critique of the English-language newspaper article as part of the final report of the Congressional Commission on the Ukraine Famine. Mace qualified his criticism by noting that, despite the shortcomings of the article, its publication "represents a major shift in the official Soviet position on the Famine."[9] In a later article, Mace also criticized Kulchytsky's scholarly article of 1988 but observed that this first essay on the famine written in Soviet Ukraine reflected

---

5   Ibid. See also Kulchytsky, "James Mace's Role in Exposing Stalin's Greatest Crime," *The Day*, June 15, 2004, Internet edition, https://day.kyiv.ua/en/article/history-and-i/james-maces-role-exposing-stalins-greatest-crime, accessed July 5, 2017. In the same article, Kulchytsky recalls an incident that took place in 1966, when he and a colleague were instructed by the first secretary of the Communist Party of Ukraine, Petro Shelest, to mention the famine in an article they had been commissioned to write on Soviet Ukrainian economic development. The passage on the famine was never printed, however, as no one dared to sanction it without written permission from Shelest, which was never obtained. This incident is also discussed in Stanislav Kul'chyts'kyj, "Il tema della carestia nella vita politica e sociale dell'Ucraina alla fine degli anni Ottanta," in *La morte della terra: La grande "carestia" in Ucraina nel 1932–33: Atti del Convegno, Vicenza, 16-18 ottobre 2003*, ed. Gabriele De Rosa and Francesca Lomastro (Rome: Viella, 2004), pp. 433–44.

6   Kulchytsky, "Why did Stalin exterminate the Ukrainians?"

7   See "Do otsinky stanovyshcha v sil's'komu hospodarstvi USRR u 1931–1933 rr.," *Ukraïns'kyi istorychnyi zhurnal*, 1988, no. 3: 15–27.

8   The English-language article, "Historical Experience: Vital Today," appeared in the newspaper *News from Ukraine*, January 1988, no. 2: 7. The Ukrainian-language article appeared under the title "Do stanovyshcha v sil's'komu hospodarstvi Ukraïny (1931–1933)" in two January 1988 issues of the newspaper *Visti z Ukraïny*.

9   See *Investigation of the Ukrainian Famine, 1932–1933*, pp. 62–66. Kulchytsky later wrote that Mace's critique was "objective" and that he had "deliberately excluded materials that had already been discovered in party archives from this article, which in fact was in my report to the CC CPU." See Kulchytsky, "Why did Stalin exterminate the Ukrainians?" https://day.kyiv.ua/en/article/history-and-i/why-did-stalin-exterminate-ukrainians-2, accessed July 10, 2017.

"the limited possibilities of a period which still considered the Soviet system and 'the socialist transformation of agriculture' as sacred cows."[10]

Kulchytsky continued to study the famine in a political environment that was rapidly changing. In early 1989 he published a four-part article in *Literaturna Ukraïna*, a newspaper that regularly produced new revelations about Stalin-era repressions and crimes in Ukraine in the years leading up to Ukrainian independence.[11] As Mace noted, the contents of the article showed that Kulchytsky's views on the famine had evolved. Mace concluded his analysis with the observation that Kulchytsky had begun his study of the famine "as a Soviet historian whose work was as much political as scholarly. As his archival access was broadened, he was ceasing to be a Soviet historian and becoming simply a historian."[12] Kulchytsky stressed in the article that "The famine of 1933 was the result of the attempt to build socialism by War-Communist methods."[13]

In the period leading up to Ukraine's independence, other Ukrainian scholars also began to study the famine. In 1989 Kulchytsky familiarized himself with documents on the famine gathered from Communist Party archives in Moscow and Kyiv that were being prepared for publication by Ruslan Pyrih and others. Although, according to Kulchytsky, some of the documents contained enough information to level accusations of genocide against Stalin, their importance was not understood at the time. Nevertheless, a political struggle broke out at the highest levels of the Communist Party leadership over the question of publishing the documents. Considered an expert on the famine, Kulchytsky was called before a Politburo meeting on January 26, 1990 to render his opinion. Not long afterward, a resolution of the Central Committee of the Communist Party of Ukraine was issued approving publication.[14] The resolution, reflecting the spirit of the changing times, recognized that the famine was "the result of the criminal course of Stalin and his closest circles (Viacheslav Molotov, Lazar Kaganovich) in regard to the peasantry."[15]

In March 1991, several months before the declaration of independence, Kulchytsky's first major study on collectivization and the famine of 1932–33 was

---

10 James E. Mace, "How Ukraine Was Permitted to Remember," *Ukrainian Quarterly* 49, no. 2 (Summer 1993): 121–51, here 122–24. In a popular article written later, Mace, referring to Kulchytsky's scholarly article and to subsequent radio interviews given by him in Ukraine, wrote that Kulchytsky "said what it was possible to say at the time." See his "History as Exhumation," https://day.kyiv.ua/en/article/close/history-exhumation, accessed July 10, 2017.

11 The four-part article "1933: Trahediia holodu" was published in *Literaturna Ukraïna* on January 12, 19, 26 and February 2, 1989. Mace analyzed the article in "How Ukraine Was Permitted to Remember," pp. 130–34. It was reissued as a brochure in a print run of more than 62,000 copies. See S. V. Kul'chyts'kyi, *1933: Trahediia holodu* (Kyiv: Tovarystvo "Znannia" Ukraïns'koï RSR, 1989). Further references are to the reprint edition.

12 Mace, "How Ukraine Was Permitted to Remember," p. 134.

13 Kul'chyts'kyi, *1933: Trahediia holodu*, p. 48. Kulchytsky has continued to stress the connection between building communism and the famine in his subsequent writings. He also characterized as criminal the activities of the grain-requisition commissions (headed by Viacheslav Molotov, Lazar Kaganovich, and Pavel Postyshev) sent by Joseph Stalin to Ukraine, the North Caucasus, and the Saratov region (ibid., p. 34).

14 Kulchytsky, "Why did Stalin exterminate the Ukrainians?"

15 See "Pro holod 1932–1933 rokiv na Ukraïni ta publikatsiï pov'iazanykh z nym arkhivnykh materialiv," in *Holod 1932–1933 rokiv na Ukraïni: ochyma istorykiv, movoiu dokumentiv*, comp. Ruslan Pyrih et al. (Kyiv: Vydavnytstvo politychnoï literatury Ukraïny, 1990), p. 4.

published. Here he used the term Holodomor—a neologism that denotes a manmade famine used as a means of killing. He concluded that as a result of the policies and actions sanctioned by Stalin, famine and genocide in the Ukrainian countryside were inevitable. Genocide, however, was committed not against Ukrainians targeted because of their ethnicity but against the Ukrainian peasantry. The famine that broke out in 1932 was due to excessive grain requisitions but was transformed in late 1932 by Stalin under the guise of continued grain collection, extending to the confiscation of all foodstuffs, into a "terror famine." Essentially, this was a "new famine." Its purpose was to entrench the collective-farm system, whose imposition had provoked mass resistance, and teach the peasants that they must work conscientiously on the collective farms.[16]

Kulchytsky's conclusions about the famine in his study of 1991 show the rapid evolution of his views in the very short period that had elapsed since he began serious study of it. Importantly, he stressed the differences between the famine of early 1932 and the one that broke out in late 1932 and their causes. He has continued to do so in his subsequent writings. Although Kulchytsky has revised and refined his views, taking account of newly available sources and literature, they do not differ radically from those presented in the 1991 study.[17]

In addition to his research on the Holodomor, Kulchytsky began to write on the doctrine of communism and its practice in Ukraine. His first major work on

---

16 Stanislav Kul'chyts'kyi, *Tsina "velykoho perelomu"* (Kyiv: Vydavnytstvo "Ukraïna," 1991), pp. 302, 358, 416–17. Some of Kulchytsky's conclusions in this study are similar to those presented by Robert Conquest in his *The Harvest of Sorrow: Soviet Collectivization and the Terror-Famine* (New York and Oxford: Oxford University Press, 1986).

17 Changes in Kulchytsky's views on the Holodomor since the publication of *Tsina "velykoho perelomu"* in 1991 can be found in his numerous subsequent articles and major studies. A major change in Kulchytsky's assessment of the Holodomor relates to his taking into account the national dimensions of the famine following the publication of *Tsina "velykoho perelomu."* Kulchytsky mentions this in "Holodomor 1932–1933 rr. v Ukraïni iak henotsyd," in *Problemy istoriï Ukraïny: fakty, sudzhennia, poshuky: mizhvidomchyi zbirnyk naukovykh prats'* (2005), vyp. 14: 255. In a 2016 interview, Kulchytsky said that it took him twenty years of study to understand the "mechanism of the Holodomor," which he characterized as a "carefully masked punitive operation." See "Stanislav Kul'chyts'kyi: 'Ia pyshu zaraz pro te, shcho z namy vidbulosia za ostannie stolittia, z revoliutsii 1917 r.'" Available at http://uamoderna.com/jittepis-istory/kulchytsky, accessed July 29, 2017. Print version in *Istoryk na zlami epokh*, comp. I. Kuz'mina and O. Iurkova, pp. 375–83. Kulchytsky discusses the evolution of his understanding of the famine on pp. 378–81. His views after twenty years of study are presented in the extended essay "Holodomor 1932–1933 rr. v Ukraïni iak henotsyd," also published in book form in Ukrainian and Russian as *Holod 1932–1933 rr. v Ukraïni iak henotsyd/Golod 1932–1933 gg. v Ukraine kak genotsid* (Kyiv: Instytut istoriï Ukraïny, 2005). See also, in Ukrainian, the more thorough treatment in Kul'chyts'kyi, *Holodomor 1932–1933 rr. iak henotsyd: Trudnoshchi usvidomlennia* (Kyiv: Nash chas, 2008). For a more recent article in Russian, see his "Ukrainskii Golodomor kak genotsid" in *Sovremennaia rossiisko-ukrainskaia istoriografiia goloda 1932–1933 gg. v SSSR*, ed. V. V. Kondrashin (Moscow: ROSSPĖN, 2011), pp. 107–94. In English, see his essay "Holodomor in Ukraine 1932–1933: An Interpretation of Facts" in *Holodomor and Gorta Mór: Histories, Memories and Representations of Famine in Ukraine and Ireland*, ed. Christian Noack et al. (London, New York, and Delhi: Anthem Press, 2012), pp. 19–33. See also the more recent "The Holodomor of 1932–1933: How and Why," in *Contextualizing the Holodomor: The Impact of Thirty Years of Famine Studies*, ed. Andrij Makuch and Frank Sysyn (Edmonton and Toronto: CIUS Press, 2015), pp. 88–111. The evolution of Kulchytsky's views on the famine to 2005 is also discussed in Valerii Vasyl'iev, "Evoliutsiia pohliadiv S. Kul'chyts'koho na holod 1932–1933 rr. u konteksti novitnikh tendentsii ukraïns'koï istoriohrafiï," in *Problemy istoriï Ukraïny: fakty, sudzhennia, poshuky: mizhvidomchyi zbirnyk naukovykh prats'* (2007), vyp. 16: 277–86.

the subject was a coauthored book on Stalinism published in 1991.[18] In 1996 he published a major study of communism in Ukraine in the 1920s and then a more general history of Ukraine (including the western Ukrainian lands) covering the entire interwar period.[19] Kulchytsky completed his long-term study of communism in Ukraine with the publication of a three-volume work in 2013. It begins with a discussion of Marxism and covers communist rule in Ukraine from 1917 to the collapse of the Soviet Union in 1991. The second volume, covering the interwar period, is the most thorough.[20]

Besides his many scholarly articles and monographs, Kulchytsky has written or coauthored textbooks for students and participated in developing curriculum for students of Ukrainian history. Such material was sorely needed in Ukraine after independence. Kulchytsky has also served on numerous editorial boards and edited many publications, including an important volume of documents on collectivization and the famine.[21] Governments have called on him to render opinions on highly disputed historical topics such as the famine. Kulchytsky has advocated strongly for recognizing the Holodomor as genocide, for which he has been criticized.[22]

Since Ukraine's independence, Kulchytsky has also written many popular articles on historical topics, a good number of which have dealt with the Holodomor and collectivization. These have often been published in such authoritative newspapers as *Den'* (The Day) and *Dzerkalo tyzhnia* (Weekly Mirror). In this way Kulchytsky has reached out to the broader public, presenting not only new revelations and factual material but also new interpretations to meet the needs of a post-Soviet society and a newly independent country. This kind of writing is particularly important, as

---

18   V. M. Danylenko, H. V. Kas'ianov, and S. V. Kul'chyts'kyi, *Stalinizm na Ukraïni: 20–30-ti roky* (Kyiv: Lybid', 1991). Kulchytsky discusses the causes of the famine on pp. 120–21.

19   See *Komunizm v Ukraïni: Pershe desiatyrichchia (1919–1928)* (Kyiv: Osnovy, 1996); *Ukraïna mizh dvoma viinamy (1921–1939 rr.)*, Ukraïna kriz' viky, vol. 11 (Kyiv: Al'ternatyvy, 1999).

20   See Stanislav Kul'chyts'kyi, *Chervonyi vyklyk: Istoriia komunizmu v Ukraïni vid ioho narodzhennia do zahybeli*, 3 vols. (Kyiv: Tempora, 2013). This study, dedicated to the generation of Kulchytsky's parents, may be seen as a synthesis of much of his scholarly work over the past thirty years.

21   See *Kolektyvizatsiia i holod na Ukraïni, 1929–1931*, comp. H. M. Mykhailychenko and Ie. P. Shatalina, 2d ed. (Kyiv: Naukova dumka, 1993). Kulchytsky was editor in chief of the volume and cowrote the introduction with Shatalina.

22   See Heorhii Kas'ianov, *Danse macabre: holod 1932–1933 rokiv u polityrsi, masovii svidomosti ta istoriohrafii (1980-ti–pochatok 2000-kh)* (Kyiv: Nash chas, 2010). See esp. the chapter "Istoryk i tema: S. V. Kul'chyts'kyi," pp. 162–89. In his study of memory politics and historiography, Kasianov criticizes and accuses Ukrainian historians, including Kulchytsky, of drawing up a "canonical version of the Holodomor" that more or less follows the "'genocidal' version of the famine of 1932–1933" which forms the basis of James Mace's and Robert Conquest's accounts (pp. 112–13). While some Ukrainian historians who have studied the Holodomor agree with the conclusions of Mace and Conquest, even Kasianov admits that new archival materials unearthed during the campaign to discredit their writings largely support the basic facts set forth by the two Western historians (p. 117). Logically, if the basic facts are supported by archival documents, then the conclusions of some, if not most, Ukrainian historians can be expected to resemble those of Conquest and Mace. Kasianov claims that Kulchytsky's views evolved in the context of the "nationalization" of Ukrainian historiography and increasing state intervention in memory politics. Kulchytsky's biography, Kasianov concludes, "is an interesting example of the dynamics of the interaction between professional historiography and politics, between research and propaganda, between the researcher and state authorities" (p. 189).

...continued on p. xvii

historical stereotypes inherited from the Soviet period persist to this day, more than a quarter century after Ukraine gained its independence.[23]

Throughout his long career Stanislav Kulchytsky has lived through several periods and episodes of significant political change, some dramatic, notably the collapse of an empire along with its ideological underpinnings and the emergence of a new state whose history had been suppressed, distorted, and subsumed under an imperial narrative. Although Kulchytsky began by interpreting historical events from a Marxist-Leninist standpoint, his study of the famine of 1932–33, beginning in 1986, caused him to rethink and change his views.[24] These changes occurred in the context of major geopolitical and ideological shifts that were taking place in his newly emerging country.

Following Ukraine's independence, Kulchytsky established himself as a leading scholarly authority on the Holodomor who also influenced public opinion through his popular writings. Moreover, he has become noted for his studies of communism and its practice in Ukraine and is acknowledged as the leading authority on the interwar period in his native land. These are remarkable achievements, considering that Kulchytsky began intensive work on those subjects around the time he turned 50. They testify—especially if one also takes into account his many accomplishments as an academic administrator—that he met the challenges of turbulent times: not only to remain productive and relevant but also to become a leading figure in the scholarly life of post-independence Ukraine.

(footnote 22, continued from p. xvi)

It is difficult to agree with Kasianov's conclusions. While Ukrainian historiography was undergoing a process of "nationalization"—a logical outcome of independence—Kulchytsky's views were more probably evolving mainly as a result of and in the context of his own research, as he claims. Also, Kasianov's use of the term "propaganda" to characterize Kulchytsky's popular writings on the Holodomor is misleading, given the difference between popular writings and propaganda. In his review of Kulchytsky's *Holod 1932–1933 rr. v Ukraïni iak henotsyd/Golod 1932–1933 gg. v Ukraine kak genotsid*, John-Paul Himka notes that an aim of Kulchytsky's book is to define the Holodomor as genocide. According to Himka, the basis on which Kulchytsky reaches his conclusion of genocide is the same as in Terry Martin's study, *The Affirmative Action Empire: Nations and Nationalism in the Soviet Union, 1923–1939* (2001). Both Kulchytsky and Martin, writes Himka, "see the famine as the result of grain requisitions that were set too high." Yet, as Himka notes, Martin does not conclude that the famine was genocidal. In his book, however, Kulchytsky clearly distinguishes the famine of early 1932 and its causes from those of the famine that broke out in late 1932/early 1933 (that is, the period of greatest mass starvation and death, called the Holodomor). Although Kulchytsky asserted that the famine of 1932 was caused by grain requisitions of the 1931 harvest, he went on immediately to write that the famine of early 1932 should not be regarded as the Holodomor. The latter, he goes on to explain, came after "the total confiscation of grain from the harvest of 1932, following which all other stored foodstuffs were removed" (p. 29). In his review, Himka overlooked or ignored this distinction and argument made by Kulchytsky. One might conclude that the enforcement of excessive grain requisitions, which caused the famine of 1932, was reckless (and might not qualify as genocide), but that the subsequent confiscation of all grain and then of all stored foodstuffs certainly implies intent to starve—that is, to commit mass murder by means of starvation. Himka also thinks that Kulchytsky underestimated Stalin's paranoia and exaggerated the sentiment for independence in Ukraine (pp. 690–91). This is an opinion, in my view, that underestimates the national factor in the famine. See John-Paul Himka, "Johan Dietsch, Making Sense of Suffering: Holocaust and Holodomor in Ukrainian Historical Culture," *Kritika* 8, no. 3 (2007): 683–94. See esp. pp. 688, 691–92. Cf. *World History in Context*, link.galegroup.com/apps/doc/A167980112/WHIC?u=edmo69826&xid=a3569a96, accessed July 22, 2017.

23 Kulchytsky strongly advocates informing the public about Soviet-era practices and crimes, including the Holodomor, as a means of breaking stereotypes inherited from the Soviet period. See, for instance, "Holodomor 1932–1933 rr. v Ukraïni iak henotsyd," p. 267.

24 Kulchytsky has commented repeatedly on how the study of the Holodomor changed his world view. See, for instance, "Holodomor 1932–1933 rr. v Ukraïni iak henotsyd," pp. 247, 257.

To the Reader

Dear Friend,

I first visited the West a quarter century ago, but so far I have met only with professional colleagues, almost exclusively on the topic of the Holodomor. It is only now that I have the opportunity to offer the Western reader a book on this topic in English. I hope that it can complement or correct prevailing impressions of the greatest tragedy in the thousand-year history of the Ukrainian people.

This monograph is a revised and updated translation of my study *Ukraïns'kyi holodomor v konteksti polityky Kremlia pochatku 1930 rr.* (The Ukrainian Holodomor in the Context of Kremlin Policy in the Early 1930s), published in 2014 by the Institute of Ukrainian History, National Academy of Sciences of Ukraine. The original text is available in electronic format at http://resource.history.org.ua/item/0009313.

Stanislav Kulchytsky

Much has been written about the famine of 1932–33 in the Soviet Union—so much that it is difficult even for specialists to find their way to the truth. More often than not, the famine is associated with Ukraine, but demographic statistics show that half the victims perished beyond its borders. There is a notion that only peasants died of hunger, but there were victims of the famine among the urban population as well. Finally, the all-Union famine of 1932–33 must be distinguished from the Ukrainian Holodomor and mass starvation in several other regions of the Soviet Union, which claimed 10–15 times more victims. They also occurred in 1932–33 but have a different character.

In the first half of 1932, the famine that existed in the rest of the Soviet Union was also present in Ukraine. That famine was caused by the confiscation of the 1931 grain harvest. Having realized that practically all their crop was being confiscated, the peasants effectively stopped working on the collective farms: as a result, a significant portion of the 1932 harvest was lost before the state could appropriate it. An extraordinary grain-requisition commission sent to Ukraine by Joseph Stalin under the leadership of the head of the Soviet government, Viacheslav Molotov, confiscated all that remained of the harvest but did not stop there. Stalin launched a punitive action in hundreds of collective farms and villages blacklisted in November–December 1932; in January 1933, the operation was extended to Soviet Ukraine as a whole. It had four components: confiscation of all available produce from private plots under the pretext of grain requisition; barricading of peasants in their villages; an information blockade; and state assistance to starving peasants. That is exactly what happened: for several weeks the countryside hovered between life and death, and when millions began dying, the state began providing ration support to the starving through collective and state farms still capable of taking part in the sowing campaign. Terror by famine was used to force the peasantry to work for the state on collective farms.

At the time, few starving peasants could make sense of the intricacies of Stalin's policy. The difficulties of Western scholars are also understandable. They decline to recognize the Holodomor as a genocide when they see how much aid the state provided to the starving. Moreover, the confiscation of everything edible took place under an information blockade, while every instance of aid was trumpeted in the media.

There is another reason why the essence of Stalin's terror by famine is misunderstood. When we assert that a genocide took place, we are rebutted: hold on, why were Ukrainians killed only in 1932–33, and not before or after? Why in 1932–33 were Ukrainians killed only in Soviet Ukraine and the Kuban, whose population wanted to be reunited with Ukraine, and not in Moscow or the Far East? Such questions come up only because the Ukrainian Holodomor is associated, even unconsciously, with the Jewish Holocaust. I repeat, however, that the Holodomor had a different character. To understand it, one must analyze the nature of communist construction in the Soviet Union from two points of view: a) What plan guided Vladimir Lenin and Joseph Stalin, and why did its realization drive the country to the brink of economic collapse in both 1920 and 1932?; b) How did the Bolshevik leaders adjust communist doctrine on the fly in order to overcome the crisis? By analyzing the theory and practice of communist construction, we come to understand the nature of the all-Union famine and the catastrophic famine of 1932–33 in a number of Soviet regions, including the Holodomor in Ukraine.

This book has an evidentiary basis that helps answer these questions. The evidence was gathered in bits and pieces over thirty years, or from the time that I stopped studying the history of the working class and industrialization, which had awarded me all my scholarly degrees, and took on issues related to the history of the peasantry and the collectivization of agriculture. I undertook this not of my own volition but as an assignment from the Central Committee (CC) of the Communist Party of Ukraine (CPU). The Chekists, or secret police, were alarmed that the Ukrainian diaspora in North America had attracted world attention to the famine of the early 1930s, evidence of which was suppressed in the USSR, and had also achieved the seemingly impossible—the creation of a US Congressional Commission to investigate the tragic events that had occurred half a century earlier on the other side of the globe. But as Mikhail Gorbachev's *perestroika* (restructuring) got under way, the commission struck rather hastily in the Ukrainian SSR Academy of Sciences under the direction of Academician Arnold Shlepakov ceased its activity because it became convinced that the "Ukrainian bourgeois nationalists" were right.

That decision did not lead me to stop working on the famine, and I even appealed to the CC CPU to acknowledge that the famine had taken place. I found it abnormal that members of the older generation, who knew about the famine, were afraid to talk about it even in their own family circles. If such behavior seems strange to you, the Western reader, I advise you to consider why nearly a third of the famine survivors who testified before the US Congressional Commission did so anonymously. In many cases they still had relatives in Ukraine, which made their decision completely understandable. Others, however, were simply afraid. They were still afraid fifty years after the Holodomor and, let me emphasize this again, on the other side of the globe.

Like everyone else, I did not immediately understand the nature of the Holodomor. The authors of my Russian-language Wikipedia biography delight in enumerating the erroneous points I made on the subject in the early stages of my work. This is their way of saying: "Look, he used to write as decent people do, but now he's sold out to the Banderites!"

The topic of the Holodomor has changed my view of communist doctrine. More precisely, not of the doctrine per se but of the methods used to realize it and the effects that came from depriving society of the basis of human civilization—private property. In the abstract, I still have no real problems with the doctrine itself. The official document of the Communist Party of the Soviet Union, "The Moral Code of the Builder of Communism," is composed entirely of biblical truths.

Convinced that the Holodomor cannot be comprehended in isolation from other phenomena of Soviet life, I began analyzing the socioeconomic and national aspects of Kremlin policy and, in 1996, I published a monograph on the first decade of communism in Ukraine (1919–28). In 2013, I published a three-volume work on the history of Soviet communism in Ukraine from birth to death. The monograph here presented to the Western reader is a synthesis of those general works.

I belong to the oldest living generation and consider it my duty to tell everyone about one of the most horrific episodes in the tragic fate of the first generation of Soviet people—my parents' generation. The two decades in which the Soviet system took shape turned out to be the most difficult for that generation. Most people scattered about the countries of the post-Soviet space and the entire world probably have a relative who suffered in those times. A few months after my birth in the ill-omened year 1937, my father was sent to the Gulag. I do not know how my grandfather, a worker in a small Odesa printshop, died. My grandmother, who actually raised me and saved me during the years of the Romanian and German occupation of Odesa, used to say that he died of lead poisoning in the spring of 1933. I now know that small business owners were deprived of ration-card access to the centralized food-supply system, and that mortality from the famine increased sharply in the cities. I also know that the authorities prohibited reporting starvation as a cause of death. Finally, I know that an information barrier was set up between adults and children by article 58 of the Criminal Code (on anti-Soviet activity). This may seem strange to the foreign reader, but the barrier stood for a long time.

We want the United Nations to acknowledge the Ukrainian Holodomor as a genocide. This is no mere caprice: it is necessary for the healing of national memory. No matter how much we say that the current war in Ukraine is not a civil war but a Russo-Ukrainian war (actually the third, after those of 1917–18 and 1918–19), there is an element of civil strife in it. One need only consider the situation from that perspective to get a sense of the degree to which both Ukrainian and Russian society are contaminated by the remnants of communism—first Russian and then Soviet. Over the last quarter century, most Ukrainians have rid themselves of what journalists and political scientists call "sovokism" (from the Russian *sovetskii stroi*, "Soviet order"), but a minority have retained many salient features of the past. After the Berlin Wall came down, the West heaved a sigh of relief: Russia was becoming democratic, the leaders of the Communist Party had renounced dictatorship, and the people had regained the sovereignty lost after the Bolshevik coup in the autumn of 1917. The Cold War was coming to an end, and one could always reach agreement with a people that no longer submitted to dictatorial rulers but chose its leaders in free elections. The only remaining fear was that of the dispersal of nuclear-armed missiles across the post-Soviet space. That is why the American leadership effectively supported the efforts of Boris Yeltsin's government to remove the deadly weapons that threatened humanity from the other post-Soviet states and concentrate them in Russia alone.

In the twenty-first century, however, the world is gradually returning to a previous reality. Moldova, Georgia, and Ukraine have lost parts of their territory. Along with the Baltic states, Belarus, and Kazakhstan, they find themselves under threat of being swallowed up by Vladimir Putin's Russia. Western leaders still believe that the present-day Russian Federation, with its tremendous nuclear potential, differs substantially from North Korea. Although Russia was indeed the first to dismantle the Soviet Union and begin establishing democratic values in daily life, the ominous communist monster has now been reborn there under a different ideological cloak, this time tsarist.

We are compelled to take up this new, no longer red but tricolor challenge. We should respond in worthy fashion. The battle is being waged on several fronts: for our territory, for our own national memory, for our right to join Europe and not turn into Little Russians, that is to say, second-class Russians. International acknowledgment of the Holodomor as a genocide will help us in that struggle.

Kyiv, August 2017

Preface

The Ukrainian Holodomor of 1932–33 was the result of a certain conjunction of time and place. What were those circumstances? They must be sought at the intersection of the Kremlin's socioeconomic and nationality policies. It is probably not worth trying to figure out which of these two factors was the decisive one. It is clear that after establishing their dictatorship, the leaders of the Bolshevik Party set themselves to building a socioeconomic order whose contours were prescribed not by life but by human imagination. This utopian experiment could be brought to life only through violence directed against social strata and national communities.

The Bolshevik Party set about realizing the speculative recommendations offered by Karl Marx and Friedrich Engels in their *Communist Manifesto* (1848) in the spring of 1918, even before those recommendations had been reduced to a system in the program of the Russian Communist Party (Bolsheviks),[1] which was ratified in March 1919. The building of communism proceeded by trial and error. The errors were covered up, while successes along the way were presented to society by the party's propaganda machine as the consistent implementation of the objective laws of communist construction as formulated by Marxism-Leninism.

The leaders of the Bolshevik Party were far from covering up their violence against society. Quite the opposite: it was propagated and glorified. Class struggle was presented as the main driving force of social progress, and violence in its various forms as the highway to the "bright future," or communism.

Communism was being built in a multinational country. The Bolshevik leaders were decisive in fanning the flames of class struggle up to its most destructive form—civil war. But they masked their negative attitude toward the peoples that resisted their experiment. Resistance was quashed by various forms of violence, including the most horrific, but the "proletarian internationalists" always veiled their repressive nationality policy in the rhetoric of class struggle.

It is sometimes believed that a stone wall divides the Ukrainian Holodomor from the all-Union famine of 1932–33. This notion simplifies what happened in reality. The all-Union famine of 1932–33 in the countryside was the result of the state's appropriation of grain. Peasants who had no other sustenance because of the lack or insufficiency of private garden plots either took refuge in the cities or died. The Holodomor of 1932–33 in the Ukrainian Socialist Soviet Republic (Ukrainian SSR, renamed the Ukrainian Soviet Socialist Republic in 1937) and catastrophic famines in several other regions of the country were the result of *absolute starvation* caused by the state's requisitioning of all available provisions and barricading the dispossessed peasants in their villages. For some time, the famine in Soviet Ukraine did not differ in causes or character from the all-Union famine, but, for several reasons to be discussed below, it was still substantially harsher than in other regions (with the exception of Kazakhstan). During the last two months of 1932, however,

---

1 "Programma Rossiiskoi kommunisticheskoi partii (bol'shevikov)" in *Vos'moi s"ezd RKP(b). Mart 1919 goda. Protokoly* (Moscow: Gosudarstvennoe izdatel'stvo politicheskoi literatury, 1959), 390–411.

in a limited area (specifically, in blacklisted villages), this famine took on a new, nightmarish form. In January 1933, all Ukraine as well as the Kuban and certain localities in the North Caucasus were blacklisted. According to objective testimony available in historical sources (not researched by me), some places in the Lower Volga region were also subjected to this. The conditions that brought about the all-Union famine continued to operate in Ukraine, but there appeared a new condition that transformed a famine with a high mortality rate into the Holodomor, with its fifteenfold greater total of victims. Stalin and the higher party functionaries subordinate to him began confiscating not only grain but all non-grain provisions from those whom they considered saboteurs of agriculture on the collective farms. In a few short weeks, Chekists carried out the confiscation with the help of activists sent from the cities and local committees of poor peasants. This took place under the guise of a grain-procurement campaign and under conditions of a total blockade of rural localities, both informational and physical. All of a sudden, the rural population found itself reduced to absolute starvation. In mid-February, however, the state began furnishing the starving villages with loans of foodstuffs, animal feed, and seeds to provide for the spring sowing campaign.

In contrast to the silence shrouding the confiscation of provisions, state aid was provided with much fanfare. Hence, the claims of scholars who accuse Stalin's government of committing a genocide of its own people are hardly persuasive to those wishing to understand the nature of the Holodomor. "Is it really possible," they muse, "to bring charges of genocide against a government that gave the lion's share of state aid to the regions suffering most from the famine—Ukraine and the North Caucasus—in the first half of 1933?"

Holodomor researchers have had to work hard to show the public that the two phases of Stalin's action—the confiscatory measures and, a few weeks later, the life-saving ones—should be seen as a single whole. The result of his punitive action was the death of millions of peasant farmers. Food aid was given not to everyone but only to those still physically capable of working on collective and state farms to prepare for the sowing campaign.

Such, in a few words, is the outline of the Ukrainian Holodomor. The present work seeks to demonstrate that the reason for the all-Union famine was the course taken by the leaders of the Bolshevik Party to build communism. The essence of communist construction was the expropriation of private property from members of society by the communal state, which was created after the Bolshevik coup with the goal of establishing a political dictatorship. The expropriation of society did not lead to the advent of socialized property, as was proclaimed from all rostrums. What emerged was state property, that is, property owned by the communal state created by Vladimir Lenin in order to bring about communist transformations of society. Owing to those transformations, as the Soviet state consolidated its political dictatorship it also gained an economic dictatorship. In other words, society ended up slavishly dependent on the state, which was controlled by a small band of Bolshevik chiefs and senior leaders—members of the omnipotent Politburo of the Central Committee (CC) of the Bolshevik Party.

The members of the urban and rural proletariat, the very social strata that had no private property, were the Bolsheviks' basis of support in bringing about their communist socioeconomic transformations. Large landowners and smallholders opposed the transformations both actively, in the civil war, and passively, in sabotage. To overcome society's resistance, the communal state employed a broad range of violent measures up to and including genocide. In the course of these transformations, it encountered not only resistance from non-proletarian social strata but also difficulties (that did not initially seem insuperable) in the comprehensive implementation of communist doctrine. The essence of the doctrine lay not only in the expropriation of large (bourgeois) and small (peasant) owners but also in the total liquidation of commodity-money relations. This meant the substitution of barter exchange carried out by institutions of the communal state for trade on the free market. Efforts to bring about the full-fledged realization of the socioeconomic order born in the minds of Marx and Engels led to economic crises that sometimes threatened the very existence of Soviet rule. The Bolshevik leadership was building communism by trial and error.

The all-Union famine of the early 1930s (including the famine in Ukraine in the first half of 1932) was the most noticeable sign of the crisis induced by the communist onslaught that Stalin led in 1929. The essence of the onslaught lay not only in the forced industrialization of the country and the implementation of the total collectivization of agriculture, as is often thought. Like Lenin before him in 1920, Stalin made it the goal of his onslaught to replace uncontrolled market commodity circulation ("market forces") with state-regulated product exchange. Whereas the Bolsheviks managed to use state institutions to organize product exchange in the industrial sector, in their relations with the village they had to make a concession to the peasants as early as March 1930, in the first stage of total collectivization. At that time, the peasants' right to a garden plot, a cow, small livestock, and fowl was recognized. Garden plots were a masked form of private property and thus a step back from communist doctrine.

Stalin took another step back in January 1933, when the Council of People's Commissars (Sovnarkom) of the USSR and the CC of the All-Union Communist Party (Bolsheviks) (AUCP[B]) adopted a resolution "On the Mandatory Delivery of Grain to the State by Collective Farms and Individual Farmers." With this resolution, the communal state renounced the appropriation of arbitrary quantities of grain and obliged the peasants to set aside a predetermined quantity of their grain production for the state to be paid as a tax in kind. This was an acknowledgment, also in masked form, of the peasants' right to ownership of the fruits of their labor after the payment of taxes; concurrently, their right to sell that produce on the open market was proclaimed. The replacement of trade with barter was thus inconspicuously postponed to the second, wholly utopian phase of communism in which material wealth was ostensibly to be divided among all members of society according to their needs.

The Soviet Union managed to overcome the economic crisis, the greatest manifestation of which was the all-Union famine of 1932–33, but that took more than the Soviet leaders' retreat from the immediate and comprehensive implementation of communist doctrine. Intent on preventing a social explosion in the country's principal grain-producing regions, which had suffered most from the economic policy of 1929–32, Stalin delivered what he called a "crushing blow" (*sokrushitel'nyi udar*) to the rural areas of Ukraine, the North Caucasus, and the Lower Volga. Extraordinary grain-procurement commissions were sent to those regions under the leadership of the general secretary's closest henchmen—the head of the Sovnarkom USSR, Viacheslav Molotov, and secretaries of the CC AUCP(B) Lazar Kaganovich and Pavel Postyshev. The essence of the "crushing blow" lay in the confiscation not only of grain but of all reserves of foodstuffs accumulated by the peasants. In Ukrainian historiography, Stalin's "crushing blow," which caused the death of millions of peasants by starvation, has been given the name "Holodomor."

How and why did the Ukrainian Holodomor happen? The logistics of its creation can be reconstructed on the basis of available documents, since civil servants of various ranks who were employed "under cover of darkness" (in the language of the Chekists) required concrete instructions. Still, we are unlikely to find documents in the Kremlin archives that shed light on the motives for Stalin's deeds. The dictator may not have explained his actions even to his closest circle.

Nevertheless, we can reconstruct the situation in which Stalin found himself and establish the motives that prompted him to resort to this nightmarish punitive campaign. And then we will be in a position to understand that the "precipitate" comes down to one thing only—Stalin's ambition to remain in power at the cost of the death of millions of Soviet citizens.

In Ukrainian society there are quite a few people who accuse Russia, not the Kremlin, of organizing the Holodomor. In this connection, reference is often made to the movie *A Very English Murder* (*Chisto angliiskoe ubiistvo*, 1974, director Samson Samsonov, based on the novel *An English Murder* by Cyril Hare), which is popular in Ukraine. In the film, a woman murders the relatives of her husband's professional rival who works in the House of Commons, seeking to ensure that the rival will inherit the title of lord and be obliged to give up his government post. Such a motive for murder could only exist in England, where membership in the House of Lords was extraordinarily prestigious but precluded holding a government post. The Ukrainian Holodomor can be called an essentially Soviet mass murder. It was the consequence of a particular chain of events that could only have happened in the Soviet Union. The all-Union famine was caused by the insistent efforts of Bolshevik Party chiefs to bring about a utopian socioeconomic order. This party created the strongest political regime known to history—Soviet rule—and then attempted to use it in order to proletarianize a society consisting mainly of smallholders. At the same time, Soviet rule brought to the surface of political life a dictator who stopped at nothing—including the organization of terror by famine and other repressive measures—in order to maintain his position in a situation of economic crisis that he himself had caused.

1. THE BIRTH OF THE COMMUNAL STATE

If the Holodomor was an essentially Soviet mass murder unlike the Holocaust or any other kind of genocide, then we must begin to analyze the causes that brought it about by elucidating the nature of the state that the Bolsheviks created. Scholars, first and foremost experts from the West, have always found this particularly difficult.

When scholars approach the study of the history of the USSR with a standard toolbox, they find it hard to understand that this approach does not work in complicated cases. They are used to dealing with a past that unfolds like a natural historical process. The Soviet system, however, was first born inside someone's mind. Some elements could be brought to life by coercive or propagandistic measures; others remained unrealized because they were unrealizable. The latter elements were either hushed up or reinterpreted as efforts to accomplish something else. One example is the communist onslaught (*shturm*, literally "storming") of 1918–20, which set off a civil war, several interethnic wars, an economic collapse, and the famine of 1921–23, which was exacerbated by the drought of 1921. In bringing a halt to that onslaught, with its millions of victims, Vladimir Lenin called his three-year policy "war communism," in other words, the kind of communism necessitated by a war, not the result of doctrine. But the state sector, which came to include the "commanding heights" of the economy, remained in existence after the onslaught.

In 1929, Joseph Stalin undertook another onslaught under the slogan of "full-scale socialist construction on all fronts." This onslaught also led to an all-Union famine in the early 1930s. Stalin then halted the further transformations prescribed by the Russian Communist Party (Bolsheviks) (RCP[B]) program of 1919, pretending that all objectives had been achieved, and proclaimed the triumph of socialism.

In putting an end to the onslaught, Lenin returned to a normal economic policy, although with certain limitations, which was now called a "new" policy. When Stalin ended his onslaught, he resorted to horrific means to force the already established artificial economy to function. Among those means were such punitive actions as the Ukrainian Holodomor of 1932–33 and the Great Terror (or Great Purge) of 1937–38.

Leninist-Stalinist economics proved ineffective but had colossal mobilizing potential that fully manifested itself in a country endowed with great natural and human resources. Making use of those resources, the Soviet Union contributed decisively to routing Hitler's Germany, created an atomic-missile shield in the postwar period, built housing on a tremendous scale for its urbanizing population, and raised education and science to new heights in order to compete, above all in armaments, with the countries of the West, which were already entering the post-industrial era. Nevertheless, the command economy proved unable to continue responding indefinitely to the challenges it encountered.

Such is the history of the Soviet Union in brief outline, with the all-Union famine and the Ukrainian Holodomor as integral elements. In studying the Ukrainian famine, which escalated into the Holodomor, one cannot limit oneself to facts that appear obligingly before one's eyes, even if they are found in the Kremlin archives. The Holodomor requires a comprehensive study of the political, social, and national aspects of "full-scale socialist construction on all fronts." Moreover, every aspect has to be approached with the realization that appearance belied reality.

In particular, the Soviet authorities positioned themselves as representatives of the workers and peasants, and so they appeared at first glance. In the final analysis, however, they showed themselves to be an oligarchic dictatorship with a tendency to turn into a personal despotism. The transfer of private property into the hands of the nation/society was proclaimed as the result of the socioeconomic transformations, when in fact society was expropriated, and the political dictatorship of the party chiefs was complemented by an economic dictatorship. Finally, according to its constitution, the USSR was a federation of sovereign national republics enjoying equal rights, but in reality it existed as a supercentralized unitary state.

The Bolshevik leaders avowed that they were building socialism. They presented communism to the people as the "bright future" eulogized by propagandists—a society that would distribute material wealth according to need. Until the early 1930s, they were convinced that socialism differed from communism only in the distribution of goods, not in their production. When the famine of 1932–33 forced them to halt their efforts to eliminate commodity-money relations, they postponed the final liquidation of the free market to the second phase of communism—the "bright future."

The famine of the early 1930s is usually associated with the Bolshevik leadership's modernizing efforts. The great majority of resources in a country trapped in a hostile (officially, capitalist) encirclement is assumed to have been dedicated to the goal of forced industrialization. This approach encourages scholars to consider the Soviet system in a global context. But the term "capitalist encirclement" itself suggests that the accustomed Westernization of prerevolutionary times was linked in the Soviet Union with efforts to create a completely different world—an attractive one, according to the propagandists' assurances, but a monstrous one in actuality. The famine was associated precisely with insistent efforts to realize the RCP(B)'s utopian program of 1919, which was based on the revolutionary Marxism of the era of the *Communist Manifesto* (1848).

In the *Manifesto*, Karl Marx and Friedrich Engels described the activity of the working class after coming to power as follows: "The proletariat will use its political supremacy to wrest, by degrees, all capital from the bourgeoisie, to centralize all instruments of production in the hands of the state, i.e., of the proletariat organized as the ruling class, and to increase the total productive forces as rapidly as possible."[1] Here the expression "the state, i.e., of the proletariat organized as the ruling class," is striking. It turns out that the first Marxists did not differentiate hierarchically structured

---

1   Karl Marx and Friedrich Engels, "Manifesto of the Communist Party," in Karl Marx, *The Revolutions of 1848*, ed. David Fernbach (Harmondsworth: Penguin, 1973), 86.

human communities (parties, armies, states) from human communities without an internal skeleton (societies, nations, classes). This conflation of communities different in principle meant that the recommendations of revolutionary Marxism were left hanging in the air, including the recommendation that guaranteed the advent of communism: "The theory of the communists may be summed up in the single sentence: Abolition of private property."[2]

The *Communist Manifesto* appeared a few weeks before the outbreak of the revolutions of 1848–49. Its opening line caused a global stir: "A specter is haunting Europe—the specter of communism." But after the revolutions, the situation in Western Europe stabilized, and the specter of communism vanished. It appeared in Eastern Europe instead.

The arrival of the specter of communism in Russia was influenced by objective and subjective factors alike. The former included the extraordinary tension in relations between the tsarist regime and society, between peasants and landowners, between the proletariat and the bourgeoisie, as well as the situation caused by World War I and its negative effect on daily life. In the course of the war, millions of scattered and politically unorganized peasants were mobilized into the army and, as such, transformed into an organized armed force capable of standing up to the autocratic landowner system. The subjective factors included the political force guided by the revolutionary Marxist platform of the era of the *Communist Manifesto* and its leader, who knew how to implement the communist doctrine, which was directed against peasant interests. By using soviets—councils of workers' and soldiers' deputies that emerged during the Russian Revolution and dispatched the 300-year-old Romanov autocracy in a week—as a fulcrum, in one year Vladimir Lenin managed to direct a gigantic country that did not understand what was happening to it onto the path of communist construction.

The specter of communist revolution appeared in Russia as early as April 1917. After Lenin returned to revolutionary Petrograd from the emigration, he spoke at meetings of Bolsheviks who were taking part in the All-Russian Conference of Soviets of Workers' and Soldiers' Deputies (April 11–16, 1917). On April 20, the Bolshevik newspaper *Pravda* (Truth) published ten theses set forth in his speech—the famous April Theses. Unlike Lenin's specific and detailed recommendations on the struggle for power, the plan of action after the establishment of the "dictatorship of the proletariat" was presented in veiled form as a short list of tasks. There were four such tasks, and they all shared a single vector—the building of communism. They were: renaming the Bolshevik Party from social-democratic to communist; the party's acceptance of a new, communist program; building the communal state; and uniting parties with similar programs from other countries in the Communist International.[3] Does this mean that the chain of cause and effect culminating in the Holodomor began with the Russian Revolution of 1917? One should not jump to that conclusion.

In Soviet historiography, communist transformations were portrayed as demands of the working masses that found expression in the people's revolution

---

2   Ibid., 80.

3   V. I. Lenin, "O zadachakh proletariata v dannoi revoliutsii," *Polnoe sobranie sochinenii* (Moscow: Izdatel'stvo politicheskoi literatury, 1974), 31: 116.

and were implemented by the Bolsheviks. To substantiate this view, the Russian Revolution was divided into two—the February bourgeois-democratic revolution and the October proletarian revolution. The October Revolution marked the beginning of the communist transformations. It is important, however, to distinguish the Bolsheviks' coming to power from their initiation of the course for the building of communism. Even though that thesis made its appearance in April 1917 as a goal for the Bolsheviks to fulfill after coming to power, it was not associated with the Russian Revolution. One can go even further: an abyss separated the idea of the communal state from the Russian Revolution.

The political parties that took part in the revolution were represented by two blocs, liberal and socialist. The term "socialism" must be understood in its original meaning, which has nothing in common with later interpretations, be they Lenin's (socialism as the first phase of communism) or Hitler's (National Socialism). The liberal bloc, led by the Constitutional Democratic Party (Cadets), was less radical, and the socialist (primarily Mensheviks and Socialist Revolutionaries [SRs]) more so. During the revolution, both blocs constituted a single democratic camp and were in agreement that the country needed to hold a constituent assembly. In addition to the political parties, there was yet another participant in the revolutionary activities—a popular camp of the lower strata in the form of soviets (councils). Unlike the parties, these soviets demanded the immediate expropriation of landowners and of the bourgeoisie. Thus they were talking not only about liquidating ruling institutions and redistributing property, as in revolutions known to historians, but also about destroying social classes. The soviets' extreme demands were the result of Russia's unique and acute social confrontation, multiplied by the burden of the grueling world war.

The great majority of the working class represented in the soviets (including those in the Ukrainian provinces) supported the Menshevik Party, which took a European social-democratic position on reconciling the interests of labor and capital through negotiations. Among the representatives of the peasants and soldiers in the soviets, the Socialist Revolutionaries were particularly influential. They, too, wanted to end the revolution on the basis of legitimately established laws, that is, with a constituent assembly. These parties curbed the anarchic and destructive soviet camp. They regarded the soviets as temporary organizations whose task was to prevent the mobilization of counterrevolutionary forces.

In the first few months after the revolution, the Bolsheviks had only limited success. Under their own slogans, they were unable to gain popularity among the lower strata that followed the soviets. Therefore, in August 1917 Lenin temporarily renounced his own slogans and armed himself with soviet ones. Instead of calling for the transformation of the imperialist war into a civil war, the Bolsheviks supported the country-wide demand to conclude a separate peace. Instead of demanding that landowners' estates be turned into soviet state farms, they supported the peasant slogan of "black repartition." It did not occur to participants in the Russian Revolution to destroy private property as such. Peasants, who made up the great majority of the population and the largest element in the soldiers' soviets, sought to increase their own property at the landowners' expense. To use a modern term, workers wanted to privatize the enterprises in which they worked. The October coup that brought the Bolsheviks to power was carried out under soviet, not communist slogans. However, after the Bolsheviks expanded their power over most of the country, Lenin again formulated his most important task: "to create a state of the commune."[4]

"The state organized as the ruling class," "the communal state," "the state of the commune"—these were the names for the state established by the Bolsheviks according to the promptings of the *Communist Manifesto*. Lenin understood how to unite an unstructured community (class) with a structured one (the state). For him, the soviets were the fulcrum, and their network had to be converted into the foundation of the worker-peasant state. On the first day he appeared in revolutionary Petrograd, he put forward the slogan "All power to the soviets!" The Bolshevik leader set out to implement communist doctrine by a tried-and-true method: "revolution from above." That was how the Russian tsars had imposed capitalism with the goal of modernizing the country.

The communal state was to serve as the instrument for the imposition of communism. Who stood behind it, and what was the actual meaning of the expression "dictatorship of the proletariat," first formulated in the *Communist Manifesto*?

Lenin called the working class a "class in itself," capable in its own milieu of developing nothing more than a trade-unionist consciousness. He gave assurances that an organization of revolutionaries directed by an intelligentsia recruited from diverse strata of the population could transform the workers into a "class for itself." In his opinion, only the party he had created could be such an organization. He called it a "new type of party," and he was right: unlike existing political parties, it was based on the principle of "democratic centralism." The party masses had to render unquestioning obedience to their leaders, low-level leaders to their superiors, and superiors to the party chiefs.

Lenin had outlined the role and place of the soviets in the system of state power as early as November 1905 in an article titled "Our Tasks and the Soviets of Workers' Deputies." He considered it "inexpedient to demand that the [St. Petersburg] Soviet of Workers' Deputies accept the social-democratic program and join the Russian Social Democratic Labor Party." The most important thing was that the soviet consider itself the germ of a provisional revolutionary government or aim for the creation of such a revolutionary government.[5] Knowing Lenin's steady focus on winning political power, it is hard to imagine that he intended to remove his party from the St. Petersburg Soviet, which was poised to become a revolutionary government. Already in 1905, he regarded the soviets as an administrative structure inseparably tied to the dictatorship of his party. How was the sought-after inseparability achieved?

First of all, the soviets had to be organizationally separated from the Bolshevik Party. Second, the party's undivided control over the soviets had to be ensured. This meant that the Bolsheviks had to force competing parties out of the soviets and fill them with their own ranks and sympathetically inclined independent deputies. As a result, the Bolshevik Party began to exist in two forms: first as a political party that,

---

4 V. I. Lenin, "Doklad ob ocherednykh zadachakh Sovetskoi vlasti na zasedanii VTsIK 29 aprelia 1918 g.," *Polnoe sobranie sochinenii* (Moscow: Izdatel'stvo politicheskoi literatury, 1974), 36: 264. Cf. https://www.marxists.org/archive/lenin/works/1918/apr/29.htm.

5 V. I. Lenin, "Nashi zadachi i Sovet rabochikh deputatov," *Polnoe sobranie sochinenii* (Moscow: Izdatel'stvo politicheskoi literatury, 1972), 12: 62–63. Cf. https://www.marxists.org/archive/lenin/works/1905/nov/04b.htm.

under the guise of the dictatorship of the proletariat, established its own dictatorship (more precisely, the dictatorship of communist party chiefs); second as soviets that had administrative functions but were deprived of political influence. Hence the dictatorship of the party chiefs relied on a firm authority that grew from the midst of the people but was independent of them.

It was no accident that the Communist Party/soviet tandem came to be called "Soviet rule" (despite the rules of orthography, the word "Soviets" in the plural and "Soviet rule" were written with capital letters). It was impossible to doubt the popular roots of this authority, especially as it took its cadres from the lower strata of society. Worker or peasant origin became an emblem of higher social status, similar to noble origin in the past. Possible misunderstandings between the party and soviet apparatuses were avoided by allowing only Bolsheviks to occupy positions of authority in soviet institutions.

As head of the Soviet government, Lenin announced in December 1917 that "The state is an institution for coercion. In the old days, it was the coercion of the whole people by a handful of moneybags. We want to turn the state into an institution enforcing the will of the people. We want to institute coercion in the working people's interests."[6] Two weeks later, the head of the Sovnarkom established the All-Russian Extraordinary Committee (*Vserossiiskaia chrezvychainaia komissiia*, VChK), the organ that would come to embody the dictatorship of the communist leaders under various names: Cheka, OGPU, UGB-NKVD, MGB and MVD, and KGB.

The system of rule was built up once and for all in the course of Stalin's socioeconomic transformations, also achieved by means of onslaught. Society's horizontally structured organizations were either destroyed or verticalized, that is, converted to the principles of "democratic centralism." Party and government power verticals were rooted in the thick of the popular masses by means of "transmission belts"—the ramified system of soviets that provided the power vertical with executive committees at various levels: the Young Communist League (Komsomol) with its subordinate Pioneer and Little Octobrist organizations, the trade unions with their millions of members, and hundreds of various civic organizations. The Bolshevik Party was also turned into a "transmission belt" when its internal party of leaders (the *nomenklatura*) separated from it. The vertical of state security, officially subordinate since its inception to the Soviet vertical, but actually to the party vertical, was freed from the control of local party committees and came under the direct control of the general secretary of the CC AUCP(B). Just like the party and Soviet verticals, it was rooted in society by hundreds of thousands (in Ukraine) and millions (in the USSR as a whole) of its "secret collaborators" (*seksoty*). Unlike previous societies, Soviet society gained a skeleton, as a result of which it started to behave like a hierarchical structure similar to a party or an army. As early as April 1917, this skeleton had its own name—the communal state. Unlike traditional, totalitarian, and democratic states, separated from society by definition, the communist state merged with its society through all its institutions, thereby gaining colossal power. Only this kind of state was capable of achieving all that could be done in a communist utopia,

---

6   V. I. Lenin, "Doklad o prave otzyva na zasedanii VTsIK 21 noiabria (4 dekabria) 1917 g.," *Polnoe sobranie sochinenii* (Moscow: Izdatel'stvo politicheskoi literatury, 1974), 35: 110. Cf. https://www.marxists.org/archive/lenin/works/1917/nov/21.htm.

specifically, expropriating society and augmenting its political dictatorship with an economic one.

It is worth repeating the already cited phrase from the *Communist Manifesto*: "The theory of the communists may be summed up in the single sentence: Abolition of private property." Does this mean that the "expropriation of the expropriators" led to the emergence of communist, that is, common property? Common property within the framework of the country had to be collective, belonging to the whole people.

Karl Marx lived another 35 years and Friedrich Engels another 47 after their *Manifesto* came out. Their work has found a worthy place in the intellectual treasury of humanity. But neither of them found time to clarify the *Manifesto*'s main riddle: how private property, on which the whole history of civilization is based, was to be transformed into common, collective property of the whole people. Without renouncing the predictions made in the *Manifesto*, they focused on studying the society of their day, which they called "bourgeois." Moreover, Marx's principal work, *Capital*, contained a fundamental postulate that contradicted the revolutionary impatience of the *Manifesto*: "[Society] can neither clear by bold leaps, nor remove by legal enactments, the obstacles offered by the successive phases of its normal development." Marx insisted that the development of productive forces and production relations, which he united in an integrated socioeconomic formation, was a natural historical process.[7]

An analysis of the *Manifesto* leads one to surmise that the young Marx and Engels associated the future of humanity with the absorption of the state by the revolutionary proletariat, which was becoming the main element of society with the development of large-scale mechanized industry. They believed that under these conditions society would assume the functions of the state. It turned out precisely the other way around: *the communal state entered society without losing its identity* and, having eliminated independent civic organizations, became capable of quashing expressions of citizens' will from within their own community.

The founders of Marxism asserted that in the course of "expropriating the expropriators," private ownership of the means of production would be socialized, that is, it would pass into the hands of society. They also assured their readers that nationalized property would pass into the hands of the nation. But nations and societies do not have "hands," whereas the state as a hierarchical structure does. After the communist transformations, society as a totality of owners large and small found itself proletarianized and therefore helpless in the face of the communal state, in whose hands the means of production were concentrated.

The nationalization or socialization of the means of production led to state ownership. Yet in no way does this assertion define the nature of that ownership, for there are too many kinds of states. Lawyers distinguish many kinds of ownership, since it has three independent functions (possession, use, and control) that appear in various combinations in two environments (state and society). Historians should reduce these to two basic forms, private and collective. After the expropriation of society, ownership of the means of production does not become the possession of the whole people, which means that it remains private. Owing to the maximum

---

7   Karl Marx, *Capital: A Critique of Political Economy,* vol. 1 (New York: International Publishers, 1967), 10.

centralization of governance in the communal state, private property was concentrated at the top of the power pyramid. But one should avoid simplifying the function of the economic dictatorship, as if the members of the Politburo of the CC AUCP(B) were owners of factories, railroads, and steamships. They were satisfied with having their names attached to particular sites or even cities. The leaders' economic dictatorship manifested itself in such actions as the apportionment of national income between consumption and accumulation, spheres and branches of production, regions, and so on.

When we study the formation of grain-procurement plans, which were directly related to the rural famine of the early 1930s, we see that in the all-Union total an exorbitant amount was set for grain procurements. Stalin did not even conceal this approach to directive planning, calling it "spurring the country on" (*podkhlëstyvanie*).[8] But it is impossible to determine what criteria he used in apportioning plan targets among the regions. One can only surmise that the requisitioning of agricultural produce (*prodrazvërstka*) was used not only for its intended purpose but also as an instrument of the Kremlin's nationality policy.

Communist construction was accompanied by fanning the flames of civil war, and the Bolsheviks showed no small aptitude for making it even more intense. But they were not prepared to combat the national-liberation movement at the same time. On the contrary, they strove to ally themselves with the oppressed peoples' liberation movements, the better to overcome the resistance of the social strata opposed to building communism. Their success in restoring the empire that had disintegrated after the fall of the autocracy was ensured by the dual nature of the Soviet state—a combination of the administrative authority of the soviets' executive committees, which was specified in their constitutions, with the dictatorship of the party committees, which was nowhere to be found in any constitution. When they proclaimed Soviet rule in the ethnic borderlands of the former empire, the Bolshevik leaders were even prepared to give them the status of independent states. *Nevertheless, every state sovietized according to the party line was subordinate to a single center.* This strategy turned out to be more effective than the primitive use of force chosen by the White generals to restore the "one and indivisible" Russia.

To Bolshevize the urban soviets, it sufficed to set "workers" against "non-workers" and "exploiters" against "the exploited." This approach worked because it took account of the objective difference between the working class and the bourgeoisie. All it took was the promotion of class warfare instead of class peace—in other words, the principle of revolutionary Marxism that formed the basis of Leninism. To Bolshevize the village soviets, disparities of property among the peasants had to be presented as class-based. This division also had an objective basis, since the figure of the kulak had appeared in prerevolutionary times as part of the process of transforming the peasantry from a social estate into a class. But the Ukrainian peasantry was wealthier than the Russian, so this attempt to divide peasant ranks did not always work. The Bolsheviks therefore had to resort to restricting the rights and competence of the soviets by creating a parallel organization of poor peasants and

---

8   I. Stalin, "Itogi pervoi piatiletki. Doklad 7 ianvaria 1933 g. na ob"edinennom plenume TsK i TsKK VKP(b)," *Sochineniia* (Moscow: Gosudarstvennoe izdatel'stvo politicheskoi literatury, 1951), 13: 185. Cf. https://www.marxists.org/reference/archive/stalin/works/1933/01/07.htm.

endowing it with rights taken from the soviets. These Committees of Poor Peasants (*Komitety nezamozhnykh selian*) remained in existence until 1933 and played an infamous role in the terror-famine organized by the authorities.

The soviets created in the non-Russian regions held the plenitude of administrative power, just like the soviets in central Russia. If the Bolsheviks based the social organization of power in Russia on the ancient Roman principle of "divide and rule," they had to come up with something different for the non-Russian regions in order to minimize the danger that Soviet institutions there might be exploited for separatist aims. *The principle of politicizing ethnicity was such an invention*, and it became the basis for the political and territorial division of the country for administrative purposes.

In Russia, Lenin's government left the established division of regions into provinces (*gubernii*), but in the non-Russian lands it created ethnically based political or territorial administrative units. Each unit was named after the nationality that made up the majority population. Ukrainians (within the Ukrainian SSR), Moldavians (in the Moldavian Autonomous SSR within Ukraine), and members of other nationalities in ethnic regions established in Ukraine (Russians, Greeks, Bulgarians, Poles, Germans, and Jews) became titular nations. People of a given nationality were considered members of the titular nation within its own administrative borders and members of national minorities without any rights outside them. The status of Russians in Ukraine was ambiguous: officially they were a national minority within the boundaries of the republic as a whole, but the titular nation in eight Russian national regions. Unofficially, the Bolshevik leaders saw them as the titular nation of the entire USSR. At an official Kremlin banquet held on May 2, 1933, Stalin stood on a chair and made a toast in which he allowed himself a departure from the official "internationalist" jargon: "Setting aside questions of equal rights and self-determination, the Russians [*russkie*] are the world's principal nationality. They were the first to raise the flag of the soviets against the whole world. The Russian [*russkaia*] nation is the most talented nation in the world."[9]

Ukrainians in the Soviet Union had three different statuses: representatives of the titular nation within the Ukrainian SSR, contenders for titular-nation status if the Ukrainized regions of the North Caucasus were to be annexed to the Ukrainian SSR, and national minorities in all other regions. When it comes to studying the question of who was the target of the terror-famine in the Ukrainian SSR and the North Caucasus, such nuances are worth taking into consideration.

What was the status of Soviet titular nations? The proving ground for the development of nationality policy was Ukraine. In December 1919, the Eighth Congress of the RCP(B) held a debate "On Soviet Rule in Ukraine" and wrote in its resolution: "Members of the RCP(B) on Ukrainian territory must put into practice the right of the working masses to study in their native language and speak it in all Soviet institutions."[10] Lenin argued for the principle of "speaking and studying

---

9 "Konspektnaia zapis' dvukh tostov Stalina I. V. na prieme v Kremle 2 maia 1933 g., sdelannaia R. Khmel'nitskim," Rossiiskii gosudarstvennyi arkhiv sotsial'no-politicheskoi istorii (Russian State Archives of Sociopolitical History, hereafter RGASPI), fond 558, op. 11, d. 1117, l. 10.

10 V. I. Lenin, "Rezoliutsiia TsK RKP(b) 'O Sovetskoi vlasti na Ukraine,'" *Polnoe sobranie sochinenii* (Moscow: Izdatel'stvo politicheskoi literatury, 1974), 39: 335. Cf. https://www.marxists.org/archive/lenin/works/1919/nov/x01.htm.

in one's native language" in such frank polemics with Russian Bolsheviks that he thought it best not to publish the speech he had given at the conference. It remains unpublished today.[11]

The peoples whom the Kremlin allowed to live in formally independent Soviet republics and, after the formation of the USSR, to earn the constitutional right to leave the federation, were titular nations with sovereign status. Any separatist inclinations among them were quashed by the party committees in charge of implementing the dictatorship. All other titular nations had to be satisfied with the principle of "speaking and studying in one's native language" without the accoutrements of statehood. The difference between the titular nations of the Union republics and all others was that the party dictatorship prevented the former from becoming full-fledged nations, while the latter were officially considered ethnonations.

The concept of a titular nation required the implementation of an indigenization (*korenizatsiia*) campaign, or the rooting of Soviet rule within the bounds of ethnically based administrative units. This campaign promoted indigenous cultural development among the titular nations, even though the state was counting on it first and foremost to strengthen its rule in the given society. The wager paid off. Soviet rule, established in Ukraine after three attempts in 1917–19, was able to shed the appearance of an occupying regime precisely because it managed to find common ground with the local population.

Non-Soviet Ukrainian historiography remains firmly attached to the erroneous view of the Soviet authorities as occupiers in Ukraine from the beginning of their rule to 1991. It must be realized that the virus of communism, once implanted in society from without, destroys or deforms all of society's horizontally organized structures—political parties, trade unions, civic organizations, and centers of spiritual life, including the church. Society is atomized and verticalized; everyone finds himself in a state of absolute economic, cultural, and ideological dependence on the three verticals of authority—the Communist Party, the Soviet state, and the security organs. People are securely isolated from external sources of information. By means of state terror, parents are prevented from passing negative information about the authorities to their children, whom the responsible institutions raise in the spirit of communism. The authorities turn the innate feeling of belonging to one's nation to their own account by putting local people in charge of official institutions, promoting the native language in all spheres of activity, and propagandizing thoroughly bowdlerized elements of national culture.

There is no doubt that from beginning to end Soviet Ukraine was a quasi-state. Yet Soviet Russia had still fewer rights than other Soviet republics in the pseudo-federation that was the Soviet Union. In forming the all-Union Communist Party and Soviet center, the builders of the USSR were concerned to prevent the emergence of a rival center of power in Moscow or Leningrad. Citizens of all the Union republics were equally disenfranchised in the face of the all-Union center of power. Under these conditions, a sense of being occupied could have been felt only by observers

---

11 Stanislav V. Kul'chyts'kyi, "Restavratsiia Ukraïns'koï SRR" in *Narysy istoriï Ukraïns'koï revoliutsiï 1917–1921 rokiv*, vol. 2 (Kyiv: Naukova dumka, 2012), 325–26. The contents of the unpublished speech can be surmised from numerous responses to it on the part of conference delegates who spoke later, as well as from Lenin's concluding statement and from the resolution that he wrote, "On Soviet Rule in Ukraine," which the conference approved without amendment.

not integrated into the hellish framework of Lenin's communal state. Even after the self-destruction of Soviet rule, the remains of communism, that is, the so-called "Sovietness" (*sovkovost'*, from the Russian *sovetskaia vlast'*, "Soviet rule") survived at least for the lifetime of an entire generation. In the present-day Russian Federation, *sovkovost'* has served as the basis for the regeneration of the Soviet order beneath a different ideological cloak.

During the Russian Revolution, the Bolshevik Party became a mass organization (including in the Ukrainian provinces) by no means because those who joined its ranks were starting to adhere to communist doctrine. The doctrine became reality gradually and inconspicuously, both for the party itself and for the society in which the party existed. That reality was masked by Lenin's radical measures, which had nothing in common with communist doctrine. The Bolshevik leadership took up the "black repartition" in agricultural policy, thereby gaining the support of the proletarianized strata of both the Russian and the Ukrainian peasantry. This helped the leaders garner the support of the all-Russian party of leftist Socialist Revolutionaries and turn their own party into the ruling one. Influenced by prevailing peasant moods, some of the Ukrainian Socialist Revolutionaries, with a greater membership than any other party in Ukraine, also switched to a communist platform, which helped the Bolsheviks gain control of Ukraine.

The initial feeling of being occupied by the Soviet authorities that indeed remained among a considerable portion of Ukrainian society vanished once and for all as the second generation of Soviet citizens was brought up. But in regions where the people were suddenly thrust into a foreign communist order (the western provinces of Ukraine and Belarus, the Baltic states, and East-Central Europe), a sense of alienation from the authorities, which could be characterized as a feeling of being occupied, remained until the end. This explains the speed of their transition from a command to a market economy, from dictatorship to democracy.

Even though the Kremlin always stressed only the principle of "speaking and studying in one's native language," Ukrainization was Janus-faced. What mattered to the party leaders, however, was something entirely different: the copying of the communist regime in the non-Russian regions by "local people" (as Stalin put it). The acknowledgment that this campaign had two faces and the attachment of an appropriate name to each face (Bolshevik or "Petliurite") occurred only after the Ukrainization of the North Caucasus had been brought to a halt. "Petliurite" Ukrainization was an unwelcome side effect of the indigenization campaign. It encouraged a national resurgence, running counter to the regime's intention of returning the nation to the state of an ethnos. The resolution of the CC AUCP(B) "On the Progress of Grain Procurements in Ukraine, the North Caucasus, and the Western Province," dated December 14, 1932, initiated a terror-famine in a territory already marked by the emergence of a "second Ukraine" within the USSR. It put an end to the "thoughtless, non-Bolshevik 'Ukrainization' of almost half the districts [*raiony*] of the North Caucasus, which did not proceed from the cultural interests of the population."[12] The Ukrainization of those districts of the North Caucasus created

---

12 "Postanova TsK VKP(b) ta RNK SRSR pro khlibozahotivli na Ukraïni, Pivnichnomu Kavkazi ta u Zakhidnii oblasti" in *Holod 1932–1933 rokiv na Ukraïni: ochyma istorykiv, movoiu dokumentiv*, ed. Ruslan Ia. Pyrih (Kyiv: Politvydav Ukraïny, 1990), 292.

objective conditions for its reunification with the Ukrainian SSR. The prospect of further increasing the resources and human potential of the largest non-Russian republic was extremely unwelcome to the Kremlin.

Along with the concept of titular nations and the campaign to indigenize Soviet rule, the third component of the principle of politicizing ethnicity was the official determination of the individual's ethnic allegiance, that is, the notorious "point five" in Soviet documents (in internal passports, which were introduced for residents of cities and new settlements in 1933, this point was fourth). In order to keep society under strict control, the communal state had to know two basic characteristics of every individual: social origin and nationality.

2 THE FIRST ONSLAUGHT

Marxism had quite a few basic distinctions from the credo that was called Marxism-Leninism in the USSR. The main one was probably that Karl Marx considered communist society the natural product of the objective historical development of humanity. We do not come across the notion of "building communism" in his works. Lenin believed, on the contrary, that it was not worth waiting for communism to mature naturally. He saw it as the main task of the proletarian party (his and none other) to build communism after it came to power.

It was no accident that the Bolshevik leaders, starting with Lenin, wanted to dress the communist experiment of their own design in the cloak of the people's revolution of 1917. This allowed them to present their experiment as the longing of the popular masses. And the Bolsheviks were the party called to realize that longing.

Many of Lenin's contemporaries believed that the Bolsheviks really intended to build a system founded on the principle "from each according to his ability, to each according to his needs." They strove to convince Lenin's party of the utopianism of that conception. But the Bolshevik propagandists redoubled their efforts to prove it possible to construct a society in which people would avail themselves of material and spiritual goods according to their needs. That is why, in the consciousness of several generations of Soviet people, that understanding of communism became tightly fused with the principle "to each according to his needs." *In actual fact, however, the essence of communism was determined by the ownership of property, not by its distribution.* Following Marx, West European Marxists identified communism with a society of the remote future in which the state would have become extinct. Lenin, for his part, demanded that communism be built immediately. With this as their aim, under the guise of nationalization (the return of ownership to the nation) or socialization (the return of ownership to society), the Bolsheviks were supposed to transfer the ownership of all means of production to the Soviet communal state. This meant the transfer of the means of production to the ownership of the state party or, more precisely, to the private ownership of its leaders.

The transformation of the power gained during the Bolshevik coup into a dictatorship and its expansion, under the slogan of "The Triumphant March of Soviet Rule," across most of the former empire was under way by the spring of 1918. In March 1918, the Seventh Congress of the Bolshevik Party ratified the Treaty of Brest-Litovsk, signed with Germany and its allies by the Sovnarkom, and the Russian Social Democratic Labor Party (Bolsheviks) was renamed the Russian Communist Party (Bolsheviks)—the RCP(B). In an article by Lenin on "The Immediate Tasks of Soviet Rule," which was published in April 1918, communist transformations were proclaimed the immediate tasks of the Soviet authorities. This meant the transfer of large-scale manufacturing to national (that is, state) ownership, the de facto expropriation of small manufacturing, the liquidation of commodity-money relations, and the creation of a centrally planned economy on the ruins of the market economy.[1]

The upper echelon of the Bolsheviks well understood the grandiosity of such transformations. At the All-Russian Congress of Economic Councils in May 1918, Lenin characterized them as follows: "We must organize the deepest foundations of the existence of hundreds of millions of people on entirely new lines."[2] These huge numbers show that the leader of the world proletariat, as he was already being called in Soviet newspapers, thought on a global scale. We see the repercussions of such a scale in the Constitution of the Ukrainian SSR, which was ratified by the Third All-Ukrainian Congress of Soviets in March 1919: "The Ukrainian Socialist Soviet Republic hereby announces its firm resolve to join the ranks of the One International Socialist Soviet Republic as soon as conditions for its emergence are brought about."[3]

The main task of the communist transformations was to change the social character of the vast peasantry. That change could be brought about only through the total collectivization of agriculture. Post-Soviet historiography emphasizes that the program of transforming the overwhelmingly agrarian country into an industrial one required the mobilization of the peasants' financial resources, which could be accomplished only by means of rural collectivization. But a weightier factor is not stressed: there was absolutely no place for the peasant-owner in the communal state. Party leaders needed an industrially developed country capable of equipping the Red Army with sophisticated weapons. But above all, they needed an obedient country, with every citizen in a state of political, economic, and ideological dependence on the communal state.

A resolution of the Eighth Congress of the RCP(B) emphasized that the "organization of state farms...support to societies and cooperatives...support to agricultural communes...regarding all these measures as the only road to the absolutely necessary raising of the productivity of agricultural labor, the party strives to secure the most complete realization of these measures."[4] But the thesis on the productivity of labor was a guise. Large agricultural enterprises in the form of state farms and communes solved another problem—that of linking the non-commoditized peasant economy with the nationalized "commanding heights." In raising the issue of changing the social status of those whom the Bolsheviks contemptuously called the petty bourgeoisie—small manufacturers and small

---

1   V. I. Lenin, "Ocherednye zadachi Sovetskoi vlasti," *Polnoe sobranie sochinenii* (Moscow: Izdatel'stvo politicheskoi literatury, 1974), 36: 165–208.

2   V. I. Lenin, "Rech' na Pervom Vserossiiskom s"ezde sovetov narodnogo khoziaistva 26 maia 1918 g.," *Polnoe sobranie sochinenii* (Moscow: Izdatel'stvo politicheskoi literatury, 1974), 36: 378. Cf. https://www.marxists.org/archive/lenin/works/1918/may/26b.htm.

3   "Konstytutsiia Ukraïns'koï Sotsialistychnoï Radians'koï Respubliky" in *Istoriia Radians'koï Konstytutsiï v dekretakh i postanovakh Radians'koho uriadu, 1917–1936* (Kyiv: Vydavnytstvo TsVK URSR "Radians'ke budivnytstvo i pravo," 1937), 114.

4   "O proekte programmy" in *Vos'moi s"ezd RKP(b). Mart 1919 goda. Protokoly* (Moscow: Gosudarstvennoe izdatel'stvo politicheskoi literatury, 1959), 385. Cf. https://www.marxists.org/history/etol/newspape/isr/vol22/no04/rcpb.html.

farmers—Lenin stressed: "The main problem of the revolution is how to fight these two classes. In order to be rid of them, we must adopt methods other than those employed against the big landowners and capitalists."[5] Although different methods were demanded, the goal was still "to be rid of them."

In order to liberate the country from peasant owners, the Sovnarkom prepared a decree whose character and goal were revealed in its very title: "On Socialist Land-Tenure Regulations and Measures for the Transition to Socialist Agriculture." The text of the decree contained the portentous phrase: "All types of individual land usage must be regarded as fleeting and moribund."[6] A second party program, adopted a month later, allowed for only two kinds of farming in the countryside: the state farm and the commune.[7]

The restoration of Soviet rule in Ukraine coincided with this radical turn. The republic, in which large landowners were still present, was thus destined to be transformed into a proving ground for the process of collectivizing the peasantry. Vladimir Meshcheriakov, the commissar of agriculture in the Ukrainian SSR, asserted that there was no reason to repeat in Ukraine the path taken by Russia: apportion all the land, pull it apart and divide it, and then establish communes and state farms in that empty space.[8] As early as March 1919, the Soviet Ukrainian government began converting a portion of the landowners' estates into state farms and communes.

The Ukrainian peasantry responded to this agrarian policy with a powerful insurrection. The Red Army, composed at the time of insurgent units that had arisen in the course of the struggle against the German-Austrian occupiers, lost its battle-readiness. Detachments of "internationalists" put together to help Soviet Hungary were thrown into battle to put down the peasant uprisings. As a result, the ambitious dreams of the "leaders of the world proletariat," Vladimir Lenin and Leon Trotsky, to penetrate Europe never came true. Moreover, the Red Army was defeated in the Donbas, and in the summer of 1919 Anton Denikin's armies, having occupied Ukraine in a lightning maneuver, set out for Moscow.

The Bolsheviks managed to fend off the threat of the White Guard, and in the autumn of 1919 Trotsky's three armies reentered Ukraine. Lenin had learned his lesson with the opposition of the peasantry, and in a resolution titled "On Soviet Rule in Ukraine," which the Eighth All-Russian Conference of the RCP(B) adopted in December 1919, Bolshevik agrarian policy took on a fundamentally different appearance from that prescribed by the party program. The party conference approved the following measures:

– total liquidation of the large landholdings restored by Denikin, to be replaced by the transfer of land to landless and insufficiently landed peasants;

– establishment of state farms only on a scale proven necessary, taking account of the vital needs of the local peasantry;

---

5 V. I. Lenin, "Doklad o taktike RKP na III kongresse Kommunisticheskogo internatsionala 5 iiulia 1921 g.," *Polnoe sobranie sochinenii* (Moscow: Izdatel'stvo politicheskoi literatury, 1974), 44: 41. Cf. https://www.marxists.org/archive/lenin/works/1921/jun/12.htm.

6 *Izvestiia VTsIK* (Moscow), 23 February 1919.

7 "Programma Rossiiskoi kommunisticheskoi partii (bol'shevikov)" in *Vos'moi s"ezd RKP(b). Mart 1919 goda. Protokoly* (Moscow: Gosudarstvennoe izdatel'svto politicheskoi literatury, 1959), 390–411.

8 *Tretii z'izd Komunistychnoï partiï (bil'shovykiv) Ukraïny, 1–6 bereznia 1919 roku* (Kyiv: Parlaments'ke vydavnytstvo, 2002), 101.

– abandonment of the policy of forcing peasants into communes and cooperative associations except by free choice of the peasants themselves, with severe punishment for any attempts to do so by coercion.[9]

Thus, the departure from the "black repartition" proclaimed in the Decree on Land of the Second All-Russian Congress of Soviets[10] was written off as an initiative of the local authorities. Lacking the resources to make sense of the intricacies of the Kremlin's agrarian policy, peasants welcomed the Bolsheviks after Denikin's defeat even as they called the communists "plunderers." In the vocabulary of Ukrainian peasants, the word "commune" began to be associated with something loathsome.

Lenin heeded the reaction of the Ukrainian peasants to the idea of collectivization as he considered the prospects of agrarian policy for the whole country. In December 1920, at the Eighth All-Russian Congress of Soviets, he indicated that "We must base ourselves on the individual peasant: we must take him as he is, and he will remain what he is for some time to come, and so it is no use dreaming about going over to socialism and collectivization at present."[11]

Where was the Bolsheviks' forced renunciation of the collectivization of agriculture leading? Again and again we find ourselves having to repeat that collectivization was promoted not with the aim of increasing the productivity of peasant labor (although that was the Bolshevik propagandists' only argument) but to bond the village economy to the nationalized urban economy. The communist onslaught could not bypass the village even when the political authorities renounced the imposition of state farms and communes. While leaving agricultural producers economically independent (a brand-new term appeared at this time—*odnoosibnyky*, individual farmers), *the state still had to obtain provisions to feed the army and workers at nationalized enterprises.*

Under normal conditions, urban and rural goods producers came together on the basis of market principles. Prices for industrial and agricultural products were established by the law of supply and demand. By its very existence, however, the Soviet communal state destroyed the market and created an urgent need for state regulation of relations between the city and the village. The problem was that instead of innumerable manufacturers in the cities, there appeared a single producer who did not even want to call his products "goods" and put them on the market. The state's demand for agricultural production rose sharply, as it was building a vast army to ensure its victory in the civil war and, given the opportunity, to provide "international assistance" to the like-minded in Europe, who were being recruited by the Comintern at an unprecedented rate. On the other hand, the nationalization of enterprises caused profound economic devastation, and the city had almost nothing to offer the village by way of natural barter. One thing remained: to implement the requisition of peasant produce.

---

9   V. I. Lenin, "Rezoliutsiia TsK RKP(b) 'O Sovetskoi vlasti na Ukraine,'" *Polnoe sobranie sochinenii* (Moscow: Izdatel'stvo politicheskoi literatury, 1974), 39: 337.

10 *Dekrety Sovetskoi vlasti*, vol. 1 (Moscow: Gosudarstvennoe izdatel'stvo politicheskoi literatury, 1957), 17–18.

11 V. I. Lenin, "Rech' pri obsuzhdenii zakonoproekta SNK 'O merakh ukrepleniia i razvitiia krest'ianskogo sel'skogo khoziaistva' na fraktsii RKP(b) VIII s"ezda Sovetov 24 dekabria 1920 g.," *Polnoe sobranie sochinenii* (Moscow: Izdatel'stvo politicheskoi literatury, 1974), 42: 181. Cf. https://www.marxists.org/archive/lenin/works/1920/8thcong/ch03.htm.

Prodrazvërstka—the requisitioning of agricultural produce—bore no direct relation to the building of communism but was the inevitable consequence of the efforts of the communal state to liquidate private ownership of the means of production. The logic of the communist transformations demanded the simultaneous abolition of private ownership, both large and small, in town and country alike. Removing the haute bourgeoisie from production proved rather simple. The authorities had the support of the working class, which was gaining substantial rights in the management of nationalized property through factory committees and trade unions. Identical transformations in the countryside were associated with the creation of Soviet farms (Russ. *sovkhoz*, Ukr. *radhosp*) out of landowners' estates and communes through the amalgamation of peasant farms. With factories, Soviet farms, and agricultural communes at its disposal, the communal state acquired—or so its leaders thought—the capacity to liquidate the free market and introduce direct product exchange instead of the trade between town and country that had existed for ages. Lenin announced his intention to bring about these transformations in his April Theses of 1917, and provision was made for them in the communist program adopted by the RCP(B) in March 1919.

But the effort to introduce these changes was a failure from the start. Peasants and soldiers mobilized in the countryside would not hear of Soviet farms and demanded the "black repartition." Lenin's government was forced to satisfy their demands and found it necessary to replace direct product exchange between town and country with some other way of turning workers' and civil servants' wages into material means of existence. The attempt to retain a portion of the landowners' estates as Soviet farms and give priority to the communes during the "black repartition" in war-torn Ukraine proved deadly for Soviet rule.

Under the resulting conditions, the Sovnarkom outlawed free trade and requisitioned the quantities of produce it needed from the peasants under the guise of mandatory duties. For fulfilling those duties, peasants received only symbolic remuneration. First and foremost, the communal state had to support the buildup of the Red Army to unbelievable numbers. Second, industry ended up in a state of partial collapse because of attempts to replace market relations in the state sector of the economy with a system of orders by directive. Third, the state became militarized and made the fulfillment of military needs its first priority.

On May 9, 1918, the All-Russian Central Executive Committee (VTsIK) issued a decree "On Granting the People's Commissariat of Food Supply Extraordinary Powers in the Struggle with the Peasant Bourgeoisie, Which Is Concealing Its Grain Reserves and Profiteering with Them."[12] It was announced that peasants were required to surrender their grain reserves only at prices set by the state. Market trade in grain was outlawed as speculation. On November 21, 1918, the Sovnarkom of the Russian SFSR approved a decree "On the Organization of Supplies for the Population of All Products and Objects of Personal Consumption and the Home Economy."[13] According to the decree, the state in the form of the Sovnarkom took responsibility for procuring and distributing all that the population had previously acquired by trade, which was now illegal. Based on existing needs, the requisitioners

---

12   *Izvestiia VTsIK* (Moscow), May 10, 1918.
13   *Izvestiia VTsIK* (Moscow), November 24, 1918.

began imposing mandatory duties on peasants, later allocating them by county, *volost* (subdivision of a county), and village. Finally, on January 11, 1919, a decree was issued on the requisition of grain and feed. In Ukraine, which had maintained formal independence, communist requisition and distribution were introduced by a decree of the All-Ukrainian Central Executive Committee (VUTsVK) "On Statewide Inventory and Distribution of Products and Objects of the Home Economy" dated April 12, 1919.[14]

As peasants ascertained that the state was appropriating everything they intended to sell on the market for itself, they lost interest in work. The amount of seeded land, especially that of non-edible crops, fell sharply. The land received after the distribution of the landowners' estates lay fallow.

Once again, it turned out that the greatest resistance to grain requisition was offered by the Ukrainian peasantry. In the spring of 1920, when radical agrarian reforms were enacted (in the spirit of the "black repartition"), they supported the Soviet authorities. Accordingly, Symon Petliura's efforts to start an all-Ukrainian peasant uprising after the capture of Kyiv by Józef Piłsudski's armed forces proved futile. By the autumn of that year, however, peasant masses angered by requisitions began fighting units of the Red Army that were directly involved in taking produce from them. "Kulak banditry," as Bolshevik agitators called the new outbreak of civil war after the liquidation of the Polish and Wrangel fronts, washed over Ukraine in a broad wave. In order to keep Ukraine under control, Soviet Russia had to maintain a million-strong force of Red Army men mobilized in other regions.

The Eighth All-Russian Congress of Soviets, held in December 1920, ratified the plan proposed by the State Commission for the Electrification of Russia (GOELRO) for the reconstruction and development of basic spheres of the economy. Lenin spoke at the congress, voicing the hope that requisitions would provide the state with no less than 300 million poods (1 pood = 16.38 kg) of grain in 1921, and noting furthermore that "Without such a supply, however, it will be impossible to restore the country's industry...impossible even to approach the great task of electrifying Russia."[15] Thus, the leader of the Bolshevik Party was prepared to implement the GOELRO plan, calculated for a period of ten to twenty years, with the help of requisitioned peasant produce. Would it be possible to force the peasants to agree to requisitions if the state did not first succeed in driving them onto collective farms?

Again, Lenin was counting on force. On his orders, the government prepared a bill "On Measures to Strengthen and Develop Agriculture" and submitted it to the VTsIK for review at the Eighth All-Russian Congress of Soviets. The bill provided for supplementing the requisition of peasant produce with requisitioned sowing and cultivation of land. It was believed that the double requisition would make it possible to prevent the expected catastrophic reduction of seeded land in 1921. In his speech at the congress, Lenin characterized the document as follows: "In substance, the bill proposes that practical measures should at once be taken to assist individual peasant

---

14   *Zbirnyk uzakonen' USRR*, 1919, no. 36, art. 430.

15   V. I. Lenin, "Doklad Vserossiiskogo Tsentral'nogo Ispolnitel'nogo Komiteta i Soveta Narodnykh Komissarov o vneshnei i vnutrennei politike na VIII Vserossiiskom s"ezde Sovetov 22 dekabria 1920 g.," *Polnoe sobranie sochinenii* (Moscow: Izdatel'stvo politicheskoi literatury, 1974), 42: 149–50. Cf. https://www.marxists.org/archive/lenin/works/1920/8thcong/ch02.htm.

farming, which is the predominating system, and that this assistance should take the form not only of encouragement but of compulsion as well."[16]

On 23 December 1920, the bill became law. It is hard to say whether the delegates to the congress gave any thought to the fact that by approving the "farming lessons" to be delivered to every peasant household by the state, they were returning the peasants to the status that had prevailed before 1861. Aimed at the building of communism, the official line was pushing the party toward the establishment of serfdom.

The implementation of this law could easily have ended in catastrophe for Soviet rule. Lenin understood this and canceled the requisitions. Peasants were given the opportunity freely to enter the market after paying the state a certain tax, initially in kind. In the first half of 1921, the government switched to the New Economic Policy (NEP), which made it possible to put a quick end to the economic devastation. The only spoils of the first communist onslaught were the "commanding heights" of the economy. The economic foundation of Soviet rule proved yet unbuilt. Lenin's communal state had failed to make everyone economically dependent on it.

---

16 V. I. Lenin, "Rech' pri obsuzhdenii zakonoproekta SNK 'O merakh ukrepleniia i razvitiia krest'ianskogo sel'skogo khoziaistva' na fraktsii RKP(b) VIII s"ezda Sovetov 24 dekabria 1920 g.," *Polnoe sobranie sochinenii* (Moscow: Izdatel'stvo politicheskoi literatury, 1974), 42: 179. Cf. https://www.marxists.org/archive/lenin/works/1920/8thcong/ch03.htm.

3. THE GREAT BREAK

The purpose of the socioeconomic transformations imposed on the country was to establish control over society by the Communist Party, which had merged with the state into a single whole. In order to establish that control, it was necessary to make every citizen not only politically but also economically dependent. In 1919, Nikolai Bukharin expressed this goal in one short sentence: "The *political* dictatorship of the working class must inevitably also be its *economic* dictatorship."[1]

Nikolai Bukharin (1888–1938). Member of the Politburo, Central Committee of the AUCP(B), 1924–29; leader of the party's "right deviation."
[Photo by M. Svishchev-Paol (Fotokhronika TASS)].

Under the terms of the NEP, however, the communal state had to maintain market equilibrium between town and country. After paying taxes, tens of millions of peasant owners sold their produce freely—something natural in a normal society but unnatural in a Soviet one. The so-called nepmen, who appeared after the communist onslaught had been halted, posed no threat to the government. It was the peasantry that posed a threat, simply by existing and producing goods essential to the city outside the bounds of the communal state.

In 1921–22 Lenin sought to persuade the party that the NEP was only a temporary retreat from the course taken in 1918. In a pamphlet of April 1921, *The Tax in Kind*, he recommended using this retreat to develop cooperatives in the countryside. The leader was convinced that deliveries of agricultural produce to the cities through the channels of cooperative capitalism were more advantageous to the government than the development of individual trade. "The cooperative policy," he wrote, "if successful, will result in raising the small economy and in facilitating its transition, within an indefinite period, to large-scale production on the basis of voluntary

---

1 N. I. Bukharin, "Teoriia proletarskoi diktatury," *Izbrannye proizvedeniia* (Moscow: Politizdat, 1988), 20.

association."[2] As required by the RCP(B) program of 1919 that Lenin himself had written, he associated the incorporation of rural producers into the communist economy with the development of state farms and communes. Taking account of the sharply negative reaction of Ukrainian peasants, whom the party had tried to force into state farms and communes in 1919, he did not make the establishment of large-scale agricultural production a task for the near future. *"An indefinite period"* was the expression that limited his plans on the matter.

During the NEP years, the dogmas of communist theory came into contradiction with practical politics. The attitude of party leaders, starting with Lenin, toward the collective farms that still existed or even began to reappear (because members of communes still enjoyed privileges) therefore became contradictory. Hryhorii Petrovsky generally expressed the view (before the introduction of the NEP at the Fifth Conference of the Communist Party (Bolsheviks) of Ukraine [CP(B)U] in November 1920) that "the highest form of agriculture in the future should not be the collective farm, and especially not the commune, which works only for itself, but the Soviet farm."[3]

What was the general party line regarding "capitalist" cooperatives and "socialist" collective farms? At times when the first priority was increasing agricultural productivity—something to which cooperatives were so well suited and collective farms so fatally unsuited—the party behaved pragmatically. In a circular from the CC RCP(B) of March 18, 1922 "On Agricultural Cooperatives," party committees were recommended to encourage the establishment of joint collective farm-cooperative associations.[4] This recommendation included convolutions of an impossible hybrid—"a collective farm-cooperative form of ownership." It was precisely in 1922 that this oxymoron began to be formulated, later to become one of the categories of the political economy of socialism and the most lasting stereotype in the distorted consciousness of the Soviet people. Until the period of total collectivization, this pairing was explained by expectations that thriving cooperatives would keep the collective farms organizationally associated with them "above water." Nevertheless, the cooperative was considered a lower form of collective association, and the collective farm (in three forms, depending on the degree of alienation of property: associations for joint cultivation of land, cooperative associations, and communes) was considered higher.

After Lenin was removed from affairs of state because of his mortal illness, he expressed his final will in letters and articles that he dictated from late December 1922 to early March 1923. In an article titled "On Cooperation," he outlined a cooperative plan—an original alternative to the previously propagated idea of the collectivization of agriculture. Lenin now considered the development of cooperatives adequate for the growth of socialism. Unlike collective farms, cooperatives could only exist under market conditions. This sensational assertion was thus a significant retreat from communist doctrine. Lenin was always a pragmatist in adapting the main

---

2   V. I. Lenin, "O prodovol'stvennom naloge (znachenie novoi ėkonomicheskoi politiki i ee usloviia," *Polnoe sobranie sochinenii* (Moscow: Izdatel'stvo politicheskoi literatury, 1974), 43: 226. Cf. https://www.marxists.org/archive/lenin/works/1921/apr/21.htm.

3   Stanislav V. Kul'chyts'kyi, *Tsina "velykoho perelomu"* (Kyiv: Vydavnytstvo "Ukraïna," 1991), 18–19.

4   *Direktivy KPSS i Sovetskogo pravitel'stva po khoziaistvennym vosprosam*, vol. 1 (Moscow: Politizdat, 1958), 317.

Vladimir Lenin in his last year of life. L-r: German neuropathologist Dr. Otfrid Förster, Vladimir Lenin, and Dr. Fedor Getie, 30 June 1923.
[Photo by Maria Ulianova, Gorky].

idea of revolutionary Marxism about the abolition of private property to the realities of his own country. Having run up against the unconquerable force of peasant resistance, in his article "On Cooperation" Lenin identified cooperatives simultaneously with the market and with socialism, after which he noted: "Now we are entitled to say that for us the mere growth of cooperation...is identical with the growth of socialism, and at the same time we have to admit that there has been a radical modification in our whole outlook on socialism."[5] From the moment he published the pamphlet *The Tax in Kind*, the patriarch of Bolshevism underwent a striking transformation in his understanding of the communist perspective.

No matter how often Bolshevik propagandists avowed that the collectivization of agriculture would be voluntary, it was impossible to believe that the peasant owners were capable of partially (in the case of associations for joint cultivation of land or cooperative associations) or fully (in the case of the communes) surrendering their farms without external pressure. But they had been joining cooperatives quite freely since prerevolutionary times. Hence it was no accident that Lenin asked a stenographer to italicize key words in his article: cooperation made the "transition to the new system by means that are the *simplest, easiest, and most acceptable to the peasant.*"[6]

This change in thinking about cooperation allowed Lenin to predict how long the agricultural transformations would take without hiding behind the expression "an indefinite period," since "socialist transformation" was no longer understood to mean collectivization, which the peasant owners fiercely resisted, but cooperation achieved even without help from the state. Not only was cooperation to proceed without pressure from the state, but it was to be initiated by the goods producers themselves. "But it will take a whole historical epoch to get the entire population into the work of the cooperatives through NEP," dictated Lenin. "At best we can achieve this in one or two decades."[7] In other words, the time required for the establishment of the "system of civilized cooperators" would be determined by the length of time needed to carry out the GOELRO plan.

---

5 V. I. Lenin, "O kooperatsii," *Polnoe sobranie sochinenii* (Moscow: Izdatel'stvo politicheskoi literatury, 1975), 45: 376. First published in *Pravda*, May 26–27, 1923. Cf. https://www.marxists.org/archive/lenin/works/1923/jan/06.htm.

6 V. I. Lenin, "O kooperatsii," *Polnoe sobranie sochinenii* (Moscow: Izdatel'stvo politicheskoi literatury, 1975), 45: 370. Cf. https://www.marxists.org/archive/lenin/works/1923/jan/06.htm.

7 Ibid., 372.

Chapter 3. The Great Break

Since cooperative socialism remained an unrealized alternative to the outline of strategic actions embedded in the RCP(B) program, it is hard to say anything definite about it. Its very existence as an idea has to be established by a careful comparison of the dissimilar approaches to the NEP and cooperation taken by RCP(B) leaders at various times.[8] However, given the course of developments in the party and state after Lenin, the concept of cooperative socialism is of great interest.

After Lenin's death, the struggle between members of the Politburo of the CC RCP(B)-AUCP(B) unfolded on both personal and doctrinal levels. Members of the collective leadership had to answer the main question: What to do with the peasantry? The documents dictated by the founder of the party and the communal state demanded changes to the structure of power that would adapt it to society's existing economic foundation. But only three members of the Politburo out of seven were inclined in that direction—Nikolai Bukharin, Aleksei Rykov, and Mikhail Tomsky. The other four (Grigorii Zinoviev, Lev Kamenev, Joseph Stalin, and Leon Trotsky) were disposed to adapt society to the dictatorship of their design. After a six-year struggle, the winner was the one who, because of his functional duties, had the opportunity to put together the personnel of the ruling party and government apparatus.

As early as 1925, Stalin set a course for establishing rural enterprises based on the alienation of peasant property, whether fully (in the communes), intermediately (in the cooperative associations), or only initially (in the associations for joint cultivation of land). Under pressure from him, the task of collectivizing 20 percent of peasant sowing by the end of the first five-year plan was added to the directives of the Fifteenth Congress of the AUCP(B) concerning the development of a prospective plan for the economy.[9]

Grigorii Zinoviev (Radomyslsky) (1883–1936). Member of the Politburo, Central Committee of the AUCP(B), 1921–26; a leader of the opposition to Stalin.

The general secretary of the Central Committee did not object to the establishment of collective farms of a fundamentally different type—cooperatives in which the right of peasants to own their means of production and their output was not violated. But rural cooperation ran counter to communist doctrine. Consequently, those in the party leadership who, following Stalin, were getting ready to put an end to the NEP and revive the communist onslaught considered the cooperative movement merely a preparatory measure for the collectivization outlined in the RCP(B) program of 1919. In response to Bukharin's statements that the party was forgetting Lenin's

---

8   See, e.g., S. V. Kul'chyts'kyi, "Kontseptsiia 'kooperatyvnoho sotsializmu,'" *Ukraïns'kyi istorychnyi zhurnal* (Kyiv), 1995, no. 2: 3–17.

9   I. V. Stalin, "Politicheskii otchet Tsentral'nogo komiteta XV s"ezdu VKP(b)," in *Piatnadtsatyi s"ezd VKP(b). Dekabr' 1927 goda. Stenograficheskii otchet* (Moscow: Gosudarstvennoe izdatel'stvo politicheskoi literatury, 1961), 1: 63–65.

cooperative plan, Stalin published an article in *Pravda* on June 2, 1928 with the following conclusion: "The collective-farm movement is sometimes contrasted with the cooperative movement, apparently on the assumption that collective farms are one thing and cooperatives another. That, of course, is wrong. Some even go so far as to contrast collective farms with Lenin's cooperative plan. Needless to say, such contrasting has nothing in common with the truth. In actual fact, the collective farms are a form of cooperatives, the most striking form of producers' cooperatives."[10]

It should be noted that Lenin himself made it easier to falsify his political will. Had the Bolsheviks critically considered their experience with the onslaught of 1918–20, it might have forced them to think about the prospects for the country's development. But the cover-up notion of "war communism" that Lenin came up with prevented them from understanding that the communist doctrine was utopian by its very nature. And while Lenin propagated the economic and political benefits of the party's course for cooperation on peasant farms in his article "On Cooperation," he wrote not a single word there about collectivization or collective farms. One could only have guessed that he had had a change of heart concerning the slogan of collectivization, but party members were accustomed to clear ideological postulates.

To the degree that the fullness of dictatorial power came to be concentrated in the hands of General Secretary Stalin, on the agro-peasant issue he began following the course set out in the RCP(B) program. When he met with delegations of foreign workers that traveled to Moscow on the eve of the tenth anniversary of the October Revolution, Stalin was asked, "How do you intend to achieve collectivism in the peasant question?" He answered: "Along… the line of organizing the individual peasant farms on a cooperative basis [and] the line of organizing peasant farms, mainly the farms of poor peasants, in producers' cooperatives." Here he found it necessary to deny what he had not been asked about: "we have not yet reached…all-embracing collectivization…and are not likely to reach it soon."[11] The notion of "all-embracing collectivization" was a neologism and, on the eve of the second communist onslaught, revealed Stalin's plans for the countryside.

Joseph Stalin (Dzhugashvili) (1878–1953).

The first practical step toward what the general secretary called "all-embracing collectivization" was taken just a few weeks later. The Central Committee's political report, which Stalin presented in December 1927 at the Fifteenth Congress of the AUCP(B), noted that the tempo of rural economic development could not be called satisfactory. After that, Stalin posed a question to the delegates: What was the way

---

10 "Na khlebnom fronte," *Sochineniia* (Moscow: Gosudarstvennoe izdatel'stvo politicheskoi literatury, 1949), 11: 90. Cf. https://www.marxists.org/reference/archive/stalin/works/1928/may/28.htm.

11 I. Stalin, "Beseda s inostrannymi rabochimi delegatsiiami 5 noiabria 1927 g.," *Sochineniia* (Moscow: Gosudarstvennoe izdatel'stvo politicheskoi literatury, 1949), 10: 221–22. Cf. https://www.marxists.org/reference/archive/stalin/works/1927/11/05.htm.

out for agriculture? Perhaps in slowing the pace of industrial development? An "obvious" answer was presented: the way out lay in the transition from small and scattered peasant farms to great associations on the basis of joint cultivation of land, in the transition to collective cultivation on the basis of new and better technology.[12]

Having gained control of the economy's commanding heights, the Soviet government took up the burden of provisioning the labor force employed in those sectors. *Thus the urban population found itself dependent on the communal state for produce, and the state became economically dependent on the peasants.* The supply crisis brought about by the peasants' unwillingness to sell grain to the state at low prices in 1927–29 affected the material condition of the working class. Workers took it as the unwillingness of peasants to consider their interests. And that was exactly how the powerful propaganda apparatus interpreted the grain-procurement crises that were really caused by the forced pace of industrialization, with the authorities putting currency into circulation that was not backed by goods.

The Kremlin continued its policy of "divide and conquer" in the countryside as well. Once the leveling division of land was complete (in Ukraine, it took place in 1923), the concept of the "kulak" had ceased to be used in legislation and propaganda. Now it reappeared. In the winter of 1927–28, significant numbers of senior officials from the towns were mobilized for grain requisition. Insisting that they resort to extraordinary measures in order to overcome the grain-procurement crisis, Stalin demanded the "arrest of speculators, kulaks, and other disorganizers of the market and price policy, to put them on trial immediately, and to mobilize as many party and government workers as possible for grain procurement."[13]

When the new party chief, like all other members of the Politburo of the CC AUCP(B), traveled deep into the countryside in January 1928, he wasted no time. In his speeches to the rural party workers of Siberia, he laid out the following plan of action:

– to demand that the kulaks deliver all their grain surpluses immediately at state prices and, in case of refusal, to take extraordinary measures and confiscate the surplus;
– to conduct partial collectivization of agriculture over the next 3–4 years;
– to conduct total collectivization following the partial one.[14]

The ebulliently prosperous country was suddenly seized by violence and famine. The winter grain procurements of 1928–29 completed the dissolution of the NEP. The shortage of produce artificially created by the accelerated pace of industrialization worsened the problem of grain procurement to the point of impossibility. The party was being pushed down the slippery slope of a new communist onslaught. In April 1929, Stalin spoke at the joint plenum of the CC and the Central Control

---

12 I. V. Stalin, "Politicheskii otchet Tsentral'nogo komiteta XV s"ezdu VKP(b)," in *Piatnadtsatyi s"ezd VKP(b). Dekabr' 1927 goda. Stenograficheskii otchet* (Moscow: Gosudarstvennoe izdatel'stvo politicheskoi literatury, 1961), 1: 63.

13 "Direktiva TsK VKP(b) partorganizatsiiam o khlebozagotovkakh, 5 ianvaria 1928 g." in *Tragediia sovetskoi derevni. Kollektivizatsiia i raskulachivanie. Dokumenty i materialy*, vol. 1 *(mai 1927–noiabr' 1929)*, ed. Viktor P. Danilov, Roberta Thompson Manning, and Lynne Viola (Moscow: ROSSPĖN, 1999), 136–37.

14 I. Stalin, "O khlebozagotovkakh i perspektivakh razvitiia sel'skogo khoziaistva. Iz vystuplenii v raznykh raionakh Sibiri v ianvare 1928 g. (Kratkaia zapis')," *Sochineniia* (Moscow: Gosudarstvennoe izdatel'stvo politicheskoi literatury, 1949), 11: 4.

Commission of the AUCP(B), devoting his attention to substantiating the "Ural-Siberian method" of grain procurement he had come up with. "Grain procurements must be *organized*," he said. "The poor and middle peasant masses must be mobilized against the kulaks, and their public support organized for the measures of the Soviet government to increase grain procurements."[15]

In 1918–20, the Kremlin had carried out two separate campaigns in the countryside: collectivization and requisition. The know-how that Stalin displayed in the "Ural-Siberian method" united them into one whole. As Stalin explained the advantages of this method to the party leadership, he emphasized that "Firstly, we extract the grain surpluses from the well-to-do strata of the rural population and thereby help to supply the country; secondly, we mobilize on this basis the poor and middle peasant masses against the kulaks, educate them politically, and organize them into a vast, powerful political army supporting us in the countryside."[16]

The first course of the new policy in the countryside was tactical: the state was requisitioning available agricultural produce. The second course was strategic: the social tension necessary to achieve total collectivization was being created in the countryside. Collectivization, in turn, proved necessary to ensure the continuous production of agricultural produce on terms established by the state. The main drawback of requisitioning in the uncollectivized countryside was well known: peasants stopped producing goods and limited production to their own needs. On the collective farm, Stalin expected, that course would no longer be available to them.

The practical application of the "Ural-Siberian method" unfolded as the 1929 harvest ripened. The grain-procurement system that would exist until the end of 1932 took shape at that time. In order to make sense of the circumstances that led to the famine of 1932–33 in the USSR, that system must be thoroughly studied.

On June 28, 1929, the VTsIK and Sovnarkom of the RSFSR adopted a resolution "On Expanding the Rights of Local Soviets to Promote the Fulfillment of National Tasks and Plans."[17] On July 3, it was duplicated by the VUTsVK and Radnarkom of the Ukrainian SSR.[18] These resolutions introduced mandatory plan targets for grain delivery with requisitions in every village according to the principle of self-taxation. If a farmer evaded supplying the state with the quota of grain established at village meetings, the village soviet was allowed to fine him five times the value of the grain he was supposed to deliver. If the fine was not paid, the debtor's property was auctioned off in his own village. Group resistance to requisitions or group evasion of selling grain after the imposition of fines would result in a charge under Articles 57 and 58 of the Criminal Code of the Ukrainian SSR, which provided for the confiscation of property and deportation of those convicted to far-off regions of the USSR. A quarter of the revenue from fines or the auction of property was transferred

---

15   I. Stalin, "O pravom uklone v VKP(b)," *Sochineniia* (Moscow: Gosudarstvennoe izdatel'stvo politicheskoi literatury, 1949), 12: 88. Cf. https://www.marxists.org/reference/archive/stalin/works/1929/04/22.htm.

16   Ibid., 88–89.

17   *Sbornik uzakonenii RSFSR* (Moscow), 1929, no. 60: 589.

18   *Zbirnyk zakoniv USRR* (Kharkiv), 1929, no. 18, art. 153.

to funds for the cooperatives and the collectivization of the poor. This measure gave poor peasants a vested interest in implementing the new laws.[19]

The breakup of the NEP was accompanied by the degradation of commodity-money relations. Much like Lenin, who in 1920 had prepared a series of decrees intended to do away with money, Stalin aspired to establish a direct production linkage (not mediated by money) between town and country. As he began to do away with the NEP in December 1927, he managed to include a thesis in the resolution of the Fifteenth Congress of the AUCP(B) to the effect that, as socialism was successfully built, trade would increasingly be transformed into barter exchange, and the trade apparatus would be replaced by that of the "socialist distribution of products."[20] Starting in 1929, the network of state trade began to turn into a distribution apparatus that supplied grain and other provisions only to those to whom the state had given ration cards. The sale of grain at the bazaar was outlawed because of its negative effect on grain procurement. Manufactured goods destined for rural consumers were transferred to a grain-procurement "redemption" fund on the basis of contracts.

The contract was entered into between the state and the collective (primarily the trade cooperative) or the individual farmer. It contained mandatory obligations for the peasants to supply the state with a certain quantity of produce or raw materials. The state's reciprocal obligation to supply manufactured goods was carried out on the basis of the existing stock of goods. But there were not enough goods for the village, and the state confined itself to paying with devalued rubles. Under these conditions, the contract came down to the ordinary *prodrazvërstka* (Ukr. *prodrozkladka*), or requisition.

A plenipotentiary of the USSR People's Commissariat of Agriculture (Narkomzem), M. N. Yukhnovsky, described the process of entering into a contract as follows: "In some villages, the practical procedure of establishing contracts and the method of presenting [tasks] to every household resulted in a dry, bureaucratic form of administration. Peasants call it *prodrazvërstka*. The contract is established in this way: a province [*okrug*] gives a quota to the district [*raion*] and, with an additional amount (to cover itself), the district gives it to the village soviet. With an additional amount (to cover itself), sometimes as much as 50 percent, the village soviet apportions the district quota to peasant households."[21] The picture painted here must be clarified. Yukhnovsky was not talking about "some villages" but about standard practice in all regions. Moreover, when the harvest proved greater than expected, the quotas established in the contracts were adjusted accordingly.

In a resolution of the CC AUCP(B) "On Basic Results and Further Objectives with Regard to Contracts for Grain Crops" adopted on August 26, 1929, victory

---

19 S. V. Kul'chyts'kyi, "Narodzhennia radians'koho ladu (1917–1938)" in *Ukraïna i Rosiia v istorychnii retrospektyvi*, vol. 2, *Radians'kyi proekt dlia Ukraïny*, ed. Vladyslav Hrynevych, Viktor Danylenko, and Stanislav Kul'chyts'kyi (Kyiv: Naukova dumka, 2004), 78.

20 "O direktivakh po sostavleniiu piatiletnego plana narodnogo khoziaistva. II. Problema piatiletnego plana i khoziaistvennaia politika partii" in *Piatnadtsatyi s"ezd VKP(b). Dekabr' 1927 goda. Stenograficheskii otchet*, vol. 2 (Moscow: Gosudarstvennoe izdatel'stvo politicheskoi literatury, 1962), 1449.

21 Tsentral'nyi derzhavnyi arkhiv vyshchykh orhaniv vlady i upravlinnia Ukraïny (Central State Archives of Supreme Organs of Government and Administration of Ukraine, hereafter TsDAVO Ukraïny), fond 27, op. 11, spr. 104, ark. 20; Kul'chyts'kyi, *Tsina "velykoho perelomu,"* 85–86.

over the market, which seemed very close to the party leaders, was marked by a terminological revolution. Goods were already being called "products." The contract was seen as a "means of organizing planned barter between the city and the village."[22] The state had no desire at all to enter into contractual relations with the "kulaks." They were given fixed quotas ("tasks") (*tverdi zavdannia*, whence the name *tverdozdatchyky*) on the basis of expert evaluations of every single farm (whence the name *ekspertnyky*). The village soviets conducted the expert evaluations together with the poor peasants and hired workers, representing the "community." In a letter of October 29, 1929 addressed to provincial and district party committees, the general secretary of the CC CP(B)U, Stanislav Kosior, explained what portion of every village should be the object of "community" attention—from 7 to 10 percent of all farms.[23] This was also requisition, but of farms, not grain. Whoever ended up in the "wealthy kulak tier of the village" immediately felt the colossal pressure of the tandem of lower state functionaries and marginalized strata of the village. The Kremlin calculated that under these conditions, the "kulaks" would be unable to mount effective resistance to the policy of total collectivization, which was already becoming the order of the day.

Stanislav Kosior (1889–1939). General secretary (from 1928) and, from 1934, first secretary of the Central Committee of the CP(B)U.

The contract did not extend to the indigent portion of the rural population because those farms held no economic significance for the state. But they had great practical significance: direct requisitions or those conditioned by contractual obligations were carried out in the countryside with the help of the committees of poor peasants.

The criteria used to define the "exploitative upper tier" of the village were kept deliberately nebulous by the architects of the collective-farm system. They could declare every more-or-less prosperous peasant a "kulak." On the other hand, not even utter indigence could save anyone who spoke out against collectivization: party workers used the neologism "kulak henchman" (Russ. *podkulachnik*, Ukr. *pidkurkul'nyk*) to crush them.

The historiography of the Great Break (Russ. *velikii perelom*, Ukr. *velykyi perelom*) has been well developed.[24] Here it is important to dwell only on the aspects related to the all-Union famine and the Ukrainian Holodomor.

---

22 *Kollektivizatsiia sel'skogo khoziaistva: Vazhneishie postanovleniia Kommunisticheskoi partii i Sovetskogo pravitel'stva, 1927–1935*, ed. Polina Sharova, comp. L. F. Kuz'mina (Moscow: Politizdat, 1987), 196–97.

23 *Holod 1932–1933 rokiv v Ukraïni: prychyny ta naslidky*, ed. Volodymyr Lytvyn (Kyiv: Naukova dumka, 2003), 348.

24 See, e.g., Kul'chyts'kyi, *Tsina "velykoho perelomu,"* 432.

Scholars seeking to establish the root cause of the all-Union famine refer to the events of November 1929, in particular the publication of Stalin's article "The Year of the Great Break"[25] and the decision by the plenum of the CC AUCP(B) to go over to the forced collectivization of agriculture.[26] But the destruction of the traditional rural way of life by forced collectivization can be considered a cause of the famine only to a certain extent. The root cause was the attempt (only an attempt!) of the communal state to go over from market to extramarket forms of economic relations between town and country. In practice, this manifested itself in a) the suppression of the free market, and b) the transition to obtaining agricultural produce (in order to supply the urban population and the army or for export) by forced requisition. In the winter months of 1927–28, requisition emerged in the form of extraordinary measures, but by the next winter of 1928–29, those extraordinary measures had become standard.

It was no accident that the transition to extramarket relations was only called an attempt. The attempt was not taken so far as to eliminate commodity-money relations. The cause of the famine, which became the most acute form of the crisis, and the cause of the economic crisis itself is to be discerned in the political authorities' ambition to create an economic foundation adequate for their purposes by implementing the RCP(B)'s program of 1919. It must be admitted that the party leaders managed to create a socioeconomic model that was utopian from the outset and remained in the force field of the dictatorship for seven decades—a model to which the third Soviet generation became completely accustomed. But they did not achieve a complete victory over the market. If the count starts from the moment the extraordinary measures were introduced, then the struggle to the death against the market lasted five years and ended in a compromise. The peasantry agreed—after all

Presidium of the XII All-Ukrainian Congress of Soviets. From left to right: Hryhorii Petrovsky, Stanislav Kosior, Panas Liubchenko. Kharkiv, February 1931.

---

25   I. Stalin, "God velikogo pereloma. K XII godovshchine Oktiabria," *Sochineniia* (Moscow: Gosudarstvennoe izdatel'stvo politicheskoi literatury, 1949), 12: 118–35.

26   "Materialy noiabr'skogo plenuma TsK VKP(b), 12, 14–15 noiabria 1929 g." in *Tragediia sovetskoi derevni*, 1: 746–64.

conceivable and inconceivable forms of violence had been used against it (here one calls to mind the Holodomor in Ukraine and the catastrophic famines in the main regions of commodity agriculture)—to work on the collective farms, and the government resigned itself to the autonomous existence of a collective-farm system based on commodity-money relations within the communal state. As will be shown below, the abolition of requisitions in January 1933 was no accident. *Stalin renounced the attempt to bring the full scope of the communist utopia into being under the influence of the all-Union famine of 1932–33.*

The theses formulated above are rather abstract and may therefore slip past the reader unnoticed. But they must be established before we proceed to an analysis of the factual material in order to prevent that material from being arranged into a familiar chain of cause and effect. We are overly accustomed (here I mean the older generation) to accepting the "building of socialism" as the fulfillment of a successive series of tasks, each of which was anticipated in some wise plan that was at the disposition of the Bolshevik Party. When Lenin retrospectively turned his communist onslaught into "war communism," the RCP(B)'s communist program of 1919 was forgotten by propagandists and scholars alike. Gavriil Popov recalled it out of the blue during Gorbachev's *perestroika*, but only as a topic for a journalistic essay.[27] We must understand that the leaders of the communal state indeed had a plan of action, but rather than being wise, it was utopian, and that plan was the RCP(B) program. Leninism can be distinguished from that other current and even highly popular term, "Stalinism," only in the sense that Lenin stopped halfway in his implementation of the program he had written in 1919, while Stalin continued building communism where his predecessor had left off. Lenin backed down in the face of a crisis whose most striking external manifestation was the famine of 1921. A catastrophic drought and the preceding series of wars helped him mask the threat posed by the full-scale implementation of the RCP(B)'s communist program. When Stalin picked up the implementation of the party program, he ran headlong into the famine of 1932–33.

Why should the Great Break be dated not from the resolution of the CC AUCP(B) plenum of November 1929 but from the introduction of the extraordinary laws on grain procurement? Historians are in a unique position to compare two communist onslaughts that differed in character, Lenin's and Stalin's. Separated by the seven years of the NEP, they took place under different conditions but had a common basis—requisition. The fundamental flaw in confiscating products from free producers was that *in the next production cycle, output was reduced to a level that provided only for one's own needs*. But the communal state was obliged to feed the urban population that depended on it; hence it again resorted to confiscating foodstuffs produced for the village's own internal needs. This created the preconditions for famine both in the village, which was plundered with the help of workers' brigades and local committees of poor peasants, and in the city. That led to a standoff between town and country because propagandists persuaded the urbanites that the kulak saboteurs wanted to strangle the proletarian revolution with the "bony

---

27 In 1996, Popov rewrote his first article and substantially expanded its scope. See Gavriil Kh. Popov, "Programma, kotoroi rukovodstvovalsia Stalin" in his *Teoriia i praktika sotsializma v XX veke* (Moscow: ROSSPĖN, 2006), 15–29.

hand of hunger." It also led to a standoff in the village itself, for the technique of requisition was based on self-taxation. Having identified three groups of property owners and given them class labels, the state was guided by the following principle when confiscating agricultural produce: from the poor, nothing; from the middle peasantry, in moderation; from the kulaks, a great deal. By the second or third year of requisition, when it gave rise to the inevitable supply crisis, the Soviet authorities no longer divided producers according to class. They took whatever grain they could find in any peasant household.

In Ukraine, requisitions involved particular difficulties. In order to overcome them, in 1920 the Kremlin resolved on an exceptional measure, creating a peasant organization endowed for some time with political and administrative powers—the Committees of Poor Peasants. These committees were used as instruments to extract provisions from fellow villagers during the Holodomor, after which they were immediately disbanded.

A socioeconomic model based on the mutual hatred of social strata pitted against each other by the political authorities was unstable and even dangerous to the authorities themselves. That is why the party leadership sought ways and means of completing the transformations undertaken in 1918 by integrating the free producers in the countryside into the planned command economy. Various paths were taken to that end during the first and second onslaughts.

After the Bolsheviks came to power, they did not immediately dare to pose the question of turning large agricultural estates into state farms. The peasantry demanded the "black repartition" and received practically all the landowners' holdings. By 1919, however, Bolshevik rule had become strong enough that they attempted to organize a certain number of state farms and communes in Ukraine, which they had just conquered, after which they promptly lost the republic. Having learned from bitter experience, Lenin renounced efforts to collectivize the countryside and, as we have seen, attempted to limit the freedom of goods producers in another way, by making the sowing and cultivation of fields mandatory. His further actions on the agrarian question came down to a pragmatic capitulation to the peasantry. Stalin, however, chose a different path and decided that the peasantry had to capitulate to the communal state. He calculated that putting peasant producers into the straitjacket of collective farms would give the state freedom of action in determining quotas for requisitioning provisions from the village.

Stalin's propagandists characterized the imposition of collective farms as a movement from below. The numbers of collective farm workers did indeed grow, thanks to poor peasants tempted by the material benefits. By October 1929 there were 477,000 households in the collective farms of the Ukrainian SSR, and the proportion of collectivized arable land had reached 8.8 percent.[28] Yet peasant owners, who had something to lose, did not join the collective farms.

Stalin's above-mentioned article "The Year of the Great Break: On the Occasion of the Twelfth Anniversary of the October Revolution" proclaimed that peasants were joining the collective farms "by whole villages, volosts, and districts." Local officials had the impression that they were lagging behind their neighbors: they

---

28 *Komunistychna partiia Ukraïny v rezoliutsiiakh i rishenniakh zʹïzdiv, konferentsii i plenumiv TsK*, vol. 1 (Kyiv, 1976), 659.

had only collectivized an insignificant percentage, but the general secretary of the Central Committee was asserting that the middle peasants had all joined.

Stalin's article was timed to coincide with the plenum of the CC AUCP(B), which announced the party's transition to a policy of total collectivization of agriculture. The question of what would befall the wealthiest peasants was resolved by the apparatus. The November 1929 plenum of the CC proclaimed the need to create an All-Union People's Commissariat (Narkomat) of Agriculture and appointed its director, Yakov Yakovlev, as head of a commission that decided to proceed to a policy of "liquidating the kulaks as a class" in totally collectivized districts. Stalin first made the committee's decision public on December 27, 1929 at the All-Union Conference of Agrarian Marxists.[29]

Yakov Yakovlev (Epshtein) (1896–1938). USSR People's Commissar of Agriculture from December 1929.

Fomenting social tension and dekulakizing wealthy farmers undermined the productive forces of the village, which had been restored during the years of the NEP. The top echelon of the party deliberately proceeded with this policy because its goal was to impose collective farms as a mandatory element of the command economy. Peasant owners would accept collectivization only under the threat of losing everything: the example of one's neighbor being "dekulakized" made the individual farmer more tractable.

The practical transition to the policy of total collectivization took place in January 1930. On January 5, the CC AUCP(B) adopted a resolution "On the Rate of Collectivization and State Measures to Assist the Development of Collective Farms" that established an order for achieving total collectivization by region. Ukraine was supposed to complete collectivization by the autumn of 1931 or the spring of 1932.[30]

On January 30, the CC AUCP(B) adopted a secret resolution "On Measures to Liquidate Kulak Households in Districts with Total Collectivization." "Kulak activists," who were subject to immediate liquidation by imprisonment in concentration camps or execution, were assigned to the first category of such households. Deportation to far-off regions of the country awaited those in the second category. People who fell into the third category were to be resettled in new villages outside collectivized lands.[31]

---

29 I. Stalin, "K voprosam agrarnoi politiki v SSSR. Rech' na konferentsii agrarnikov-marksistov 27 dekabria 1929 g.," *Sochineniia* (Moscow: Gosudarstvennoe izdatel'stvo politicheskoi literatury, 1949), 12: 166.

30 *Kommunisticheskaia partiia Sovetskogo Soiuza v rezoliutsiiakh i resheniiakh s"ezdov, konferentsii i plenumov TsK*, vol. 5 (Moscow: Politizdat, 1984), 72–75.

31 "Materialy komissii politbiuro TsK VKP(b) pod predsedatel'stvom V. M. Molotova po vyrabotke mer v otnoshenii kulachestva, 15–30 ianvaria 1930 g." in *Tragediia sovetskoi derevni, vol. 2 (noiabr' 1929–dekabr' 1930)* (Moscow: ROSSPĖN, 2000), 116–31.

In Ukraine, the Committees of Poor Peasants participated actively in dekulakization. By early spring of 1930, they had established 7,762 groups to promote collectivization.[32] Chekists carried out the operation, which lasted from February 18 to March 10 and encompassed 29 provinces of the Ukrainian SSR. A total of 19,531 households comprising 92,970 people were resettled. By April 1, preliminary work on resettling 15,000 individuals from eleven border provinces ("the counterrevolutionary and anti-Soviet element and kulaks") was to be completed. The deportation of another thousand families from five eastern and southern provinces was planned for the same period.[33]

The commission headed by Yakovlev inclined to the view that the agrarian cooperative association should be recognized as the main form of collective farm organization. "Every further step toward socialization on the path to the commune," said the draft resolution sent to the Politburo of the CC AUCP(B), "should rely on the direct experience of the peasant collective farmers, on their increasing confidence in the stability, convenience, and advantages of collective forms of agriculture." The committee insisted on "preserving peasants' private property under current conditions—small implements, a few cattle, milch cows, etc., where they serve the consumer needs of the peasant family."[34]

Stalin passed the draft resolution on to the secretary of the CC AUCP(B), Viacheslav Molotov. The latter called it unsatisfactory, "with false notes here and there." It was the reasons given for the creation of cooperative associations instead of communes that Molotov considered false.[35] Stalin agreed with him, and the wording about the peasants' right to have minor implements and milch cows among their private property was stricken from the final version of the resolution, which was issued on January 5, 1930. Instead, the Narkomzem of the USSR was instructed to develop a model statute for agricultural cooperative associations "as a form of collective farm transitional to the commune"[36] as quickly as possible.

Viacheslav Molotov (Skriabin) (1890–1986). Chairman of the USSR Council of People's Commissars from December 1930. In October 1932 he headed an extraordinary grain-procurement commission of the Central Committee of the AUCP(B), which, under the pretext of grain procurement, confiscated all food supplies from the peasants of Ukraine, thereby condemning them to death from starvation. [Photo by Petr Otsup, 1930].

---

32 Kul'chyts'kyi, *Tsina "velykoho perelomu,"* 80.
33 *Tragediia sovetskoi derevni*, 2: 336–42.
34 Ibid., 2: 63.
35 Nikolai A. Ivnitskii, "Kollektivizatsiia i raskulachivanie (nachalo 30-kh godov). Po materialam Politbiuro TsK VKP(b) i OGPU" in *Sud'by rossiiskogo krest'ianstva*, ed. Iurii N. Afanas'ev (Moscow: Rossiiskii gosudarstvennyi gumanitarnyi universitet, 1996), 257.
36 *Kollektivizatsiia sel'skogo khoziaistva: Vazhneishie postanovleniia*, 259.

A month later, on February 6, the Narkomzem of the USSR and the Collective Farm Center published the model statute,[37] which was strongly influenced by the thesis of transition. The difference between the cooperative association and the commune as forms of the collective farm, so fundamentally important to the peasants, was deliberately obscured in it. A statement about the possibility of establishing kitchen gardens turned out to be an empty declaration, as the statute did not regulate the size of garden plots or establish norms concerning the right of collective farmers to keep cows and small livestock.

A qualitative leap in collectivization occurred in February 1930, as the Cheka was rolling out its program of dekulakization. It was in this month that all across Ukraine, with the exception of the Polisia region, the area of collectivized land came to exceed that of land held by individual farmers. Peasants were subjected to tremendous administrative and Cheka pressure to join the collective farms. The resistance engendered by such pressure was general, albeit disorganized. In all regions, peasants had the same reaction to the endless grain quotas, dekulakization, socialization of cows and small livestock, and destruction of churches. Incidents of civil disobedience and even armed resistance became more frequent. The situation in the country began to resemble a war. On February 7, the Politburo of the CC AUCP(B) began receiving operational reports from the OGPU (Joint State Political Directorate or secret police).[38]

On February 26, the CC AUCP(B) received a panicked telegram from Kharkiv. The secretary of the CC CP(B)U, Panas Liubchenko, and the head of the VUTsVK, Hryhorii Petrovsky, gave notice of local instances of "blatant distortion of party directives" that were precipitating a "peasant movement" against collectivization. Stalin used the telegram's terminology ("distortion," the "blockheadedness" of local officials) in his famous article "Dizziness with Success." Over the next few days, similar telegrams with messages about the movement against collective farms arrived from Alma-Ata, Voronezh, and Riazan. After a poll taken on February 28, the following decision was entered into the minutes of a meeting of the Politburo of the CC AUCP(B) on March 5: "a) a committee composed of Comrades Syrtsov, Stalin, Molotov, Kalinin, Rykov, Mikoyan, Voroshilov, Yakovlev, and Yurkin is to make the final decision on the matter of the collective-farm statute based on an exchange of opinions. Comrade Rykov will convene the meeting. They have 24 hours; the statute must be published

Panas Liubchenko (1897–1937). Secretary of the Central Committee of the CP(B)U, 1927–34. Concurrently first deputy chairman (from 1933) and chairman (from 1934) of the Council of People's Commissars of the Ukrainian SSR.

---

37   *Pravda*, February 6, 1930.
38   Ivnitskii, "Kollektivizatsiia i raskulachivanie," 269.

in the press on March 2; b) Comrade Stalin is to publish an article in the papers the same day."³⁹

In the new version of the model statute, a fundamental concession was made to collective farmers, who were given the right to keep a cow, small livestock, and poultry and to have a garden plot near their homes. The same issue of *Pravda* printed Stalin's article, "Dizziness with Success." The general secretary announced without reservations that "the main link of the collective-farm movement...is the agricultural cooperative."⁴⁰ In a harsh tone, he pointed out that promoting the "collective-farm movement" in bureaucratic fashion was unacceptable.

Following these documents published on March 2, on March 10 the CC AUCP(B) adopted a resolution "On the Struggle against Distortions of the Party Line in the Collective-Farm Movement." The name itself contained two big lies: first, local administrative bodies were not guilty of "distortions"; second, there

Hryhorii Petrovsky (1878–1958). Chairman of the Central Executive Committee of the Ukrainian SSR, 1919–38.

was no movement—peasants were dragged into the collective farms by force. The resolution was circulated to party committee secretaries down to the district level, as well as to plenipotentiaries of the OGPU, prosecutors, and members of the republican Sovnarkoms. The Politburo also suggested that the presidiums of the republican Central Executive Committees hear complaints on religious matters and correct the distortions.⁴¹

Local authorities took umbrage at the unjust accusations of "distortions," and Stalin was obliged to resort to an unaccustomed level of frankness in order to explain the situation. A confidential letter "On the Tasks of the Collective-Farm Movement in Connection with the Struggle against Distortions of the Party Line" dated April 2, 1930, addressed to lower party organizations, said the following: "In February the Central Committee received notices of mass peasant actions in the Central Black Earth province, in Ukraine, in Kazakhstan, Siberia, and Moscow province. These notices indicated a state of affairs that can be called nothing less than threatening. If measures had not been taken immediately against these distortions of the party line, we would now be facing a broad wave of insurgent peasant actions, a good half of our lower-ranking officials would have been killed by peasants, the sowing would have been disrupted, the development of collective farming would have been undermined, and we would be under internal and external threat. This called for the intervention of the CC, a change to the Statute of Agricultural Cooperative

---

39 *Tragediia sovetskoi derevni*, 2: 270, 833.
40 See https://www.marxists.org/reference/archive/stalin/works/1930/03/02.htm.
41 *Tragediia sovetskoi derevni*, 2: 305.

Associations, and the publication of Comrade Stalin's article 'Dizziness with Success' by special resolution of the CC."[42]

How true to reality was the apocalyptic picture painted in the confidential letter from the CC AUCP(B)? In his closing address at the February–March (1937) plenum of the CC AUCP(B), which marked the beginning of the Great Terror of 1937–38, Stalin recalled the events of the first months of 1930 and again confirmed their gravity: "This was one of the most dangerous periods in the life of our party."[43]

On the basis of OGPU reports, historians have been able to analyze the situation that arose in the USSR after February 26, 1930. Given all that happened afterwards, up to and including the Holodomor, one can agree with Stalin's assessment of the events that forced the Kremlin to halt its policy of total collectivization for half a year.

According to data provided by Lynne Viola, 4,098 peasant disturbances were recorded in the Ukrainian SSR in 1930, 1,373 in the Central Black Earth province, 1,061 in the North Caucasus, and 1,003 on the Lower Volga.[44] Hence there were significantly more disturbances in the Ukrainian SSR than in the three other regions of commodity agriculture put together. According to Terry Martin's account, as many as 100,000 peasants took part in the March disturbances in the border regions of Right-Bank Ukraine in 1930.[45] According to Liudmyla Hrynevych's data, proclamations by insurgents calling for the restoration of the Ukrainian People's Republic were widely circulated during the disturbances.[46] From this we can draw our first important conclusion: the order in which the regions were listed in Stalin's apocalyptic confidential letter did not expose but rather covered up the threat coming from the Ukrainian SSR. Stalin evidently understood this threat, which was doubling with the active participation of Ukrainians from the North Caucasus in the campaign to Ukrainize almost half the districts of a territory that shared a border with the Ukrainian SSR. Nevertheless, the general secretary's frankness in assessing the social consequences of accelerated collectivization was not matched by frankness in assessing the national aspects.

The confidential letter of April 2, 1930 from the CC AUCP(B) mentioned the Central Committee's sanctioning the publication of Stalin's article "Dizziness with Success." This is a striking indication of the degree of Stalin's influence on the party and society in the early 1930s. At that time he had achieved unqualified control over the party and government nomenklatura in all three power verticals that converged in the Politburo of the CC AUCP(B). Yet his influence over the party—and, all the more, over society—was rather limited. The failure of the communist

---

42 Ibid., 2: 367–68.

43 *Pravda*, April 1, 1937. (Plenums always took place at the Kremlin in Moscow; dates are specified in the text.)

44 Lynne Viola, *Peasant Rebels under Stalin: Collectivization and the Culture of Peasant Resistance* (New York: Oxford University Press, 1996), 138–39. For statistics on mass uprisings in 1930, see also *Tragediia sovetskoi derevni*, 2: 803.

45 Terry Martin, "The 1932–1933 Ukrainian Terror: New Documentation on Surveillance and the Thought Process of Stalin" in *Famine-Genocide in Ukraine 1932–33: Western Archives, Testimonies and New Research*, ed. Wsevolod Isajiw (Toronto: Ukrainian Canadian Research and Documentation Centre, 2003), 104.

46 Liudmyla V. Hrynevych, "Vyiavlennia natsional'noï identychnosti ukraïns'koho selianstva v roky kolektyvizatsiï" in *Holod 1932–1933 rokiv v Ukraïni: prychyny ta naslidky*, 421–25.

onslaught could have cost him his position as general secretary. Stalin only became the unquestioned dictator of the party and the country after two successful wars: one against his own people, the other against Hitler's Germany.

And, finally, we should dwell on the main conclusions that emerge from an analysis of the confidential letter in conjunction with an analysis of the entire socioeconomic policy during the onslaught of 1929–32. In the letter, the course toward forced collectivization taken by the party in the barely disguised form of imposing the communes was called a distortion of the party line. We know that after March 2, 1930, anyone who wanted to leave the collective farms was allowed to do so, and practically all peasant owners took advantage of this. We also know, however, that the directive letter "On Collectivization," which the CC AUCP(B) sent out to the party committees on September 24, 1930, instructed them to "achieve a decisive shift with regard to organizing a new, powerful upsurge of the collective-farm movement."[47] After this, a repeat campaign to "liquidate the kulaks as a class" was carried out in the country, with other peasants now in the role of kulaks. The collective farmers were freed from taxes, whereas individual farmers were shouldered with unbearable obligations. In short order, the new wave of dekulakization in conjunction with the tax-privilege disparity drove most of the peasantry into the collective farms. By October 1931, 72 percent of the arable land in the Ukrainian SSR had been collectivized.[48] Only six months after the publication of Stalin's "Dizziness with Success," forced collectivization was no longer considered a distortion of the party line.

---

47 *Tragediia sovetskoi derevni*, 2: 646.
48 *Istoriia kolektyvizatsiï sil's'koho hospodarstva Ukraïns'koï RSR, 1917–1937 rr.*, ed. Ivan Hanzha et al., vol. 2 (Kyiv: Naukova dumka, 1965), 554–55.

4. THE COLLECTIVE-FARM SYSTEM UNDER STALIN'S REQUISITIONS

What happened with that other element of the course for total collectivization, the disguised imposition of the communes, which was also declared a distortion? Contemporary historiography has not been interested in this question, even though it helps make sense of the causes of the all-Union famine of 1932–33, which was the backdrop and initial stage of the Ukrainian Holodomor.

As the global discussion of the Holodomor shows,[1] Kremlin policy at this time is difficult for historians to understand. First, it was aimed at realizing theoretical concepts of communism and therefore implemented by trial and error. Second, as has already been emphasized, Stalin, the chief architect of the collective-farm system, was very unforthcoming in communication, even with his own team. It takes a good deal of effort to recreate the actual sequence of his actions during the establishment of the collective-farm system from small and diverse bits of information.

Historians often consider the past from the standpoint of the reality to which they are accustomed. This understandable tendency has its own scholarly name (presentism) and leads to a distorted picture of the past. An example of such distortion is the notion that the character of Soviet collective farms during the years when the collective-farm system was taking shape (1930–32) is identical to its character in the decades that followed.

Unfortunately, post-Soviet Ukrainian historiography has focused particularly on the Holodomor and overlooked the related problem of collectivization. That is why it has failed to note the stage of trial and error in Stalin's policy, which led to

---

1   *Famine in Ukraine, 1932–1933*, ed. Roman Serbyn and Bohdan Krawchenko (Edmonton: Canadian Institute of Ukrainian Studies, 1986); *La morte della terra: La grande "carestia" in Ucraina nel 1932–33. Atti del Convegno, Vicenza, 16–18 ottobre 2003*, ed. Gabriele De Rosa and Francesca Lomastro (Rome: Viella, 2004); *Holodomor: Reflections on the Great Famine of 1932–1933 in Soviet Ukraine*, ed. Lubomyr Luciuk (Kingston, Ontario: Kashtan Press, 2008); *Holocaust-Genozid in der Ukraine 1932–1933: Sammelband der wissenschaftlichen Beiträge*, ed. D. Blochyn (Munich and Poltava: ASMI, 2009); *Holodomor and Gorta Mór: Histories, Memories and Representations of Famine in Ukraine and Ireland*, ed. Christian Noack, Lindsay Janssen, and Vincent Comerford (London and New York: Anthem Press, 2012); *The Holodomor Reader: A Sourcebook on the Famine of 1932–1933 in Ukraine*, comp. and ed. Bohdan Klid and Alexander J. Motyl (Toronto and Edmonton: CIUS Press, 2012); *After the Holodomor: The Enduring Impact of the Great Famine on Ukraine*, ed. Andrea Graziosi, Lubomyr A. Hajda, and Halyna Hryn (Cambridge, MA: Harvard Ukrainian Research Institute, 2013); *Holod v Ukraïni u pershii polovyni XX stolittia: prychyny i naslidky (1921–1923, 1932–1933, 1946–1947). Materialy mizhnarodnoï naukovoï konferentsiï, Kyïv, 20–21 lystopada 2013 r.*, ed. Myroslava Antonovych et al. (Kyiv: Instytut demohrafiï ta sotsial'nykh doslidzhen' im. M. V. Ptukhy NAN Ukraïny, Instytut istoriï Ukraïny NAN Ukraïny, 2013); *Golod 1930-kh godov v Ukraine i Kazakhstane: voprosy istoriografii i podkhody k issledovaniiu problemy (k 80-letiiu tragedii). Sbornik materialov vystuplenii, dokladov i soobshchenii uchastnikov mezhdunarodnoi nauchno-metodicheskoi konferentsii 3 dekabria 2013 goda*, ed. E. B. Sydykov (Astana: Evraziiskii natsional'nyi universitet im. L. N. Gumileva, 2014).

the development of a profound socioeconomic crisis. The famine of 1932–33 was precisely the greatest manifestation of this crisis. The fact of the matter is that Stalin publicly proclaimed the cooperative association "the basic link of the collective-farm movement" and went to great lengths in 1930–32 to strengthen cooperatives both organizationally and economically but built relations between town and country as if the communes were dominant in the countryside.

The collective farm as cooperative may be considered Janus-faced. One face (the communal farm) was turned toward the command economy, the other (the private farm) toward the market economy. The cooperative form of collective farming was indissolubly associated with commodity-money relations and the market. The market face of the collective-farm system mitigated the disproportions of the Soviet economy. It signaled to planners when and where they needed to take measures to avoid difficulties in selling their output or, on the contrary, in dealing with deficits.

The party leaders gave workers the right freely to select their place of work without any effort on their part—the result of a simple understanding of the organic shortcomings of militarizing the labor process. The experience of the onslaught ("storming"), when they had begun to unite workers into labor armies, proved wholly persuasive. The peasants, on the other hand, won their right to private garden plots after a fierce struggle. These two elements, foreign to a communist economy, are what made its sustained existence possible. The command economy always remained ineffective but gave the Kremlin the opportunity to make use of its natural mobilizing capacity. Its sustained existence can be explained by the fact that the USSR disposed of colossal human potential and almost inexhaustible natural resources.

But all this concerns the period that came after the end of the second communist onslaught and the famine of 1932–33 associated with it. We need to understand why the onslaught was stopped halfway; why Stalin, like Lenin before him in 1921, was forced to abandon his efforts to incorporate peasant agriculture completely into the command economy.

We must always study what has actually happened, and the history of Soviet collectivization is no exception. But the communist revolution had nothing to do with a historical process subject to objective laws. The history of collectivization must be studied with an eye to the initial designs in the leaders' minds. That is to say, students of the Soviet period should also take note of what did not come into being.

In order to appease the peasants, Stalin asserted in "Dizziness with Success" that the cooperative was indeed the "basic link of the collective-farm movement." A few months later, in June, he repeated this assertion in the report of the Central Committee of the AUCP(B) to the Sixteenth Party Congress but added "at this moment."[2] It was his opinion that everything could change in an instant. The general secretary's position was reflected in the congress resolution "On the Collective-Farm Movement and the Promotion of Agriculture," which emphasized that at the *given stage* the basic form of the collective farm was the cooperative but allowed that

---

2   I. Stalin, "Politicheskii otchet Tsentral'nogo komiteta XVI s"ezdu VKP(b) 27 iiunia 1930 g.," *Sochineniia* (Moscow: Gosudarstvennoe izdatel'stvo politicheskoi literatury, 1949), 12: 286.

the "collective-farm movement could be raised to a higher form—the *commune*."³ This allowance was grounded in the proposition that the cooperative could not exist in a society lacking commodity-money relations. At the time, not a single member of the Bolshevik leadership or Soviet economist could imagine that the link between the peasant cooperative and the market could work in reverse: the market would remain as long as the cooperative existed. In 1931, the twenty-eight-year-old economist Nikolai Voznesensky published a book proposing the development of a theory of labor units (*trody*) "in preparation for the time when *chervintsi* [banknotes] will be replaced by workdays." Voznesensky considered direct socialist accounting and auditing in *trody* an urgent matter.⁴

This general conviction is worth illustrating with Stalin's statement on the NEP, which was part of the Central Committee's political report to the Sixteenth Party Congress. The stenographic record gives the statement as follows: "Going over to the offensive along the whole front, we are not yet abolishing the NEP, for private trade and capitalist elements still remain; trade and the money economy still remain."⁵ Historians have not paid attention to the specific wording of this statement. But Stalin himself took note when he was preparing his *Works* for publication in 1949 and edited the statement thus: "We are not yet abolishing the NEP, for private trade and capitalist elements still remain; 'free' trade still remains."⁶ The changes he made were required to disguise the position he had taken on trade and the money economy in the early 1930s. In editing the text, he deleted the mention of the money economy and modified the term "trade" with the ironic adjective "free" (in quotation marks), meaning trade that is not controlled by the state and operates according to the law of supply and demand.

A former seminarian, Stalin sometimes borrowed expressions from the Bible. His most often repeated expression was "the first commandment." It was addressed to the peasantry and meant that the collective farm had to settle up with the state before it could divide the remaining product among the workers.

Everything looked fine on paper. The explanation for the implementation of the Model Statute of Agricultural Cooperatives offered by People's Commissar of Agriculture of the USSR Yakov Yakovlev and the head of the USSR Collective Farm Center (*Kolkhoztsentr*), Tikhon Yurkin, established grain quotas (in the form of sales at drastically low prices) to be delivered to state procurement organs. In grain-growing regions, including Ukraine, a quarter to a third of the gross yield was to be delivered, based on calculations for an average harvest; in grain-consuming regions, the quota did not exceed one-eighth of the yield. "The rest of the gross yield," according to the explanation, "remains at the complete disposal of the collective farms."⁷

---

3   *Kommunisticheskaia partiia Sovetskogo Soiuza v rezoliutsiiakh i resheniiakh s"ezdov, konferentsii i plenumov TsK* (Moscow: Izdatel'stvo politicheskoi literatury, 1970), 4: 450.

4   Nikolai A. Voznesenskii, *Khozraschet i planirovanie na sovremennom étape* (Detskoe selo, 1931), 12, 16.

5   *XVI s"ezd VKP(b). Stenograficheskii otchet* (Moscow and Leningrad: Gosizdat, 1930), 37.

6   I. Stalin, "Politicheskii otchet Tsentral'nogo komiteta XVI s"ezdu VKP(b) 27 iiunia 1930 g.," *Sochineniia* (Moscow: Gosudarstvennoe izdatel'stvo politicheskoi literatury, 1949), 12: 307. Cf. https://www.marxists.org/reference/archive/stalin/works/1930/aug/27.htm.

7   *Tragediia sovetskoi derevni*, 2: 383–84.

Chapter 4. The Collective-Farm System under Stalin's Requisitions

Yakovlev and Yurkin's explanation was approved by the Politburo of the CC AUCP(B) on April 12, 1930.[8] The next day it appeared in print in the official *Sbornik zakonov SSSR* (Collection of Laws of the USSR)[9] and was published in all newspapers. Thus, after all the cataclysms of January–March 1930, the peasants approached the sowing campaign completely at ease. Some of them worked on collective farms and others on their private farms. After the general secretary's authoritative explanation that joining a collective farm was a voluntary matter, after his assurances that collective-farm workers would be allowed their private plots, after the state's commitment to limiting the "first commandment" to very specific amounts, the peasants worked at full capacity. Moreover, the climatic conditions of 1930 were conducive to a good harvest.

In June 1930, the Ukrainian Grain Center (*Ukrzernotsentr*) calculated the grain balance on the basis of the expected harvest (in millions of poods):[10]
- gross yield: 1,355;
- consumption by rural population (based on the calculation of 16 poods per person and a population of 23.5 million): 376;
- sowing, feed, and insurance funds altogether: 515;
- reserve fund: 35;
- grain-procurement plan: between 425 and 430.

Ukraine's grain-procurement plan was established at 440 million poods but increased to 490 million in September. In October, the CC CP(B)U won a reduction of the plan to 472 million poods, but grain procurement proceeded with great difficulties. On January 27, 1931, the Politburo of the CC AUCP(B) stated that Ukraine was 34 million poods in debt. Stalin reduced that debt to 25 million and ordered the CC CP(B)U to declare February a month of shock procurement in order to fulfill the quota completely. They were still wringing the previous year's debt out of the peasants when the spring sowing began. In early May 1931 the new head of the Soviet government, Viacheslav Molotov, summoned Stanislav Kosior to Moscow and informed him that the plan for the harvest of 1930 would be reset to the previous quota of 490 million poods.[11] This was a typical "spurring" tactic of Stalin's: when the quota seemed impossibly large, it was increased in order to mobilize the peasants to fulfill the previous, less arduous one.

By the end of May 1931, the state had requisitioned 477 million poods of grain from Ukraine's harvest of 1930. On average, 4.7 quintals (470 kg) of grain were obtained from every hectare of arable land—a record output yardstick for all pre- and post-revolutionary years.[12]

In 1931, the Ukrainian Collective-Farm Center (*Ukrkolhosptsentr*) projected the harvest at 845 million poods, or 510 million poods less than that of the previous

---

8 Ibid.
9 *Sbornik zakonov SSSR* (Moscow), 1930, no. 24: 256.
10 Ivan I. Slyn'ko, *Sotsialistychna perebudova i tekhnichna rekonstruktsiia sil's'koho hospodarstva Ukraïny* (Kyiv: AN URSR, 1961), 281–82.
11 Stanislav V. Kul'chyts'kyi, "Sutsil'na kolektyvizatsiia ukraïns'koho sela" in *Holod 1932–1933 rokiv v Ukraïni: prychyny ta naslidky*, 394–95.
12 Slyn'ko, *Sotsialistychna perebudova i tekhnichna rekonstruktsiia*, 282, 285.

year. Nevertheless, the grain-procurement plan was set at 510 million poods.[13] The requisitioners were exercising primitive logic: they did it the first time we pressed them; they'll do it again. At the Sixteenth Congress of the Communist Party, Stalin asserted that the country was successfully solving its grain problem thanks to the establishment of the collective-farm system.[14]

What were the relations between the state and the peasantry, between town and country during the years of Stalin's onslaught? Under the NEP, the state bought grain. Whenever the procurement prices set by the state became disadvantageous to the peasants because of inflation, they stopped taking grain to market, and grain-procurement crises flared up across the country. Stalin planned to do away with these crises by imposing state farms (Russ. *sovkhoz*, Ukr. *radhosp*) and nationalized ones (collective farms: Russ. *kolkhoz*, Ukr. *kolhosp*) in order to promote large-scale production in the countryside. In January 1928 he announced to party workers in Siberia: "All areas of our country, without exception, must be covered with collective farms (and state farms) capable of replacing not only the kulaks but also the individual peasants as suppliers of grain to the state."[15]

Three and a half years went by, and the state had fundamentally changed the social face of the countryside. Now peasants were forced not to sell but to give up their grain, and in unspecified quantities at that. Now, as the state had shown in requisitioning the harvest of 1930, it could appropriate for itself as much of the collective-farm output as it found necessary. The grain quotas were becoming an increasingly technical matter: grain was taken directly from the collective-farm fields on trucks of the Machine and Tractor Stations (MTS) to the elevators.

Yet the architects of the collective-farm system had not taken the human factor into account. If the government was appropriating all the grain grown in the public sector for itself, then the collective farmers had no reason to work to their full potential in the fields. It was as if the state were pushing the peasants to devote the utmost attention to their private plots. That was the only way they could guarantee food for themselves.

The agricultural campaign of 1931 took place under the specter of the exhausting grain quotas of the 1930 harvest. A report prepared for party leaders on June 5, 1931 by the secret political division of the OGPU, titled "On Preparations to Procure the Grain Harvest," clearly shows how the collective farmers were doing their jobs. The Chekists warned about the possibility of a failed campaign and the threat of losing a significant portion of the harvest. According to a section on the readiness of the MTS to reap the harvest, "A behind-the-scenes inspection of the state of harvesting equipment on the collective farms of Ukraine has established that owing to careless maintenance, the available vehicles and equipment have mostly become unusable or require major repairs." As for the preparation of storage facilities for the harvest,

---

13 Iurii Babko and Mykola Bortnychuk, *Tretia Vseukraïns'ka konferentsiia KP(b)U* (Kyiv: Politvydav Ukraïny, 1968), 81.

14 I. Stalin, "Politicheskii otchet Tsentral'nogo komiteta XVI s"ezdu VKP(b) 27 iiunia 1930 g.," *Sochineniia* (Moscow: Gosudarstvennoe izdatel'stvo politicheskoi literatury, 1949), 12: 290.

15 I. Stalin, "O khlebozagotovkakh i perspektivakh razvitiia sel'skogo khoziaistva. Iz vystuplenii v raznykh raionakh Sibiri v ianvare 1928 g. (Kratkaia zapis')," *Sochineniia* (Moscow: Gosudarstvennoe izdatel'stvo politicheskoi literatury, 1949), 11: 7. Cf. https://www.marxists.org/reference/archive/stalin/works/1928/01/x01.htm.

Chapter 4. The Collective-Farm System under Stalin's Requisitions

the report stated that in many districts of Ukraine collective and state farms had not yet begun preparing storehouses. The facts noted in all sections of the report indeed supported its initial conclusion about the possible failure of the harvest campaign. Ukraine was no exception; the situation was critical in all regions.[16]

The procurement of the 1931 harvest dragged on, just as in the previous year. On December 23, 1931, the Politburo of the CC AUCP(B) examined the state of grain procurements in the presence of Hryhorii Petrovsky and Volodymyr Zatonsky, establishing that at the beginning of December Ukraine had fulfilled 74 percent of its plan. A resolution was adopted to send Molotov to Kharkiv "to assist the CC CP(B)U in improving its grain procurements."[17]

Volodymyr Zatonsky (1888–1938). People's Commissar of the Workers' and Peasants' Inspectorate of the Ukrainian SSR and head of the Central Control Commission of the CP(B)U, March 1927–February 1933.

Molotov went to Kharkiv and stayed there until early 1932, taking charge of operations on the "grain front." In essence, he led an extraordinary grain-procurement commission comprised of members and candidates for membership in the Politburo of the CC CP(B)U as well as leaders of republican agencies. Here, for the first time, and in Ukraine particularly, the Kremlin used the method of "direct" management of grain procurements. Ten months later, such "extraordinary" commissions headed by figures from the Kremlin would again be sent to the Ukrainian SSR, the North Caucasus, and the Volga region, with tragic consequences for the peasantry.

Considering that Ukraine had become the proving ground for trying out extraordinary methods of grain procurement, Molotov's visit to Kharkiv in December 1931–January 1932 requires more detailed consideration. The archives contain no documents with his signature regulating methods of confiscating grain. Yet there are reports about the activities of local leaders who, on his instructions, turned January 1932 into a "shock" month of grain procurement. Let us examine a telegram from the secretary of the Zinovievsk (renamed Kirovohrad, 1934–2016; present-day Kropyvnytskyi) city CP(B)U committee, Dmytro Mykheienko, delivered to Molotov in Kharkiv on January 1, 1932. Mykheienko reported that the measures planned for the "shock" month were "based on the resolution of the CC CP(B)U of December 29 and directives of Comrade Molotov, delivered at a meeting of district activists."[18] This CC CP(B)U resolution, adopted at a meeting of the Politburo of the Central Committee in the presence of Molotov, details the organization of grain-procurement work, the task of exacting grain over a ten-day period (for the first ten) and five-day periods (for the next

---

16   *Tragediia sovetskoi derevni*, vol. 3 *(konets 1930–1933)* (Moscow: ROSSPĖN, 2001), 137–40.
17   Ibid., 3: 217, 218.
18   Ibid., 3: 239.

twenty). The methods by which the grain would be confiscated were not specified in the resolution. What Mykheienko was talking about in his telegram was obviously part of the oral instructions given by the head of the Council of People's Commissars of the USSR (Sovnarkom), Viacheslav Molotov.

In particular, the telegram indicates that no later than January 1, every village soviet within the Zinovievsk CP(B)U committee's jurisdiction would receive a one-time cereal task for its five-day periods based on the assignments established by the CC CP(B)U, and every authorized member of the city party committee would have three hours following receipt of the message to apportion the indicated quantity of grain among its collective farms. All authorized persons were to remain in the villages until the complete fulfillment of the annual quota. Collective farms that did not fulfill their plan within three days would have their seed stocks confiscated. The authorities of the city party committee (*mis'kpartkom*) and the secretaries of the party cells were to take charge of the task of mobilizing the "grain squandered and stolen from the collective farms, considering that this is required both to fulfill the annual grain-procurement plan and to secure seed-stock material for spring sowing."[19]

The language of this telegram, which ultimately came from Molotov and was characteristic of the whole requisition period of 1930–32, is telling. Any reserves of grain found on peasant farmsteads were considered "squandered" or "stolen" for the simple reason that grain was not paid out for workdays until the grain-procurement plan was fulfilled, but there was never any chance of fulfilling the plan, as it was flexible. This "squandered" grain was that which collective farmers received through illegitimate administrative decisions, while the "stolen" grain was that which they took of their own initiative—collective farmers from the cooperative and individual farmers from their own farms. Such terminology strikingly reflected the twisted logic of Stalin and his team, who believed that all grain produced on either a collective farm or a private one belonged to the state and the state alone. When peasants attempted to consume their own production, they were declared thieves.

Such a conclusion appears paradoxical, given the Soviet government's well-known efforts to reinforce the collective farms both organizationally and economically. In January 1931, for example, there was an All-Union Conference on Organizing Work on the Collective Farms that paid considerable attention to the proper standardization of agricultural labor and developed a system of piecework valuation in fractions of workdays for every unit of labor. In March 1931, the Sixth All-Union Congress of Soviets passed a resolution "On the Development of Collective Farms" in which the workday was declared the only qualitative and quantitative measure of the results of labor in the public sector. The congress obligated heads of collective farms to ensure the universal implementation of piecework. It was emphasized in the resolution that the distribution of products was to be carried out according to the principle "whoever works better and harder gets more, and whoever does not work gets nothing."[20]

An orderly and effective payment system for work on the collective farms took shape on paper, but all those resolutions and decisions stood in sharp contradiction

---

19 Ibid., 3: 240.

20 *Ocherki istorii kollektivizatsii sel'skogo khoziaistva v soiuznykh respublikakh: sbornik statei*, ed. Viktor P. Danilov (Moscow: Gospolitizdat, 1963), 196.

to the so-called "technological" resolutions of the CC AUCP(B). In analyzing the resolutions on organizing the sowing and reaping campaigns with reference to supervision of the sowing, again and again we note a sensationally important detail: *the Central Committee of the AUCP(B) made no distinction between collective and state farms.* The produce of the collective farms was considered no less the property of the state than that of the state farms. Yet there was a basic distinction between workers on the state farms and those on collective farms (although they were the selfsame peasants): the former received a salary, while the latter did not. This would indicate that, as the Kremlin saw it, the produce that the peasants obtained from the private plots "given" to them in March 1930 was sufficient material compensation for their work in the public sector. The lack of a distinction between collective and state farms meant that the "collective-cooperative" form of ownership was tacitly transformed into state ownership. Yet the state paid the collective-farm workers no wages.

What did the collective farmers think of this? Their reaction can be judged from the many letters addressed to Hryhorii Petrovsky. For example, members of the Nezamozhnyk Cooperative in the village of Tyshkivka (Haisyn district, Uman region) recounted in a letter of November 25, 1931 that rather than grain—of which there was none, since the state had taken it all—the district official had ordered the confiscation of potatoes, leaving no more than two poods per family. "He declared," complained the collective farmers, "that if you gave every peasant five poods of potatoes and five of grain, he would wrap himself up like a spider and say nothing to anyone." But the peasants assured the head of the VUTsVK that they reserved the right to find a solution so as not to die of hunger. They concluded as follows: "Better that the one making working people die of hunger die himself."[21]

On the collective farms, the destructive effect of the Bolshevik division of the peasantry into poor peasants, middle peasants, and kulaks began to disappear. The peasantry again began behaving, according to the definition of Teodor Shanin, a discerning expert on peasant psychology, "as a social entity with a community of economic interests, its identity shaped by conflict with other classes and expressed in typical patterns of cognition and political consciousness, however rudimentary, which made it capable of collective action reflecting its interests."[22] Forced to work in the fields to raise crops destined for the state, collective farmers were so careless that grain losses increased to fantastic proportions. Refusing to work conscientiously in the fields, they focused their efforts on their individual plots, which were supposed to save them from hunger in the winter months.

During the "shock-work month" of January 1932, Molotov wrested all existing grain from the Ukrainian SSR with no concern for the morrow. In ruining the economy of the collective farm, Stalin's requisitions simultaneously plunged the whole economy into a state of crisis. The carefully worded CC CP(B)U resolution of March 28, 1932, "On the Results of the Work of Collective Farms in 1931 and the Further Tasks of Reinforcing Them Organizationally and Economically," stated the following: "In connection with the grain quotas, excesses took place with regard to

---

21 *Kolektyvizatsiia i holod na Ukraïni, 1929–1933: Zbirnyk dokumentiv i materialiv,* comp. Hanna M. Mykhailychenko and Ievheniia P. Shatalina; ed. Stanislav Kul'chyts'kyi (Kyiv: Naukova dumka, 1992), 366.

22 "Part IV: Peasantry as a Class" in *Peasants and Peasant Societies: Selected Readings,* 2d ed., ed. Teodor Shanin (Oxford: Basil Blackwell, 1987), 329.

the hardest-working farms in a number of districts, so that they actually covered up the effects of mismanagement in poorly organized cooperatives."[23] Obviously, this was not about "a number of districts." When the grain requisitioners "swept clean," they confiscated the produce of all districts and collective farms, whether they were working well or badly. From time to time, the local authorities had to increase quotas for collective farms that still retained any surplus grain at all. The CC CP(B)U operated similarly when it came to the districts. During the procurements of the 1930 harvest, the CC CP(B)U twice changed the quotas in 61 districts and once in 91 of them.[24]

The administrative chaos created by administrative-territorial reform, specifically the dissolution of provinces (*okruhy*) in September 1930, substantially affected the grain-procurement campaigns. The republican agencies found themselves with 503 administrative units under their direct administration—the Moldavian ASSR, 18 centrally run cities, and 484 rural districts.[25] Running so many subjects from one center turned out to be practically impossible, and oblasts (provinces) were created in February 1932. At the February 1933 plenum of the CC CP(B)U, Hryhorii Petrovsky announced: "For weeks or even entire months, we were unable to find out about elementary matters at the district level that should have been reported to the Central Committee or some other government agency. Our organized oblasts are not working efficiently by any means. Last year, on a trip around Donetsk oblast, I saw how the oblast organizations had not yet encompassed the districts on the management level. They had not taken care of the matter in such a way as to make the villages feel the leading role of the party."[26]

A report by USSR People's Deputy Commissar of Agriculture Andrii Hrynevych spells out the concrete effects of Molotov's directives on grain procurement that Mykheienko mentioned in his telegram. In April 1932, Hrynevych observed the progress of sowing in the Zinovievsk district. In his report he informed Yakov Yakovlev that the district was 98 percent collectivized but that 28,300 peasants had abandoned it since January 1, including all the qualified tractor drivers (in all, there had been about 100,000 people in the district). Most of those who remained were starving. The collective farms had run out of grain back in March, and there were already cases of hunger-induced swelling. The number of horses was down by half from the previous year, and the remaining ones were totally exhausted and unsuited for work.[27]

Hrynevych did not mention the people's suffering from hunger: he was only interested in economic indicators. But it emerged from his detailed report that the state's winter 1931–32 confiscation of all grain grown in the district had long-lasting economic consequences that were extremely adverse to the state itself. The Kremlin's economic policy, which undermined the productive forces of the countryside, was obviously shortsighted.

---

23   *Partaktyvist* (Kharkiv), 1932, no. 9: 2.
24   Kul'chyts'kyi, *Tsina "velykoho perelomu,"* 230–31.
25   "Postanova TsVK i RNK SRSR 'Pro likvidatsiiu okruh' vid 23 lypnia 1930 r.," *Visti VUTsVK* (Kharkiv), August 5, 1930.
26   *Holod 1932–1933 rokiv v Ukraïni: prychyny ta naslidky,* 389.
27   *Tragediia sovetskoi derevni,* 3: 363–65.

The collective farmers who were forced to starve also recognized this shortsightedness. During the days when Hrynevych was observing the Zinovievsk district, the collective farmer Davydenko from the Znamianka district remarked in a letter addressed to Stalin: "You could have said there was a poor crop or a drought, but there wasn't—the harvest was good, and as they took it away they said that the Soviet authorities wouldn't let the collective farmers perish.... In connection with which there is no grain, or perhaps the grain was sent to arid districts, or perhaps for the workers of our Union, or to build up reserves for war, or perhaps it was sent abroad in exchange for tractors, and now they sit hungry with those tractors."[28] There was only one difference between the remarks of the Ukrainian collective farmer and the deputy commissar: the former was thinking about the people, the latter about production.

There was still no all-Union famine during the first half of 1932. At that time, famine had only begun in two regions—Kazakhstan and the Ukrainian SSR. It was indirect in Kazakhstan, while in the Ukrainian SSR it was the direct result of grain procurements. These indisputable assertions lead us to pose two fundamental questions. First, why did the quotas on the harvest of 1931 directly cause famine only in the Ukrainian SSR? Second, how was it that these grain procurements led to famine when they were smaller than those of 1930?

Characterizing the scope of the grain-procurement plans in their detailed year-by-year descriptions, Robert W. Davies and Stephen G. Wheatcroft limit themselves to remarking that the extraordinarily high all-Union procurements were allocated among the republics, provinces, and districts with particular assignments for state farms, collective farms, and individual farmers.[29] The regional requisitions were an act of voluntarism, and here the two authors had to do without assumptions of their own. Yet the breakdown of regional grain quotas, which is reproduced in their book without comment, gives food for thought. Why indeed did Ukraine give the state 7,675,000 metric tons of grain when the Central Black Earth province, the Middle Volga, Lower Volga, and the North Caucasus Krai (region), taken together, gave 7,356,000 metric tons? Never—not in the years of the NEP, nor before the revolution—had Ukraine produced as much grain as those four other regions of commercial agriculture in the European part of the country put together. Not until the end of May 1931 did the republic manage to fulfill the grain quota set for the harvest of 1930. From its harvest of 1931, Ukraine gave the state 7,253,000 metric tons of grain—not significantly less than in the previous year (the other four regions of commercial agriculture taken together supplied 8,336,000 metric tons).[30] Grain procurement continued until the late spring of 1932, when many districts were left with no reserves of produce or fodder at all. The effect of this was not limited to the further erosion of agricultural productivity. In the first half of 1932, a famine began to ravage Ukraine.

Can we guess why the communal state so forcefully imposed requisitions specifically in Ukraine? It is perhaps necessary to take a closer look at the

---

28 *Holod 1932–1933 rokiv na Ukraïni: ochyma istorykiv, movoiu dokumentiv*, 153.
29 Robert W. Davies and Stephen G. Wheatcroft, *The Years of Hunger: Soviet Agriculture, 1931–1933* (New York: Palgrave Macmillan, 2004), 79–80.
30 Ibid., 470.

aforementioned regional statistics on peasant disturbances in 1930. As is well known, in March 1930 Stalin halted total collectivization for six months. He described the situation in the spring of 1930 across the country in the confidential letter of April 2, 1930 to lower party organizations, the contents of which have already been presented. But let us now look at the regional statistics on peasant disturbances in four regions of commercial agriculture (excluding the Middle Volga):[31]

Regions	March 1930	All of 1930
Ukrainian SSR	2,945	4,098
Central Black Earth province	737	1,373
North Caucasus	335	1,061
Lower Volga	203	1,003

These data speak for themselves. Situated on the European border with Western Ukraine, which was then part of Poland, the national republic with the greatest human and economic potential in the USSR particularly unnerved the party leadership. It is not hard to imagine how those in the Kremlin felt when they read OGPU summaries citing the proclamations of Ukrainian insurgents with their calls for achieving independence and restoring the Ukrainian People's Republic. Many of these facts are presented in the book *Holod 1932–1933 rokiv v Ukraïni: prychyny ta naslidky* (The Famine of 1932–33 in Ukraine: Causes and Effects).[32]

Although there could have been no written evidence of the relation between unattainable grain quotas and peasant disturbances, it is hard to deny the correlation between them. The Kremlin used the grain quotas as an instrument to punish the rebellious Ukrainian peasants. Only in Ukraine did Stalin go so far in the confiscation of grain as to deploy an extraordinary commission that reported directly to the head of the Soviet government.

When the famine started, the peasants bolted for other regions. On June 18, 1932, Stalin, who was vacationing at a resort, wrote to Kaganovich in frustration: "several tens of thousands of Ukrainian collective farmers are still traveling around the entire European part of the USSR and demoralizing our collective farms with their complaints and whining."[33] As of mid-July, noted a report from the secret political department of the OGPU, up to half the population of certain rural districts of Ukraine had left in search of food. According to the Chekists' data, 116,000 refugees had left 21 districts.[34] If we use this figure to calculate the number of refugees for all 484 rural districts of Ukraine, the total is almost 3 million. Not exactly tens of thousands...

---

31   Viola, *Peasant Rebels under Stalin*, 138–39.
32   Hrynevych, "Vyiavlennia natsional'noï identychnosti," 421–25.
33   *Stalin i Kaganovich: Perepiska 1931–1936 gg.*, comp. Oleg V. Khlevniuk (Moscow: ROSSPĖN, 2001), 179. Cf. "Letter from Stalin to Kaganovich and Molotov on organizing the 1932 grain-procurement campaign" in *The Holodomor Reader*, 233.
34   *Tragediia sovetskoi derevni*, 3: 420.

Chapter 4. The Collective-Farm System under Stalin's Requisitions

Lazar Kaganovich (1893–1991). Secretary of the Central Committee of the AUCP(B), 1928–39. In October 1932 he headed an extraordinary grain-procurement commission of the Central Committee of the AUCP(B), which, under the pretext of grain procurement, confiscated all food supplies from the peasants of the North Caucasus, especially the Kuban region, thereby condemning them to death from starvation.

This same report stated that refugees from Ukraine had settled in large numbers in other regions. The Chekists emphasized that "They have demoralized the local collective farmers with their talk: 'We ate our horses and dogs: you will have to endure the same. We had a pretty good harvest but collectivized earlier than you, and they took us in hand.'"[35]

The leaders of the CP(B)U mindlessly carried out all that the Kremlin demanded. Forced to react to a phenomenon comparable in scale to the famine of 1921, only caused not by a drought or economic collapse but by the state's economic policy, these people were at a loss. Their first reaction was to play down the scale of the famine and foist responsibility for it onto individuals in the lower administrative apparatus who were taking a "leftist course." On April 26, 1932, Stanislav Kosior wrote to Stalin: "Here we have isolated incidents and even isolated villages that are starving, but this is only the result of local bungling and deviations, especially with regard to the collective farms. All talk of 'famine' in Ukraine should be categorically disregarded."[36]

All Ukraine was starving. But when it came time to distribute food aid, urgently needed to save people from death, the Central Committee of the CP(B)U identified only 33 districts in need of assistance. In turn, the CC apparatus reduced the number of districts with mass mortality that were in need of special attention to eleven. These were Buky, Tetiiv, Bohuslav, and Rokytne in Kyiv province; Uman, Plyskiv, Babanka, and Orativ in Vinnytsia province; Dolyna and Nova Praha in Dnipropetrovsk province; and Hlobyne in Kharkiv province.[37]

The man-made famine shattered the world view of the younger generation brought up in Soviet schools. In a letter of June 18, 1932 addressed to Stanislav Kosior, the twenty-year-old student and member of the Young Communist League H. Tkachenko wrote: "You cannot imagine what is going on in the Bila Tserkva, Uman, Kyiv and other regions right now. There are large expanses of unsown land, and the yield of what is planted will be no more than 25–30 percent of what it was in 1925–28. The collective farms that had 100–150 horses now have 40–50, and they're too weak even to stand up. People are starving something terrible. I simply can't understand it, and if someone in authority had told me in 1927–28 that

---

35 Ibid., 3: 427.
36 *Holod 1932–1933 rokiv na Ukraïni: ochyma istorykiv, movoiu dokumentiv*, 148.
37 *Komandyry Velykoho holodu: Poïzdky V. Molotova i L. Kahanovycha v Ukraïnu ta na Pivnichnyi Kavkaz, 1932–1934 rr.*, ed. Valerii Vasyl'iev and Iurii Shapoval (Kyiv: Heneza, 2000), 226–27.

under Soviet rule people would die of hunger at work, I wouldn't have believed it and would have mocked or even sent him packing, considering him to be an idiot, counterrevolutionary, and what have you."[38]

In the ever-growing literature on the Soviet famine of 1932–33, more often than not only a regional picture is offered: authors focus on the study of their own regions. The lack of a comparative analysis prevents us from making the necessary generalizations. And the literature on the famine in Ukraine lacks the chronological element: the famine of the first half of 1932 merges with that of the second half of the year, and the latter runs into the famine of the first half of 1933. True, people in Ukraine were dying of a man-made famine caused by the authorities throughout both those years, but scholars need to find the line that divides death by hunger from murder by starvation. In the former case, starvation was an unexpected, and even unwanted, side effect of the authorities' actions. As much as possible, they took measures to save the starving. In the latter case, having already crossed that line, they deliberately organized the famine with the aim of killing a certain number of people. Unlike the very precise target figures for executing "enemies of Soviet rule," the number of people subjected to murder by starvation was not fixed but rather regulated by measures to save the starving. Moreover, in this case, efforts to save the starving served as persuasive evidence of the authorities' innocence of murder by starvation—an utterly repulsive and therefore camouflaged way of combating "enemies of Soviet rule."

It is worth repeating that the famine of the first half of 1932 in Ukraine was clearly unexpected and unwanted by the authorities. On March 18, the Politburo of the CC CP(B)U gave 1,000 poods of grain to feed the collective farmers of the Zinovievsk district and 1,000 metric tons of corn to the Moldavian ASSR. The scope of this aid was paltry, and Kosior's insistence that the republic's leaders did not have their own stores of provisions were not at odds with the truth. The resolution on Zinovievsk included this phrase: "Suggest that the provincial committee dispatch special comrades to organize this aid without widely publicizing it."[39] Deprived of real power by all-Union agencies, the Ukrainian leaders feared that other starving districts would take advantage of the precedent and importune them for help.

All-Union agencies first agreed to provide assistance to the starving only on April 19. At that time, 3,000 metric tons of millet were distributed from reserves held on the territory of Ukraine.[40] It turned out, however, that the all-Union agencies did not have significant reserves either, and Stalin had no desire to expend an untouchable reserve fund on current needs, even if that need was saving peasants from death by hunger. Accordingly, in late April and early May 1932, the USSR People's Commissariat of Foreign Trade was ordered to turn 15,000 metric tons of corn and 2,000 metric tons of wheat back from the ports. The corn and wheat removed from export were given to Ukraine. At the same time, 9.5 million poods of grain were purchased from China, Persia, and Canada to meet the needs of the Procurement Committee. That made it possible to stop exporting grain from Ukraine to the Transcaucasus and give 4 million poods of grain from the Central Black Earth province to the

---

38   *Holod 1932–1933 rokiv na Ukraïni: ochyma istorykiv, movoiu dokumentiv*, 184.
39   Ibid., 134.
40   Ibid., 146.

Ukrainian SSR.[41] In late May, on orders from the Politburo of the CC AUCP(B), trusts and associations of all-Union agencies (located mainly on the territory of Ukraine) contributed to the provision of food aid, after which the starving began to receive dried fish, salt sprats, and other provisions.

On May 15, Stalin addressed Kaganovich: "In my opinion, Ukraine has been given more than it needs. There is no need to provide any more grain, and there is nowhere to get it from."[42] On June 23, the Politburo of the CC AUCP(B) decided to end the transport of grain to Ukraine.[43] The new crop was ripening, and the Kremlin began preparing for its next procurement campaign.

The beginning of 1932 brought the "third collective-farm spring," as Soviet propagandists put it—time to start thinking of the new sowing campaign. In Ukraine, which was the first part of the European USSR to begin starving, few people were concerned about sowing. More precisely, their concerns were directed toward continuing the procurement campaign that was ruining the productive forces of the countryside.

On March 6, after coming to an agreement with the CC AUCP(B), the CC CP(B)U announced the end of the grain procurement. All the efforts of party organizations were focused on gathering seed for the sowing. Tens of thousands of requisitioners mobilized in the towns returned to their established workplaces.[44] They were no longer needed because they had already turned over all available grain stocks—for sowing, provisions, and fodder—to the state as part of the grain procurement.

1932 was the fourth year of the first five-year plan and the third year of the communist onslaught. Having abandoned "storming" methods in early 1933 with regard to a country besieged by hunger, Stalin found his own term for such methods—"spurring." The essence of "spurring" in the city amounted to setting an impossibly quick tempo of industrialization, with punishment of those who lagged behind. In the countryside, this policy was carried out by confiscating the greatest possible quantity of grain, followed by returning a portion of what had been confiscated in order to provide seed for the sowing campaign and reduce mortality from starvation. The policy was horrendous, in the spirit of the early Middle Ages, but the general secretary described it calmly and somewhat poetically: "The party spurred the country on, as it were, hastening its sprint forward." He used the country's industrial backwardness, which threatened it with "mortal danger" as a result of ostensibly inevitable intervention by neighboring states, to justify the necessity of "spurring."[45] Some historians make similar arguments even today.

The end result of Stalin's onslaught turned out to be the same as that of Lenin's. True, there was one difference. In the early 1920s, the peasantry was ready to unleash a second civil war. At that time, the countryside had sufficient reserves of weapons and millions of people who knew how to handle them, having just come back from a six-year war. By the start of the 1930s, the Chekists had wrested practically

---

41 *Tragediia sovetskoi derevni*, 3: 362–63, 365.
42 *Stalin i Kaganovich: Perepiska 1931–1936 gg.*, 169.
43 *Holod 1932–1933 rokiv na Ukraïni: ochyma istorykiv, movoiu dokumentiv*, 190.
44 Ibid., 123.
45 I. Stalin, "Itogi pervoi piatiletki: Doklad 7 ianvaria 1933 g. na ob"edinennom plenume TsK i TsKK VKP(b)," *Sochineniia* (Moscow: Gosudarstvennoe izdatel'stvo politicheskoi literatury, 1951), 13: 184.

all weapons from the rural localities, and in 1930–31 they deported the politically active peasants to concentration camps or resettled them in far-off places as kulaks and kulak henchmen. It seemed that the communal state was now in a position to do whatever it wanted with the peasants. But rural resistance did not come to an end; it only changed its form. Now it manifested itself in unwillingness to work in the communal economy of the collective farms or, from the authorities' point of view, sabotage.

Foreigners were struck by the scale of the sabotage. The head of the Polish general consulate in the Ukrainian SSR, Jan Karszo-Siedlewski, told his ministry of foreign affairs that on September 27, 1932 he had flown from Kharkiv to Odesa in order to get an idea of the actual state of agriculture in Ukraine. The six hours he spent in the air on a cloudless day convinced him that no more than one-sixth of the republic's arable land had been plowed and sown. Everywhere he saw only small numbers of people in the fields, even though the autumn agricultural season was reaching its end.[46] In June 1933 the Italian ambassador in Moscow, Bernardo Attolico, informed his government: "We must seek the main cause of the current famine in the peasants' loss of interest in working the land, which has ceased to be their property, and in the peasant resistance and disinclination to give the state the fruits of their labor."[47]

At the end of his life, Vladimir Lenin abandoned his plans to collectivize agriculture and suggested developing cooperatives in the countryside that would be connected to the market. Only a small number of party leaders, headed by Nikolai Bukharin, supported this revision of communist doctrine. The majority, united around Stalin, resumed the RCP(B) program of 1919 with "storming" methods. Nevertheless, after two years of "storming," the idea of correcting the chosen course, including its application to the peasantry, began to germinate even among the majority.

It may be assumed that such a correction already took place in the course of the Seventeenth Conference of the AUCP(B), which was held from January 30 to February 4, 1932. In their speeches at the conference, Aleksei Stetsky, head of Agitprop for the CC AUCP(B), and Boris Sheboldaev, secretary of the North Caucasus Krai party committee, referred to money and trade as "vestiges of the old society." Yet in the main address, delivered by the head of Gosplan, Valerian Kuibyshev—and, accordingly, in the conference resolution—the conviction was expressed that at the current stage of development direct barter could not be substituted for trade.[48]

The germination of the idea that collectivization would have to coexist for a time with market relations can be traced by the change in the Stalin government's approach to establishing collective livestock farms in 1931 and 1932. In 1931, the Kremlin assigned Ukrainian leaders the task of creating specialized livestock farms in the countryside. The June 1931 plenum of the CC CP(B)U gave the order to increase

---

46   *Hołodomor 1932–1933: Wielki Głód na Ukrainie w dokumentach polskiej dyplomacji i wywiadu*, comp. Jan Jacek Bruski (Warsaw: Polski Instytut Spraw Międzynarodowych, 2008), 126–27.

47   *Lysty z Kharkova: Holod v Ukraïni ta na Pivnichnomu Kavkazi v povidomlenniakh italiis'kykh dyplomativ. 1932–1933 roky,* comp. Andrea Hratsiozi [Graziosi] (Kharkiv: Folio, 2007), 168–69.

48   *XVII konferentsiia VKP(b): Stenograficheskii otchet* (Moscow: Partizdat, 1932), 180, 193, 211.

the herds to 251,000 head of cows on state farms and 150,000 on collective farms.[49] The lack of distinction between state and collective farms on the part of the leaders of the governing party is again striking. Dairy farms in the collective sector could be established only by collectivizing the peasants' cows. Perhaps it was still possible to hope (and, in the Kremlin, they hoped) that the collective farmers would grow grain for the state in exchange for permission to work their private plots. But what were they hoping for when they took the peasants' last cows?

Attempting to fulfill the task before them by the end of 1931, local leaders again began forcibly collectivizing large horned cattle, just as in early 1930. As a result, the situation in the countryside became explosive. Female collective farmers who had nothing to feed their children took the lead in protest actions. Stalin sensed that he needed to back off again. On March 26, 1932, with a resolution "On the Forced Collectivization of Cattle," the CC AUCP(B) condemned the practice of collectivizing cows, scapegoating local functionaries for the nth time. The resolution proclaimed: "The party's task is to make sure that all collective farmers have their own cow, small livestock, and fowl. The further expansion and development of collective farms should proceed only by farms' raising young livestock or purchasing cattle."[50] The document required collective-farm administrations to assist collective farmers to purchase and raise young livestock for their personal needs. In other words, this resolution established the right of collective farms to sell the means of production (in this case, milch cows) to their own members and, in return, to buy cattle from them. With this, the state acknowledged that in public agriculture members of cooperatives were alienated from the means of production. Practically speaking, the right to buy and sell meant a) the state's recognition of the autonomous status of the collective-farm system within the command economy and b) recognition of the impossibility of collective-farm production existing in a nonmarket form. Yet this legal qualification of production relations as they really existed was not understood by the lawmakers. For Stalin, the episodic attempt to create collective livestock farms remained just a concrete fact of everyday life and nothing more. In February 1933 he recalled it with the following words: "Of course, not so long ago, the Soviet government had a slight misunderstanding with female collective farmers. That was over cows. But now this business about cows has been settled, and the misunderstanding has disappeared."[51]

The May 6, 1932 resolution of the Sovnarkom and the CC AUCP(B) "On the Grain-Procurement Plan for the Harvest of 1932 and the Development of Collective-Farm Trade in Grain" should also be regarded as a theoretically unsubstantiated concession to the peasantry made under the influence of concrete circumstances. The resolution promised, "after the fulfillment of this grain-procurement plan and the creation of seed stocks, that is, starting on January 15, 1933, to give collective farms and collective farmers the full opportunity to engage in the unhindered sale of leftover grain at their discretion at bazaars and markets, as well as in shops of their

---

49 *Komunistychna partiia Ukraïny v rezoliutsiiakh i rishenniakh z'ïzdiv, konferentsii i plenumiv TsK*, vol. 1 (Kyiv: Politvydav Ukraïny, 1976), 734–35.

50 *Tragediia sovetskoi derevni*, 3: 298.

51 I. Stalin, "Rech' na Pervom Vsesoiuznom s"ezde kolkhoznikov-udarnikov 19 fevralia 1933 g.," *Sochineniia* (Moscow: Gosudarstvennoe izdatel'stvo politicheskoi literatury, 1951), 13: 252. Cf. https://www.marxists.org/reference/archive/stalin/works/1933/02/19.htm.

own collective farms."⁵² On May 10, the Sovnarkom and the CC AUCP(B) adopted an identical resolution on meat titled "On the Plan for Livestock Procurement and on Trading in Meat by Collective Farmers and Independent Working Peasants." We see from the title that those participating in collective-farm trade could include private farmers. Just as the Bolsheviks renamed remaining unexpropriated private property "personal" property, so free trade according to supply-and-demand prices was renamed "collective-farm trade."⁵³

Neither resolution had any real significance, as these were normative documents whose implementation was postponed. The state was promising to lift the ban on free trade only in the future, in January 1933. The harvest of 1932 was ripening, and the state was promising that after the conscientious fulfillment of the "first commandment" it would allow agricultural producers to enter the free market.

Abandoning efforts to drive peasants into communes in 1930 and promising to introduce free trade in 1932 were tactical retreats. For the leaders of the AUCP(B), the strategic goal remained that of creating a nonmarket communist economy. To the end of his life, Stalin swore devotion to the communal-state model outlined in the RCP(B) program of 1919. In his last work, "Economic Problems of Socialism in the USSR" (September 1952), he wrote: "In order to raise collective-farm property to the level of public property, the surplus collective-farm output must be excluded from the system of commodity circulation and included in the system of product exchange between state industry and the collective farm."⁵⁴ And in 1932, immediately after the resolutions on collective-farm trade were issued, he began preparing the infamous Law of Spikelets.

An undated letter, written by Stalin at a resort between July 20 and 24, 1932 and sent to Kaganovich and Molotov at the Kremlin, provides a theoretical interpretation of this law. It explains the plan to integrate the established collective-farm system into the planned-command economy, which was in place from the winter of 1929–30 to the winter of 1932–33. Stalin's argument is worth presenting in the original with all his underlines of words (single underlines are given in italics, double in bold italics): "*Capitalism* would not have been able to destroy feudalism, would not have developed and gained strength if it had not declared the principle of *private* property the *foundation* of capit(alist) society, if it had not turned *private* property into *sacred property*, the violation of whose interests was most severely punished, and for the protection of which it created its own state. *Socialism* will not be able to finish off and bury capitalist and individualist, self-seeking habits, skills, and traditions (which form the basis of theft), which undermine the foundations of the new society, if it does not declare *public* (cooperative, collective-farm, state) ownership sacred and *inviolable*."⁵⁵

A few words about the particular situation that gave rise to these theoretical postulates are in order. It was a Ukrainian situation for the simple reason that in the first half of 1932, as noted above, famine caused by grain procurements took place

---

52 *Sbornik zakonov SSSR* (Moscow), 1932, no. 31: 190.

53 *Tragediia sovetskoi derevni*, 3: 910.

54 I. Stalin, *Ėkonomicheskie problemy sotsializma v SSSR* (Moscow: Gospolitizdat, 1952), 93. Cf. https://www.marxists.org/reference/archive/stalin/works/1951/economic-problems/ch14.htm.

55 *Stalin i Kaganovich: Perepiska 1931–1936 gg.*, 240–41.

only in Ukraine. In a letter of June 10, 1932 to Molotov and Stalin, the head of the Ukrainian government, Vlas Chubar, warned: "In order to make better provision for winter this year than last, widespread theft of grain will begin. What we see now—the digging up of planted potatoes, beetroots, onions, and so on—will be replicated on a much greater scale as the winter wheat matures, since food supplies from allotted resources will last no longer than July 1." The head of the VUTsVK, Hryhorii Petrovsky, echoed him in a letter written the same day: "Another reason we need to provide aid is that the peasants will gather unripened grain out of hunger, and much of it may be lost for nothing."[56] Both letters were sent to the Kremlin after the Ukrainian leaders had traveled to the "depths" of the countryside.

Stalin's one and only conclusion was that the harvest of 1932 had to be saved from thieves for the state by unbelievably harsh measures. He knew that a very strong stimulus—hunger—was causing the "theft." He did not doubt the truth of what Chubar and Petrovsky had written, but his awareness of the reality of the situation in Ukraine drove him to one conclusion only: the starving peasants had to be terrorized with incredibly cruel punishments. On August 7, 1932, the Central Executive Committee and Sovnarkom of the USSR adopted a resolution "On Safeguarding the Property of State Enterprises, Collective Farms, and Cooperatives and Strengthening Public (Socialist) Property." Expressed in the language of Bolshevik justice, "judicial repressions of the highest degree as measures of social protection" would be meted out for "theft" of collective-farm and cooperative property—execution and the confiscation of all property. If "mitigating circumstances" were present, execution would be commuted to no less than ten years' imprisonment.[57]

The newspaper *Pravda* published this resolution twice, on August 8 and 9. In conjunction with these publications, the editors of *Pravda* and local party and government agencies organized a huge raid in Ukraine as part of the struggle against grain theft, with the participation of 100,000 "shock workers of the press" from August 7 to 17.[58]

Returning to the analysis of the theoretical questions fundamental to Stalin's communist onslaught, it must be pointed out how it differed from Lenin's onslaught. Lenin's was directed, first and foremost, against capitalist property. Acting with the full support of the general population, Lenin expropriated large owners—landowners and the bourgeoisie—but failed in his attempt to collectivize agriculture. This forced him to undertake a radical revision of his views on socialism after he left the political arena. Stalin's onslaught, if we are to consider its agrarian and peasant aspect, had only one goal: to liquidate the peasant owner. Stalin was willing to pay any price in his efforts to cut off the many millions of peasants from the market. The point was not to bring about the "expropriation of the expropriators," for which Karl Marx and Friedrich Engels had called in their initial activity, but to change the social character of the peasantry through the use of force. If the peasants were to lose

---

56   *Komandyry Velykoho holodu*, 209, 214.

57   *Tragediia sovetskoi derevni*, 3: 453–54. Cf. "Resolution On Safekeeping Property of State Enterprises, Collective Farms, and Cooperatives and Strengthening Public (Socialist) Property'" in *The Holodomor Reader*, 239.

58   Kul'chyts'kyi, *Tsina "velykoho perelomu,"* 212.

their "individualist, self-seeking" habits, skills, and traditions, strong measures on the order of the Law of Spikelets were required.

What did communism mean to Stalin and his team? In arguing for the need to adopt the Law of Spikelets, the general secretary was concerned with protecting public property and uniting cooperative, collective-farm, and state property under this concept. He was perfectly right in equating state and collective-farm/cooperative forms of property. The true owner of all means of production was not society but a small group of people at the peak of the power structure who acted in the name of the state and society. The ultimate goal of the bureaucratic "revolution from above" was to overcome society's resistance and concentrate all its material and human resources in the hands of that small group.

The official slogan that defined Stalin's communist onslaught was "a full-scale socialist offensive on all fronts." In justifying the aggressive methods leading to the famine that everyone knew about (because they were starving!) but were forbidden to speak of, in 1933 Stalin invented an unofficial appellation for this historical period—"spurring." Such an appellation could be made public only in conjunction with the announcement that the historical period in question had ended, and that its tasks had been completed. A year earlier, however, Stalin did not yet know that he would be forced to abandon his "spurring" methods and, in particular, the principle of *prodrazvërstka* (requisitioning) in relations between town and country.

Meanwhile, all party leaders could still remember how Lenin had rescinded *prodrazvërstka*. As they saw the country slipping into the quagmire of crisis, they suggested following Lenin's example. In a note of January 1932 addressed to the Central Committee, the head of the Central Control Committee of the AUCP(B) and people's commissar of Rabkrin (Workers' and Peasants' Inspectorate), Jānis Rudzutaks, insisted that the collective farms be told of the grain quotas at the beginning of the agricultural year. Rudzutaks tried to persuade Stalin that the peasants would have every reason to work hard for a good harvest if they were certain that all produce above and beyond the "state task" would be theirs. Stanislav Kosior put forward the same idea in different form in a note to Stalin on March 15, 1932. The Ukrainian general secretary proposed the following: "In the name of all-Union organizations, announce the grain quotas for the upcoming harvest, on the principle that the greater the harvest the collective farms and collective farmers achieve, the greater will be the fund to be divided and distributed for personal consumption."[59]

The suggestions were rational, and Stalin cannot have failed to understand that. Nevertheless, he dismissed them for purely doctrinal reasons. What did the concept of "state task" mean in Rudzutaks's more clearly worded formulation? It was the equivalent of a tax that throughout the ages has been a fixed amount deducted from output or assets privately owned by the taxpayer. Stalin, however, regarded collective-farm property as a form of public property that he was entitled to manage at his own discretion.

The Kremlin knew that *prodrazvërstka* had a ruinous effect on production and outraged the peasants but expected to overcome their "individualist, self-seeking habits, skills, and traditions" by means of violence. Stalin believed that this method of economic relations with the peasantry had its drawbacks, but he wrote them off as

---

[59] Nikolai A. Ivnitskii, "Golod 1932–1933 godov: kto vinovat?" in *Sud'by rossiiskogo krest'ianstva*, 336.

the consequence of incompetent apportioning of identical grain quotas to districts and collective farms regardless of size or population—the principle of "equalization." "This *mechanical equalizing* approach to the matter," he wrote to Kaganovich at the Kremlin on June 18, 1932, "has resulted in glaring absurdities, so that a number of *fertile* districts in Ukraine, despite a fairly good harvest, have found themselves in a state of *impoverishment* and *famine*" (all italics Stalin's).[60]

Oleksandr Shlikhter (1868–1940). People's Commissar of Land Affairs of the Ukrainian SSR, 1927–29; director of the Ukrainian Institute of Marxism-Leninism, 1930–33.

In 1930 and even in 1931, the state managed to obtain the necessary quantity of grain from the countryside through requisitioning. As is evident from his letter to Kaganovich, Stalin was counting on using this method to confiscate the harvest of 1932. Were there objective grounds for such calculations?

All three years proved fruitful in the main grain-growing regions of the USSR. But the crops had to be grown, reaped, and transported. With every year, the collective farms and individual peasant farms treated the agricultural campaigns with increasing indifference because they knew that the state had a simple method of combating any sign of "equalizing" in the *prodrazvërstka*: it would assign additional quotas to those who had already fulfilled the plan.

The grain-procurement plan was apportioned to regions, districts, and villages based on the crop as it stood unharvested in the fields. But as early as 1931, crop losses in Ukraine were colossal. Stanislav Kosior estimated them at 120 to 150 million poods, Oleksandr Shlikhter at 150 million, and Mykola Skrypnyk at up to 200 million poods.[61] Even without claiming to be precise, these figures gave some idea of the scale of the loss—up to half the annual fund of provisions for the rural population. But the harvest losses of 1932 were much greater. How much greater, no one knows for sure: the Ukrainian leaders no longer ventured to give summary estimates. Only individual cases, of which there are many in the archives and the press, can illustrate this.

Mykola Skrypnyk (1872–1933). People's Commissar of Education of the Ukrainian SSR, 1927–33.

---

60 *Stalin i Kaganovich: Perepiska 1931–1936 gg.*, 179. Cf. "Letter from Stalin to Kaganovich and Molotov on organizing the 1932 grain-procurement campaign" in *The Holodomor Reader*, 233.

61 Stanislav V. Kul'chitskii, "Sozdanie sovetskogo stroia" in *Istoriia Ukrainy: Nauchno-populiarnye ocherki*, ed. Valerii Smolii (Moscow: OLMA-media-grupp, 2008), 643.

Here is what the newspaper *Visti VUTsVK* (VUTsVK News) had to say on July 27, 1932: "On the Kosior State Grain Farm in Mykolaiv, the fields harvested by combines are densely covered with grain. The threshing is good for nothing, and 50 percent of the harvest is lost with the chaff. Aware of all these facts, the state-farm troika[62] has taken no measures to prevent these enormous losses." On August 19, 1932, a correspondent for *Pravda* wrote from Odesa province: "The harvest is above average and greater than last year's. There was a particularly high yield of winter wheat. But the reaping is not yet finished. Ten percent is standing uncut in the fields, and the grain is falling off the stalks. Barely 25 percent of what was reaped has been shocked and threshed. Three-quarters of the harvest is lying in the open fields." A letter from the Nove Zhyttia collective farm in the Artemivsk district published by *Visti VUTsVK* on January 4, 1933 vividly depicts the situation at that enterprise, where seven heads of administration followed one another in a single year: "Complete disorder and chaos reigned in the course of the harvesting campaign and threshing. The brigades fell apart, whoever felt like it went into the fields, and the work was not organized. We did not have any plans. Work was delayed, grain fell of the stalks in the fields, and crops requiring larger growing areas were not gathered at all. There was a wave of theft; day and night they pilfered the grain belonging to the collective farm, taking it from the fields in plain sight of everyone. There was no inventory. To this day we do not know what kind of harvest we had."

This last piece of correspondence was probably published for the sole purpose of establishing the guilt of the collective farmers themselves for the famine that seized Ukraine. Whereas in the second year of *prodrazvërstka* only the peasants felt its repercussions (with Ukrainian peasants especially hard hit), the third year was catastrophic for the country as a whole, which was in the grip of severe famine. In vain did Stalin hope that the Law of Spikelets would protect the 1932 harvest for the state. Faced with the prospect of death by hunger, the peasants paid no heed to the punishments with which they were threatened by the state. They strove to get the grain they had grown with their own hands on the fields of the collective farms and hide it for a rainy day. However, the harvest of 1932 suffered its greatest losses not because of "theft" but as a result of the peasants' natural disinclination to work without any material remuneration.

Meanwhile, the Stalin government was strongly hoping for a harvest that would mitigate the catastrophic dynamic of the Soviet balance of payments. In 1930 they were able to export 298 million poods of grain, and in 1931 exports reached their maximum for the whole post-revolutionary period—316 million poods. But the commercial results of these exports were unsatisfactory. The Great Depression of 1929–33 reduced prices for machinery much less than for agricultural produce. In order to achieve their previous level of earnings to pay for imports, they had to sell 2 to 3 times more raw materials. Yet their grain exports, on the contrary, fell significantly—to 107.9 million poods in 1932.[63] The Soviet Union, which did not recognize its prerevolutionary debts, could only count on short-term commercial paper loans. The reduction of exports threatened a default on such loans, with the

---

62 A reference to the administrative triad comprising the head of the collective or state farm, a local party secretary, and the head of the village council.

63 Kul'chyts'kyi, *Tsina "velykoho perelomu,"* 313.

prospect of foreign banks refusing credit for imports or courts deciding to confiscate ships and export cargo in ports as well as all Soviet property abroad. The hopeless state of the balance of payments was one manifestation of the impending economic catastrophe.

As the Sovnarkom of the USSR proved convincingly in 1930–31, it was capable of "shaking down" the collective farms for all their grain in order to provide for its export needs. The abrupt reduction of grain exports in 1932 is to be explained not by a desire to keep grain in the country but by the lack of grain. The crisis forced the government to reduce spending on the "sacred cows" of the budget—industry and the army. On June 14, 1932, Kaganovich wrote to Stalin that they were working hard in Moscow to find ways of increasing foreign-exchange earnings and reducing the deficit.[64] This meant, among other things, putting priceless works of world art and unique antiquities up for sale.

---

64 *Stalin i Kaganovich: Perepiska 1931–1936 gg.*, 166–67.

PHOTOGRAPHS FROM THE ALBUM OF ALEXANDER WIENERBERGER

Alexander Wienerberger was an Austrian engineer who spent years working in the industrial sector in Kharkiv, then the capital of Soviet Ukraine. In 1933 he took a series of photographs in Kharkiv and vicinity that captured the suffering and starvation caused by the Holodomor. In taking those photographs he was risking his life, as any reference to hunger, let alone material photographic evidence, was considered malicious anti-Soviet propaganda. Later that year he managed to smuggle the album of photographs out of the Soviet Union and place it at the disposal of Cardinal Theodor Innitzer, archbishop of Vienna. At the request of Metropolitan Andrei Sheptytsky, Cardinal Innitzer organized an international aid committee to provide assistance to famine victims. In December 1933 he held a conference in Vienna to inform the international community about the tragedy of the Ukrainian people.

Wienerberger's memoirs of his life and work in Soviet Ukraine were published under the title *Hart auf hart: 15 Jahre Ingenieur in Sowjetrußland. Ein Tatsachenbericht. Mit 52 Original-Leica-Aufnahmen des Verfassers* (Salzburg and Leipzig, 1939).

Alexander Wienerberger (08.12.1891–05.01.1955).
Digital photograph supplied by his great-granddaughter, Samara Pearce.
Reproduced with permission.

Photographs from the album of Alexander Wienerberger

The tragic famine in South Russia, 1933

Sr. Eminenz, Kardinal Erzbischof
Dr. Theodor Innitzer
in dankbarer Verehrung
gewidmet von
Ing. A. Wienerberger

Dedicated with grateful devotion to His Eminence, Cardinal Archbishop Dr. Theodor Innitzer, by A. Wienerberger, engineer

Die hungernden Bauern verlassen das Dorf, um Hilfe in der Stadt zu finden.

Famine-stricken peasants leaving a village in search of assistance in the city

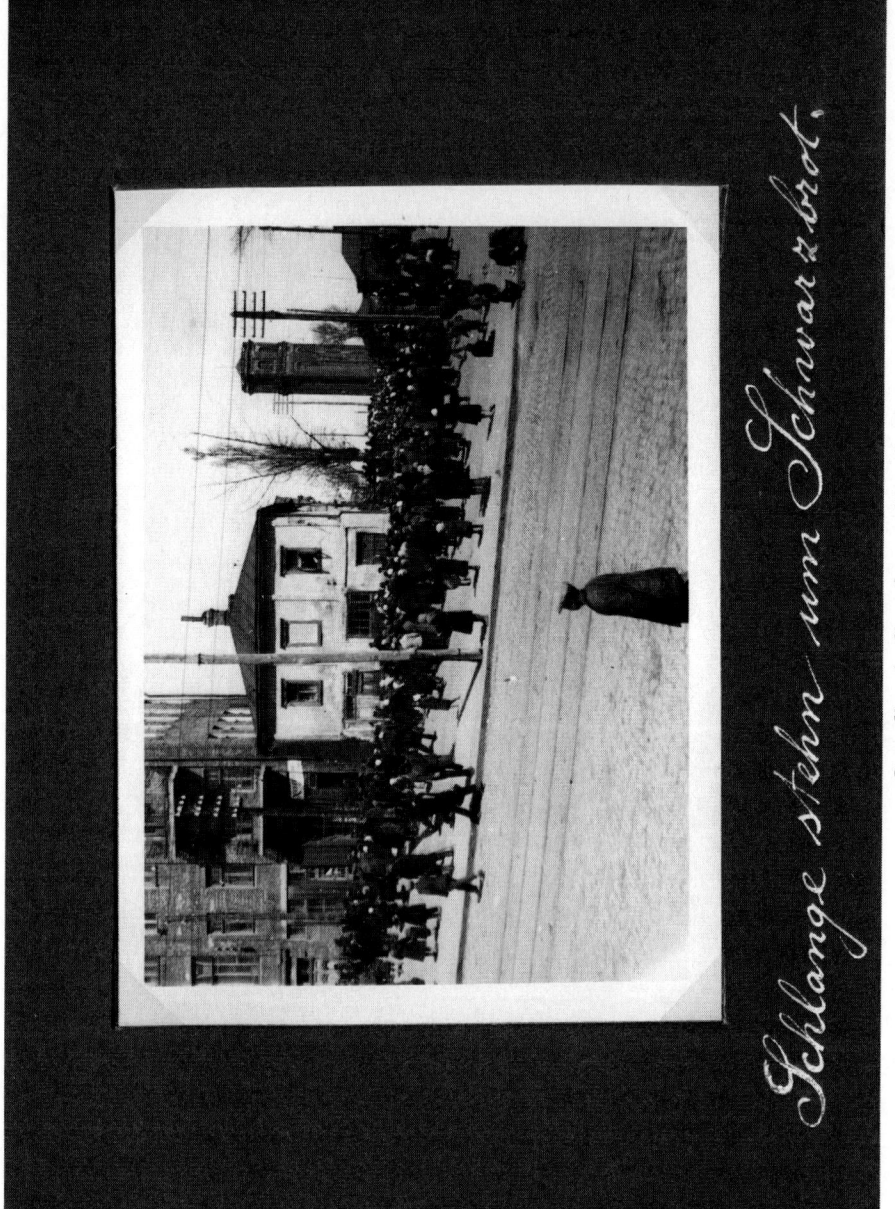

Schlange stehn um Schwarzbrot.

Standing in line for rye bread

Photographs from the album of Alexander Wienerberger

Schlange stehn um Schwarzbrot...
Standing in line for rye bread

Auch die Tiere leiden Hunger.

Animals also suffer from hunger

Photographs from the album of Alexander Wienerberger

In agony

"Verlauste Todeskandidaten."

Lice-ridden candidates for death

Child of workers from Kharkiv

Illicit trading in food

In allen Stadien des Verhungerns.

In every stage of starvation

Famine!

Photographs from the album of Alexander Wienerberger

Eines der ersten Opfer.

One of the first victims

Hungerleichen — Auf dem Markte —
Famine corpses. In the marketplace

Photographs from the album of Alexander Wienerberger

Auf den Straßen —
On the streets

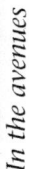

In den Alleen —
In the avenues

Photographs from the album of Alexander Wienerberger

In den Gassen.

In the alleys

Auch das Kindesalter blieb nicht verschont.
Even children were not spared

Photographs from the album of Alexander Wienerberger

81

Die Tragödie eines Bauern in vier Bildern.

I.

The tragedy of a peasant in four photos

IV. Endlich erlöst.

Deliverance at last

Massengräber für die Verhungerten.

Mass graves for famine victims

Mass graves for famine victims

Photographs from the album of Alexander Wienerberger

Ausgestorbenes Dorf.

Lifeless village

"Das Begraben von Menschen ist hier strengstens verboten"!!!

"Burials categorically forbidden here!"

5 | THE "CRUSHING BLOW"

In the early 1930s, Stalin subordinated the upper echelons of the party, government, and Cheka power verticals to himself, but not the entire party or the whole country. The Stalin who was beyond criticism only appeared after the Great Famine of 1932–33 and the Great Terror of 1937–38, with their many millions of victims, and after World War II, in which he was responsible for the deaths of as many as 30 million Soviet citizens. The economic crisis of 1932 caused by *prodrazvërstka* and the ensuing all-Union famine might easily have cost him his post of general secretary of the Central Committee. In order to protect his position at the top of the power structure, the chief was prepared to sacrifice the lives of millions of people.

The state, which was Stalin's team incarnate, presented itself to the working class as an aggregate entrepreneur obligated to pay wages and make sure that those rubles would suffice to provide adequate nutrition. The workers invested their hopes for a minimum level of nutrition under conditions of "temporary hardship" not in the peasantry but in the state, since it was the state that had destroyed the free market previously functioning between town and country in order to facilitate the confiscation of "surplus" by means of requisitioning. In 1931 and especially in 1932, however, the workers began to sense that something was going wrong in the country. Workers who belonged to the party still remembered the observations and warnings of leaders of the Right Opposition in the Politburo of the CC AUCP(B), even though those "rightist opportunists" had publicly recanted. Meanwhile, the policies of those who had ousted Nikolai Bukharin, Mikhail Tomsky, and Aleksei Rykov from the senior party leadership led to famine not only in the countryside but also in the cities. Consequently, members of the social stratum that the Chekists called "socially close" to the authorities began to pose a threat to Stalin's team.

Martemian Riutin, expelled from the CC AUCP(B) at the Sixteenth Congress in 1930 for propagandizing "rightist opportunistic views,"

Martemian Riutin (1890–1937). Secretary of the Krasnoperekopsk District Committee of the AUCP(B) in Moscow; arrested in the case of the "Union of Marxist-Leninists," 1932; author of the anti-Stalin manifesto "Stalin and the Crisis of the Proletarian Dictatorship."

came out openly against the Kremlin leadership. At his initiative, a document titled "Stalin and the Crisis of the Proletarian Dictatorship" was prepared in March 1932, along with "An Appeal to All Members of the AUCP(B)." Grigorii Zinoviev, Lev Kamenev, and a number of (recently) senior party and government officials in Moscow and Kharkiv who had suffered during the rout of the Right Opposition familiarized themselves with the documents. "An Appeal" stated in particular:

> The party and the proletarian dictatorship have been led by Stalin and his clique to a dead end without precedent and are undergoing a deadly crisis. Through deception, slander, and duping of party people, through unbelievable violence and terror, under the banner of struggle for the purity of Bolshevik principles and party unity, relying on a powerful centralized apparatus, over the last five years Stalin has cut off and removed all the best, genuinely Bolshevik members of the party from its leadership, established a personal dictatorship in the AUCP(B) and the entire country, broken with Leninism, and set out on the path of the most unbridled authoritarianism and savage personal despotism, bringing the Soviet Union to the edge of the precipice.[1]

This long quotation should illustrate the mood that was shared by a certain portion of the party membership and reflected the actual state of affairs in the country. To be sure, Stalin remained sufficiently devoted to Leninism that he did not venture (until January 1933) to reject the literal implementation of the constructions of the Soviet system that were set forth in the RCP(B) program of 1919.

The October 1932 plenum of the CC AUCP(B) held as many as thirty people liable to the party in the Riutin affair. But only a month later, Stalin had to deal with a number of individuals in the Russian government who had grouped themselves around Aleksandr Smirnov. Influenced by the growing crisis, this group began to regard the general course of the CC AUCP(B) in Stalin's implementation as a threat to the party and the country.[2]

The party and government nomenklatura did not suffer materially from Stalin's policy of "spurring." The oppositional attitudes in the middle and lower strata of government developed only because the leaders of those elements of the communist apparatus, well aware of the attitudes of the popular masses, were afraid of losing their positions in the event of a social explosion.

In describing the situation in Ukraine in his aforementioned letter of April 26, 1932 to Stalin, Kosior tried to convey optimism but still expressed the main threat to the authorities in communist newspeak: "The lack of grain and the famine are the topics around which the kulak and his agents are stoking a stormy campaign, resorting to all possible provocations." Having downplayed the destructive effects of the grain quotas, Kosior reduced them to what he claimed was the unexpected production lag in Kyiv province, especially in the former Bila Tserkva *okruh* (earlier term for province) and in Vinnytsia province, specifically in the former Uman *okruh*. At the very end, he cautiously observed: "According to what comrades who have

---

1 "O dele t.n. 'Soiuza marksistov-lenintsev,'" *Izvestiia TsK KPSS* (Moscow), 1989, no. 6: 106.

2 Aleksandr N. Iakovlev, *Reabilitatsiia: Politicheskie protsessy 30–50-kh godov* (Moscow: Izdatel'stvo politicheskoi literatury, 1991), 99, 173; *Tragediia sovetskoi derevni*, 3: 557–61.

been there are saying, the mood in those districts is despondent, and in some places highly aggravated."³

Without a doubt, the situation in the districts of the two former *okruhy* that Kosior mentioned and that Molotov had visited was simply horrible. In this case, however, the authorities' partial loss of control over the periphery after *okruhy* were abolished played a beneficent role: the destructive effects of Molotov's directives did not become manifest everywhere. Yet the incessant efforts of the grain requisitioners meant that the famine continued to spread. The "aggravated mood" spread along with it.

Reports on anti-Soviet attitudes poured into the Kremlin from near and far. The letters also contained threats. Here are a few of the shorter messages:

> "The peasants are under such an impression that it is frightening even to speak of it: if the least thing were to happen, they would immediately turn their guns against [the regime]. This is Ivan Tarasiuk, a student at the factory apprenticeship school, Dolyna station, writing to you. I am currently working for the GPU in detecting anti-Soviet activity."⁴

"Dear Comrade Stalin," wrote students at the Dnipropetrovsk Chemical and Technological College, "you must pay special attention to this, for the village folk will strike openly. They will rise up against Soviet rule and, if they remain without grain a while longer, hungry, they will simply go and destroy the collective farms, take back their belongings, and work individually, as they did before. They are being driven to this by destitution, poverty, and hunger, which is now making them swell up."⁵ A collection of unpublished correspondence (from July 6, 1932) received by the newspaper *Izvestiia VTsIK* (News of the All-Russian Central Executive Committee) contains an unsigned letter from Moscow full of the terror of an apocalyptic premonition of the Holodomor:

> "The famine in Ukraine is the result of our inept policy. Every day we trumpet our successes while the train stations fill up with refugees from the starving republics. Whole families go begging in the cities. And try as we might, there is no covering up this horror. It is rumored that less than 50 percent of Ukraine has been sown, which means that they will starve again."⁶

The country's senior leadership was inundated with messages from Chekists about society's "aggravated mood." On March 6, 1932, the following letter was tossed into the correspondence box for the newsletter of the 153rd Infantry Regiment in the Ukrainian Military District: "Woe to socialism if war breaks out in 1932. All it takes is one spark, and an unheard-of fire will flare up."⁷ On June 18 H. Tkachenko, a twenty-year-old Young Communist League member from the Brusyliv district in

---

3 *Holod 1932–1933 rokiv na Ukraïni: ochyma istorykiv, movoiu dokumentiv*, 150.
4 Ibid., 152.
5 Ibid., 158.
6 *Tragediia sovetskoi derevni*, 3: 407.
7 Liudmyla V. Hrynevych, "Sotsial'ni pochuttia ta politychni nastroï chervonoarmiitsiv v roky holodomoru" in *Holod 1932–1933 rokiv v Ukraïni: prychyny ta naslidky*, ed. Volodymyr Lytvyn (Kyiv: Naukova dumka, 2003), 641.

the Kyiv region who was studying at the Kyiv Fishery College, wrote a letter to the general secretary of the CC CP(B)U, Stanislav Kosior:

> "It seems to me that, as far as the party was authoritative at least among the broad masses, its authority is constantly declining. As soon as a spark appears among the peasantry, flames will break out everywhere.... Comrade Bukharin's theories are now gaining strength and authority."[8]

With regard to Stalin and the henchmen he appointed to the Politburo of the CC AUCP(B) in place of Bukharin, Tomsky, and Rykov, this rank-and-file Komsomol member's mention of the leader of the Right Opposition sounded like a judicial verdict.

Since Zinoviev and Kamenev were involved in the Riutin affair, it was widely publicized in the newspapers and, obviously, given the appropriate interpretation. But Chekist documents show that many senior officials in the party and government apparatus construed the struggle at the heights of the party in their own way.

In November 1932, the head of the Organizational Department of the Nosivka district party committee (in the Chernihiv region), Yaremenko, left the village of Lykhachiv, where he had worked as a grain-procurement representative, and notified the leadership of the district party committee of his intention to leave the party. He made the following statement to an individual who turned out to be an OGPU informer:

> "In my opinion, the Politburo of the CC AUCP(B) is taking the wrong course, and as a result the country will become impoverished. The peasants are groaning under the burden of excessive taxes. Those at the top do not see what is happening in the localities. The peasants are also given excessive grain-procurement quotas, and they are set against the government. The Politburo is taking a clearly counterrevolutionary line, as is shown by the departure from the Politburo of a number of people who were actually carrying out the true line (Bukharin and Zinoviev)."[9]

In December 1932, the transport division of the Ukrainian SSR GPU prepared a report on political attitudes among laborers and engineering and technical workers—party members who worked for the railroad—for the Moscow and Kharkiv leadership of the state security services. A brief selection of openly expressed statements or opinions overheard by informers suffices to indicate the depth of the abyss that had emerged between the Kremlin leaders and the rank-and-file party members.[10]

Solodov, a machinist from the Piatykhatka depot, a veteran, worker, and longtime member of the party, said to his coworkers:

> "What are we going to do? They're fleecing us to the *n*th degree. They've reduced the grain norms. We're left without grain, potatoes, or fuel for the winter. Everything's disappearing into some abyss. It's dreadful when you think what

---

8   *Holodomor 1932–1933 rr. v Ukraïni. Dokumenty i materialy,* comp. Ruslan Ia. Pyrih (Kyiv: Vydavnychyi dim "Kyievo-Mohylians'ka akademiia," 2007), 212.

9   *Holodomor 1932–1933 rr. v Ukraïni: Zlochyn vlady — trahediia narodu. Dokumenty i materialy,* comp. Volodymyr S. Lozyts'kyi (Kyiv: Heneza, 2008), 229.

10 *Rozsekrechena pam'iat': Holodomor 1932–1933 rokiv v Ukraïni v dokumentakh HPU-NKVD,* comp. Viktor Borysenko (Kyiv: Vydavnychyi dim "Stylos," 2007), 264–84.

we've lived to see and what's awaiting us. We'll probably all die like flies. And you can't say anything anywhere."

Ye. Myroshnychenko, a locksmith from the power plant at the Nyzhniodniprovsk railcar repair factory with 27 years of work experience, said:

> "They've brought the country to total ruin. The country is doomed with such a government. No wonder Trotsky spoke the truth."

S. Pidiablonsky, a worker from the Mariupol port station, said:

> "Because of Stalin's policy, people like Kamenev and Zinoviev have suffered. Stalin's clan will cause us to revolt. They're all but saying to us, 'Fools, you're dying of hunger.'"

Kobeliatsky, a machinist from the Yasynovata depot who had transport and party experience starting in 1924, said:

> "In comparison to Zinoviev, Stalin is still young. Zinoviev is a real leader. He organized the Comintern, did time in jail, and was in exile longer than Stalin, but now they're trying to hang counterrevolution on Zinoviev and Kamenev."

A smith from the factory apprenticeship school at the Znamianka station, I. Vovkodav, said:

> "Something's going to happen soon. We can't go on living like this."

After a party meeting about the expulsion of the Riutin group from the party, Pyrohov, a handcar driver from the Polohy station, said in a group of workers:

> "Workers and peasants are starving. Zinoviev, Kamenev and others saw this, took it into account, and wanted to improve the workers' situation but ended up in the opposition because of it. The party's current policy will be recognized sooner or later as subversive."

The grain deficit forced the state to reduce its norms of centralized supply in the cities and newly built-up areas. In the fourth quarter of 1932, there were 7,160,000 people on the centralized ration list in Ukraine. To ensure consistency between grain rations and available resources, on November 29 the Politburo of the CC CP(B)U found it necessary to reduce centralized grain rations for civil servants, their dependents, and workers' dependents on the special and first ration lists from 400 grams per day to 300; completely remove artisans from the list; reduce the public nutrition fund by 15 percent; and mix barley, corn and the like with the flour.[11] This led to a severe deterioration of attitudes among the urban population, as noted by the organs of state security.

At a party meeting at the Nikopol station, during a discussion about the Central Control Commission's decision to expel the Riutin group from the party, the depot joiner Kocherov said:

---

11   Stanislav Kul'chyts'kyi, *Holodomor 1932–1933 rr. iak henotsyd: trudnoshchi usvidomlennia* (Kyiv: Nash chas, 2007), 260. Primary source: Tsentral'nyi derzhavnyi arkhiv hromads'kykh ob'iednan' Ukraïny (Central State Archives of Public Organizations of Ukraine, hereafter TsDAHOU), fond 1, op. 6, spr. 268, ark. 116.

> "After this speech they'll call me an opportunist. But that would be wrong. The opposition is right. We are building heavy industry, and we have worked to the point where the workers are starving."

At a party meeting at the Melitopol station concerning the decision of the October 1932 joint plenum of the CC and CCC AUCP(B) to expel the Riutin group from the party, the machinist Nikolenko, who was in charge of the party school, said:

> "We disagree fundamentally with party policy on relations with the peasantry. They are taking grain and cattle away from the peasants; they are starving, and they have nothing to feed us with."

A foreman from the Korosten depot, I. Shavynsky, a transport worker since 1915 and party member since 1924, spoke about the expulsion of the Riutin group from the party:

> "This group was acting correctly. The same thing happened to them that happened to [Georgii] Chicherin, who was rubbed out who knows where under the guise of a disease."

An assistant machinist, a worker with twenty years' experience at the Ilovaisk station depot, A. Cherenkov, said:

> "They're writing and saying that everything's for the workers, but they're doing absolutely nothing. The opportunists were driven out of the party for naught. They spoke the truth. If they had remained in the leadership, we would not be undergoing the poverty we are now. The grain has rotted in the fields, and the remainder has been sent abroad."

A worker from the railcar shop at the Kremenchuk depot, H. Netiaha, declared to the secretary of the party cell:

> "Here are your International Red Aid [MOPR] cases and my candidate card. I no longer wish to be in the party, since the Soviet government and party are doing the wrong thing in reducing our grain rations. They have taken 100 grams away from each of my two dependents, and my mother receives nothing at all."[12]

As is evident from these statements, the workers' protest against the policy of the "government of famine" had an economic subtext. The peasant disturbances had the same subtext. On the basis of the aforementioned report from the secret political division of the OGPU, "Basic Aspects of the Political Attitudes of the Most Affected Districts," which was delivered to the Kremlin leaders in July 1932, Nicolas Werth notes that "Sixty percent of all disturbances in 1931–32 were recorded in Ukraine and the North Caucasus, that is, in the main grain-producing regions, which were strategically important to the regime from this angle."[13]

Any worker-peasant protest in the non-Russian regions of the country inevitably took on a national tint. The Kremlin leaders realized that the joint cumulative force of both forms of protest in the Ukrainian SSR, located in close proximity to Europe, was particularly dangerous to them. Given that the principle of prevention was

---

12   *Rozsekrechena pam'iat'*, 264–84.
13   Nikolia Vert (Nicolas Werth), *Terror i besporiadok: Stalinizm kak sistema* (Moscow: ROSSPĖN, 2010), 72.

central to Stalin's repressions, one might think, as has already been emphasized, that exorbitant grain quotas were imposed in the Ukrainian SSR in 1930–32 and in the Kuban region in 1932 not only as part of the all-Union policy of "spurring" but also with the goal of undermining the economic basis of the national-liberation movement.

In all likelihood, the Kremlin overestimated rather than underestimated the threat of Ukrainian separatism. Yet how could it not have done so when sparks of the flame that had blazed in 1917–20 flared up in Ukraine from time to time? On February 26, 1931, for example, the presidium of the Twelfth All-Ukrainian Congress of Soviets was presented with a declaration signed by "A group of delegates and attendees at the congress of Kharkiv factory workers." It urged that "We must build a Ukrainian Soviet state, for the time has come. The population has matured and now says little about broken fences or confiscated apartments: it is talking about the State. Ukrainian Soviet statehood must be built, for it has only just begun, and so far we have spoken only about language and culture, although they, too, are elements of statehood."[14]

On August 5, 1932, the Secret Political Division of the OGPU summed up the data on peasant protests for the seven preceding months. They paid special attention to the increasing activity of the movement against collective farms over the previous two months—June and July. The Chekists also noted a sharp rise in peasant protests in 1932 as compared to the previous year. The Ukrainian SSR was in first place with regard to the number of protests: 923 out of 1,630. Second place went to the North Caucasus, with 173 protests. They were followed by Western Siberia with 119, the Lower Volga with 95, the Middle Volga with 78, the Western province with 59, and the Central Black Earth province with 43 protests.[15] The number of protests in the Russian regions was exponentially lower.

Was the Ukrainian peasants' tenfold greater protest activity due only to their love of liberty, their propensity to revolt or, ultimately, their mentality? It would make more sense, considering the burdensome grain quota that the Kremlin imposed on Ukraine, to recognize its provocative nature: to bring the situation to the boiling point and then "respond with a crushing blow."

From time to time, data on the fulfillment of plans for the fall sowing and grain procurement in the Ukrainian SSR came across Stalin's desk. This included an OGPU USSR report on opposition to the quotas on the part of members and candidates of the CP(B)U. Information on agricultural campaigns was not passed over in silence, even though the results were disappointing. In late October 1932, the sowing campaign was supposed to have been concluded owing to weather conditions, but the sowing of winter wheat was only 82.9 percent complete. Despite the enormous army of grain requisitioners, grain deliveries as of October 25 amounted to only 39 percent of the plan.[16]

Information about the attitudes of those who carried out the grain-procurement plans was kept secret. The sentiments expressed by many functionaries from the lower ranks of the party and government apparatus would obviously have made

---

14   Hrynevych, "Vyiavlennia natsional'noï identychnosti ukraïns'koho selianstva," 426.
15   *Tragediia sovetskoi derevni*, 3: 440–41.
16   Hryhorii Kostiuk, *Stalinizm v Ukraïni (heneza i naslidky)* (Kyiv: Smoloskyp, 1995), 135.

them subject to penalties under the article of the criminal code on anti-Soviet propaganda. A summary document on opposition to grain procurements as of October 20, 68 pages in length, was prepared by the Secret Political Division of the GPU of the Ukrainian SSR. It first appeared in a collection of documents titled *The Famine-Genocide of 1932–1933 in Ukraine*, published in Canada in 2005.[17] Let us consider a few comments from this overview:

> "We will not accept the grain-procurement plan, since it is of a scope that cannot be fulfilled. And agreeing to leave people hungry again would be a crime. I'd rather hand in my party card right now than condemn collective farmers to starvation by deceit" (Yermak, the party cell secretary in the village of Nyzhni Sirohozy in the district of the same name in Dnipropetrovsk province).

> "The plan is unrealistic unless they're going to requisition people in the grain procurements too. One way or another, the peasantry will have to die of hunger.... It's obvious that there are either counterrevolutionaries or scatterbrains in power who are drafting plans in such a way as to make them impossible to fulfill" (from a speech by S. Shovkoplias, a former Red partisan, candidate for party membership, and member of the village council, speaking at a plenum of the Leninske village council in the Velyka Bilozerka district, Dnipropetrovsk province).

> "They want to leave you without any grain this year, just like last. If you fools are going to keep quiet, you'll end up with no grain. There is no need to adopt a grain-procurement plan right now; we'll see what the surplus looks like, and that's what we'll deliver" (statement of Babychev, head of the 30th Irkutsk Division Cooperative and member of the CP(B)U, before a general meeting called to approve the grain-procurement plan, Bohdanivka village council, Pavlohrad district, Dnipropetrovsk province).

> "We won't give up a single pound of grain, don't threaten us, we're not afraid, starvation is more terrible" (so said the head of the Putylovets Cooperative, a former Red partisan and candidate member of the CP(B)U, Denysenko, at a meeting of activists in the Velyka Bilozerka district of Dnipropetrovsk province).

> "I've already been living here for four months, and I've gotten used to considering myself not an authority from the district party committee but one of the local collective farmers. I'm probably going to live here for another 14 months, but there's little use in it because the grain-procurement plan cannot be fulfilled, as there's no grain even for sowing or eating" (Perederii, district party committee representative, Viuny village council, Velyka Bilozerka district, Dnipropetrovsk province).

> "This year's grain-procurement plan is unrealistic for both the district and the state farm. We'd have to relinquish all our grain in order to fulfill those plans. Again the collective farmers will starve; again the horses will be infected. Soviet rule has created conditions such that it's impossible to work either on the state farms or on the collective farms" (Birkin, director of the Bilshovyk State Farm, Novoukrainka district, Odesa province).

> "This is real theft on the part of the Soviet authorities. There aren't leaders but blockheads sitting in the district administration and higher up. Stalin, Kosior,

---

17   *Holod-henotsyd 1932–1933 rokiv v Ukraïni: The Famine-Genocide of 1932–1933 in Ukraine*, ed. Iurii Shapoval (Kingston, Ontario: Kashtan Press, 2005), 146–211.

and the others can't run this country.... I'm going to quit and go away; I don't want to rob the peasants" (Nyzkousov, district party committee representative in the village of Ivanivka and head of the Committee of Poor Peasants, Novoheorhiivsk district, Kharkiv province).

"I can't even imagine what's happening in our Soviet Union. It seems to me that a counterrevolution has taken root in the government and is mocking the people. I am well aware that the peasants have no grain. They're already eating substitutes. But you can't say anything, or they'll accuse you of opportunism and kick you out of the party. Lots of party members are working unwillingly, but you have to work" (Postnov, head of the collective farm in the village of Koptiieve, Olyshivka district, Chernihiv province).

"This year's plan is beyond our capacity, and if we fulfill it, we'll drive Ukraine to collapse and hunger" (Dubovyk, secretary of the Slovechne district Young Communist League committee, Kyiv province).

As the remarks overheard by secret collaborators (*seksoty*) show, Ukrainian peasants already foresaw what awaited them in the first half of 1933. The peasants' disorganization, deliberately brought about by the authorities, did not reduce the scope of the resistance. The situation looked all the more menacing to the Kremlin because certain elements of organization in opposition to the authorities were sometimes introduced even by functionaries from the lower ranks of the party and government apparatus.

On November 27, 1932, Stalin convened a joint session of the Politburo of the CC and the Presidium of the CCC AUCP(B) at which he raised questions about Aleksandr Smirnov's group. Denying personal responsibility for the failure of the grain procurements, he gave two reasons for the defeat: 1) the penetration of collective and state farms by anti-Soviet elements in order to organize wrecking and sabotage; and 2) the wrong attitude to collective and state farms manifested by a significant number of rural communists. In his opinion, the attitude was wrong in that it idealized those forms of agriculture, which were socialist by their very nature. The problem was the "Bolshevization" of the collective and state farms. "It would be foolish," declared the general secretary, "if communists, proceeding from the premise that collective farms are a socialist form of agriculture, failed to respond to the blow struck by these individual collective farmers and collective farms with a crushing blow of their own."[18]

Stalin's "crushing blow" was already being delivered when the higher party synod of members of the Politburo of the CC and the Presidium of the CCC AUCP(B) heard the general secretary utter this expression. The suppression of "saboteurs" was being carried out by extraordinary grain-procurement commissions. The first two were established by a decision of the Politburo of the CC AUCP(B) on October 22, 1932: the commission headed by Viacheslav Molotov (consisting of the head of administration of the USSR State Bank, Moisei Kalmanovich, the head of the all-Union Zagotzerno Association, Sarkis Sarkisov, and others) was to work in the Ukrainian SSR, and the commission under Lazar Kaganovich was to work in the North Caucasus Krai of the Russian Federation. A third commission, headed by

---

18 *Tragediia sovetskoi derevni*, 3: 559.

Mendel Khataevich (1893–1937). Secretary of the Central Committee of the CP(B)U and member of the Politburo, Central Committee of the CP(B)U, 1932.

a secretary of the CC AUCP(B), Pavel Postyshev, was created somewhat later in the Volga region.

The extraordinary commissions were organs of the Kremlin's dictatorial rule created in specific regions for a certain time. They made use of local apparatuses—party, government, and Chekist—for a grain "shakedown." Their resolutions and other binding documents were made public in the name of local government agencies. The mass media—radio, newspapers, and newsreels—broadly publicized the struggle against the "sabotage" of grain procurements. The uncovering of "black granaries" on the collective farms—grain reserves concealed from the state inventory—was an especially popular subject, as was that of uncovering pits with hidden grain in villagers' yards. This was the authorities' way of driving a wedge between the grain producers in the countryside and the grain consumers already starving in the cities.

According to instructions given by Molotov in the minutes of a meeting of the Politburo of the CC CP(B)U on November 1–5, 1932, a new directive was issued by the judicial system to provide additional assistance to the grain requisitioners. Judicial authorities were required to hear cases concerning grain procurement ahead of schedule, usually in on-site sessions, and to apply severe repressive measures. Administrative agencies were instructed to implement coercive measures promptly against debtors. The central and local press was to give broad publicity to these court cases.[19]

This decision allowed Molotov to create the necessary conditions for implementing the "draconian" (Stalin's term) resolution adopted on August 7, 1932 by the Central Executive Committee and the USSR Sovnarkom. On November 5, Molotov and the newly appointed secretary of the CC CP(B)U, Mendel Khataevich, sent the following telegram to the secretaries of provincial committees of the CP(B) U:

> Reports from the OGPU provincial authorities contain much news about theft, criminal squandering, and concealment of collective-farm grain with the participation and under the leadership of collective-farm administrations, including some communist administrators who are in fact kulak agents corrupting the collective farms. Despite this, the Central Committee of the CP(B)U is unaware of what the provincial committees are doing to combat these occurrences. Noting the inexcusable inactivity of courts and prosecutors and the passivity of the press with regard to such concrete facts, the CC CP(B) U categorically demands that the provincial committees take immediate and decisive measures to combat these occurrences, including the prompt and binding application of judicial repressions and the unsparing punishment of criminal elements in the collective-farm administrations on the basis of the well-known decree on the protection of public property, the exposure of these

---

19   Ibid., 3: 528–29.

facts in the press, and the adoption of resolutions condemning these facts at collective-farm meetings.[20]

On November 21 Molotov, Chubar, Vasilii Stroganov, and Kalmanovich appealed to Stalin with a request to give the CC CP(B)U the right, in the form of a special commission (comprising the general secretary of the CC, the head of the GPU of the Ukrainian SSR, and a representative of the Central Control Committee) appointed for the period of the grain procurements, to make the final decision when it came to the death penalty. The special commission was to report to the CC AUCP(B) on its verdicts in such cases only once every ten days.[21]

Vlas Chubar (1891–1939). Chairman (from July 1923) of the Council of People's Commissars of the Ukrainian SSR; deputy chairman (from 1934) of the USSR Council of People's Commissars.

The tried-and-true method of expropriating farms, which had long been in use, was an important element in the activity of Molotov's commission. Individual farmers who had not fulfilled their grain quotas were deprived of their chattels, crops, garden plots, and buildings. This repressive measure was almost immediately extended to include collective farmers and later perfected: all dekulakized farmers were deported to remote localities of the USSR or to concentration camps.

Officials from the party and government apparatus who were mobilized for the grain procurements wrote reports on their work. The head of the CCC of the CP(B)U and people's commissar of the Rabkrin (Workers' and Peasants' Inspectorate) of the Ukrainian SSR, Volodymyr Zatonsky, noted in his report: "I have been told that in Odesa province, particularly in Novoukrainka and Znamianka (a comrade who arrived from Nikopol told me the same thing), those exiled to the north were not so upset about it. No one deserted, many people left with their accordions, and there were even cases of 'volunteerism,' when neighbors asked to be included among those being resettled."[22] Zatonsky wrote about this with surprise, not understanding the peasants' behavior. But the explanation is simple: the peasants preferred deportation to death by hunger. In December 1932, the secretary of the Krasnopillia district party committee (in Kharkiv province) reported to the CC CP(B)U: "Almost daily, the People's Court (*Narsud*) settles grain cases in the localities. After a trial in the village of Krasnopillia, the middle peasant Oleksii Vasyliovych Besarab said, 'May they sentence us and take us away from here so that at least we won't die of starvation, but if we stay home, we'll all die no matter what.'"[23]

---

20   *Komandyry Velykoho holodu*, 236.
21   *Tragediia sovetskoi derevni*, 3: 548.
22   *Holod 1932–1933 rokiv na Ukraïni: ochyma istorykiv, movoiu dokumentiv*, 341.
23   Ibid., 289.

In Ukraine, grain procurements for the harvest of 1932 lasted until February 1933. Let us examine their results in the peasant sector by province (in thousands of metric tons):[24]

	Plan	Qty delivered	Percent complete
Northern provinces			
Vinnytsia	430.8	437.0	101.4
Kyiv	224.4	225.8	100.6
Chernihiv	144.1	128.6	89.2
Kharkiv	728.9	636.6	87.3
Southern provinces			
Dnipropetrovsk	1,138.4	844.4	74.2
Odesa	1,141.7	891.0	78.0
Donetsk	411.2	350.6	85.3
Moldavian ASSR	55.7	55.2	99.2
Entire Ukrainian SSR	4,275.3	3,569.2	83.5

The total quantity of procurements from the harvest of 1932 in the Ukrainian SSR was 4,171,700 metric tons (74.3 percent taken from collective farms and 11.3 percent from individual farmers, totaling 85.6 percent from the peasant sector, with 14.4 percent coming from the state farms). The procurements from the harvest of 1931 were 7,047,100 metric tons.[25]

Without reliable data on losses, it is impossible to determine the share of the procurements in the harvest. It is obvious, however, that in the winter of 1932–33, owing to the extraordinary commission, practically all available grain was confiscated. Nonetheless, the procurements turned out to be smaller, almost by half, than they had been the previous year. The catastrophic failure of procurements in the Ukrainian SSR and other grain-producing regions may well have forced Stalin to give serious thought to the expediency of requisitioning.

Data on the amount of grain procured from the harvest of 1932 by province before and after the appearance of the extraordinary commission cannot be compared: in October 1932 Chernihiv province, the seventh in the republic, was formed from districts in neighboring provinces. It is therefore necessary to group the data by northern and southern provinces, as in the preceding table, in order to compare the figures. The chronology of grain procurements in the rural sector was as follows (in millions of poods):[26]

---

24 Kul'chyts'kyi, *Tsina "velykoho perelomu,"* 303. Primary source: TsDAVO Ukraïny, fond 27, op. 13, spr. 1136, ark. 2, 4.

25 Procurements from the harvest of 1931 amounting to 7,047,100 metric tons are taken from the archival source cited in the preceding footnote. Using data from I. Strilever, S. Khazanov, and L. Iampol'skii, *Khlebooborot i standarty* (Moscow, 1935), 169, Davies and Wheatcroft provide a different figure: 7,253,000 metric tons. The difference is quite significant, but it is hard to say which of the two is closer to the actual. See Davies and Wheatcroft, *The Years of Hunger: Soviet Agriculture, 1931–1933,* 470.

26 Kul'chyts'kyi, *Tsina "velykoho perelomu,"* 304.

	Northern provinces	Southern provinces	Entire UkrSSR
Final (reduced) procurement plan	95.5	171.7	267.2
Procured as of November 1, 1932	51.7	84.4	136.1
Procured as of February 1, 1933	86.8	136.3	223.1
Increase in procurements in three months	35.1	51.9	87.0
Fulfillment of final procurement plan (percent complete)			
As of November 1, 1932	54.1	49.2	50.9
As of February 1, 1933	90.9	79.4	83.5

The table shows that the Ukrainian SSR had fulfilled the reduced plan only by half before the implementation of extraordinary measures. In the following three months, the authorities managed to squeeze only 87 million more poods of grain out of the Ukrainian countryside and, if the state farms are added, a total of 105 million. The thrice reduced grain-procurement quotas (the original plan for the rural sector was 356 million poods) were 83.5 percent fulfilled.

Finally, let us take a look at the progress of winter procurements by sector (in millions of poods):[27]

	As of November 1, 1932	As of February 1, 1933	Increase in procurements	
			Thousands of poods	As a percentage of procurements by Nov. 1, 1932
Collective farms	120	194	73	60.8
Individual farmers	16	29	14	87.6
Entire rural sector	136	223	87	63.9
State farms	20	38	18	88.2
Difference from 1932 harvest procurements in UkrSSR	156	261	105	67.0
Difference from 1931 harvest procurements in UkrSSR (As of Nov. 1, 1931 and Feb. 1, 1932, respectively)	334	440	106	31.7

---

27   Ibid., 305.

These data indicate that the requisitioners ran riot particularly among the individual farmers, forcing them in three months to practically double the quantity of grain they relinquished. They also cleaned out the state farms, which drastically reduced their staffs and left the unemployed with no grain. A total of 105 million poods were confiscated in the republic during the winter. Over the next three months (February–April 1933), 34 million poods were returned in the form of produce, seed, and fodder loans in order to provide for the new sowing campaign. The total confiscated came to 71 million poods. If this quantity of grain is divided by the rural population of 25 million as of early 1933, then each person accounts for somewhat less than 3 poods.

The grain procurements of the 1931 harvest were the direct cause of famine in the first half of 1932. At that time, the quantity of grain wrung out during the winter months was less than a third of the total procured in the summer and fall. In 1932–33, almost the same amount of grain was procured during the winter months as in the preceding winter of 1931–32, but now this quantity represented two-thirds of the total procured during the normal period. There is only one explanation for the fact that the state managed to squeeze the same amount of "winter" grain out of the Ukrainian countryside as in the previous year: the requisitioners worked very hard indeed.

By the fall of 1932, after relatively small procurements (they were 178 million poods lower than the previous year's procurements, or more than two times less), the Ukrainian village had already run out of food reserves. If every peasant had had 16 poods of grain until the new harvest, then the confiscation of three poods would have gone practically unnoticed. If the peasants had had half as much grain at their disposal (the constant deterioration of agriculture because of requisitioning should be borne in mind), or eight poods per person, then the confiscation of three poods would not have brought them to the brink of starvation. After all, peasant households had long-term reserves in the form of meat (livestock), *salo* (fatback), potatoes, onions, and everything they grew on their private plots. So how are we to understand the tables that show the grain procurements in all their various breakdowns? What actually happened in the Ukrainian countryside? What was the Kremlin doing there with its most trusted functionaries? What was the essence of the "crushing blow" that Stalin hinted at on November 27, 1932 at a joint session of the CC Politburo and the Presidium of the CCC AUCP(B)?

Up to this point, we have considered the socioeconomic effects of the two communist onslaughts. The leaders of the party that was building the communal state knew both successes and failures. The greatest failure was requisitioning (*prodrazvërstka*), which worsened famine in 1921 and caused it in 1932. The famine of 1932–33 affected different regions to different degrees, but up to a certain point the difference between regions was quantitative, not qualitative. The time has come to make sense of this point, which divides the all-Union famine from the Ukrainian Holodomor. Death is always death. *But we need to distinguish death due to a lack of food, resulting from actions of the regime that were not aimed directly at killing, from murder by starvation.*

Here I shall allow myself a brief digression on the topic of how difficult it is to comprehend the real essence of the Holodomor. On the one hand, we have the emotional interpretation of events, which is repudiated by serious scholars.

Chapter 5. The "Crushing Blow"

Yefim Yevdokimov (1891–1940). From 1923, plenipotentiary representative of the OGPU in the southeastern Russian SFSR, North Caucasus Krai, and Central Asia.

The emotional arguments are not made any more convincing by the outrageously high and completely unrealistic number of Holodomor victims cited to distinguish it from the all-Union famine. On the other hand, we have the utter denial of the Holodomor's distinctness from the all-Union famine. This point of view is still the one most commonly held in world historiography for two reasons. First, the all-Union famine was the background and first stage of the Holodomor. Differentiating these stages is not easy. Second, the Chekists' punitive campaign, which resulted in the Holodomor, was thoroughly covered up and carried out under the guise of grain procurements.

The essence of this digression is a request to take a careful look at the documentary remains of the Chekist campaign that were bound to be preserved and in fact were preserved. These fragments are all in scholarly circulation; they only need to be brought together, as I have done in my publications over the last ten years. In any case, they should not be passed over in silence, as is invariably the case when an alternative viewpoint on the nature of the Holodomor is presented.

The first thing to do in characterizing the essence of Stalin's "crushing blow" is to call out by name the organizers of the murder of millions of Ukrainian peasants by starvation. They can be counted on the fingers of one hand; everyone else blindly carried out their instructions without knowing the general plan of action.

Viacheslav Molotov arrived in Ukraine on October 29, 1932 and stayed in Kharkiv until November 6. He then left for Moscow to take part in the ceremonies marking the fifteenth anniversary of the October Revolution and returned to Kharkiv on November 17, staying in Ukraine until November 23.[28]

On the same day (November 27) that Stalin announced his intention to deliver a "crushing blow" to saboteurs on the collective farms, he made two senior personnel appointments to the OGPU. The OGPU plenipotentiary in Central Asia, Yefim Yevdokimov, became the plenipotentiary in the North Caucasus Krai, and the deputy head of the OGPU, Vsevolod Balytsky, became the special plenipotentiary of the GPU in the Ukrainian SSR. Both had previously worked in the regions to which they were appointed, Yevdokimov in 1924–29 and Balytsky in 1919–31. On December 1, Balytsky was inducted into the Politburo of the CC CP(B)U.[29]

---

28 *Komandyry Velykoho holodu*, 35, 36, 39.
29 Iurii Shapoval and Vadym Zolotar'ov, *Vsevolod Balyts'kyi: osoba, chas, otochennia* (Kyiv: "Stilos," 2002), 188, 388.

Lazar Kaganovich showed up in Rostov-on-Don on November 1 and spent a long time in the North Caucasus Krai. He and Yevdokimov were in charge of grain procurements in Kuban province.

On December 10 the leaders of the CP(B)U, the North Caucasus Krai party committee, and the Western provincial committee of the AUCP(B) were summoned to the Politburo of the CC AUCP(B). Stalin criticized them harshly for their liberalism and spinelessness in the struggle against saboteurs. He especially singled out Stanislav Kosior and Mykola Skrypnyk (the latter "for ties with nationalist elements").[30] Nine days later, there appeared a resolution of the CC AUCP(B) and the Sovnarkom USSR on grain procurements in Ukraine instructing Kaganovich and Postyshev "to go immediately to Ukraine to assist the CC CP(B)U and the Council of People's Commissars [Radnarkom] of Ukraine and to reside in Ukraine's crucial oblasts as special plenipotentiaries of the CC AUCP(B) and the Sovnarkom USSR, sharing the work with Kosior, Chubar, and Khataevich."[31]

Thus Stalin picked a team of his closest colleagues—Molotov, Kaganovich, and Postyshev—to carry out the plan he had come up with for

Vsevolod Balytsky (1892–1937). Chairman of the State Political Directorate (secret police) of the Ukrainian SSR (September 1923–July 1931) and plenipotentiary representative of the OGPU USSR in the Ukrainian SSR. Concurrently deputy chairman of the Joint State Political Directorate (OGPU) USSR (July 1930–July 1934), and specially authorized operative of the OGPU USSR in the Ukrainian SSR (November 1932–February 1933). People's Commissar of Internal Affairs of the Ukrainian SSR (July 1934–May 1937).

Pavel Postyshev (1887–1939). Secretary of the Central Committee of the AUCP(B), 1930–34. In early 1933, on Stalin's instructions, he was elected second secretary of the Central Committee of the CP(B)U and secretary of the Kharkiv Regional Committee of the CP(B)U.

---

30   *Komandyry Velykoho holodu,* 309.

31   *Holod 1932–1933 rokiv na Ukraïni: ochyma istorykiv, movoiu dokumentiv,* 295.

the two Ukrainian regions. The team also included two high-ranking Chekists, Balytsky and Yevdokimov.

The general secretary preferred not to leave any traces even in people's memory. With the exception of Molotov and Kaganovich, whom he trusted, the organizers of the Holodomor became victims of the repressions: Balytsky in 1937, Postyshev in 1939, and Yevdokimov in 1940. The responsibility of Yevdokimov and Postyshev did not come to light, and they were officially rehabilitated. Balytsky had committed other crimes and was not a candidate for rehabilitation. After Stalin's death, Molotov and Kaganovich, along with others in the senior party leadership, themselves spearheaded the rehabilitation process.

The Ukrainian Holodomor began with two resolutions adopted by republican agencies: the resolution of the CC CP(B)U, dated November 18, 1932, "On Measures to Intensify Grain Procurement,"[32] and the resolution of the Ukrainian SSR Radnarkom, dated November 20, "On Measures to Intensify Grain Procurement."[33] The resolution of the CC CP(B)U Politburo, signed by Stanislav Kosior, was meant for representatives of the regime and remained unpublished until it ended up in a body of documents issued according to a resolution of the CC of the Communist Party of Ukraine, dated January 26, 1990, "On the Famine of 1932–33 in Ukraine and the Publication of Archival Materials Related to It." The resolution of the Ukrainian SSR Radnarkom was signed by Vlas Chubar and published on the following day in the newspaper *Visti VUTsVK*. The similarity of titles was no coincidence: the measures to intensify grain procurements in the government resolution were copied from that of the party. But the party resolution was not adopted in Kharkiv or by the person who signed it. The set of measures was discussed in the Kremlin before Molotov's second trip to Ukraine as head of the extraordinary commission. The text of the resolution was worked out by none other than Molotov, and its contents were made known to the leading members of the CP(B)U at a meeting of Kharkiv activists. The materials of the extraordinary commissions published in 2001 by Valerii Vasyliev and Yurii Shapoval include a telegram that Molotov sent to Stalin on November 20:[34]

> "Two days had to be spent in Kharkiv.
>
> 1) The CC's new practical instructions on grain procurements were developed and have been sent to the CC AUCP(B).
>
> 2) Select Kharkiv activists were gathered to explain the tasks with regard to the grain procurements, as there are opportunist waverings on this question among a considerable portion of the Ukrainian workers."

The subtlest nuances are important here: 1) the fact that it was Molotov who prepared the resolution of the Politburo of the CC CP(B)U (of course, Kosior had to be there); 2) the fact that before it was distributed, the resolution dated November 18 went to the Kremlin for approval; 3) the fact that the measures suggested by the Kremlin for intensifying grain procurements did not arouse enthusiasm among the "select Kharkiv activists."

---

32   Ibid., 250–60.
33   *Kolektyvizatsiia i holod na Ukraïni, 1929–1933*, 548–49.
34   *Komandyry Velykoho holodu*, 239. First publication of primary source: RGASPI, fond 82, op. 2, d. 141, l. 42.

Both the party and the government resolutions signed by Stanislav Kosior and Vlas Chubar, respectively, required that the grain-procurement plan be fulfilled completely by January 1, 1933, and that seed stocks be created by January 15. Expending seed stocks created on collective farms that had not yet met their grain quotas was forbidden. In fact, all grain held in reserve was sequestered. The goal of this extraordinary measure was exposed in the following point: to give district executive committees the right to count all in-kind assets of the collective farms as part of the grain-procurement fund. Indebted cooperatives that had issued in-kind advances as payment for workdays or contributions to the public nutrition program over and above the established norm (15 percent of what had been threshed) were supposed to arrange the immediate return of the "illegally distributed grain" in order to direct it toward the fulfillment of plan quotas. District executive committees were directed to organize the confiscation of grain stolen in the course of reaping, threshing, and transportation from collective farms, individual farmers, and workers on state farms. In reality, this ominous point meant that the state sanctioned mass searches to carry out the immediate and total confiscation of all available grain reserves, for no one was about to differentiate "stolen" grain from any other.

The point about searches was only the first feature of the measures to intensify grain procurements that later developed into the Chekist campaign that caused the Holodomor. The second such feature was the point on fines in kind, which figured as point 9 in the government resolution: "In-kind fines in the form of additional meat-procurement targets shall be levied on those collective farms that have countenanced the theft of grain and are maliciously undermining grain-procurement plans: they are to supply a 15-month quota of meat from both collectivized livestock and that owned by collective farmers. District executive committees shall levy such fines with the prior permission of the provincial executive committee in every instance."[35]

The party resolution repeated point 9 of the government document but augmented it as follows: "On collective farms unsatisfactorily fulfilling grain-procurement plans, all grain harvested by collective farmers from their home garden plots shall be counted as their in-kind payment for workdays; any excess grain issued to them shall be confiscated toward grain procurements." Finally, the resolution of the CC CP(B)U contained one more important point that was not included in the considerably shorter government resolution: individual farmers who had not fulfilled their grain quotas (either contracted or "self-imposed") could be fined by the imposition of additional quotas not only of meat procurement (amounting to a 15-month quota) but also of potatoes (a one-year quota).[36]

Let us now draw conclusions on the basis of the new regulatory framework for grain procurements in Ukraine. The party and government resolutions implemented with Stalin's personal approval established the collective farmers' responsibility for the failure of the collective farms to fulfill the quotas. Debtors were to make up the shortfall by relinquishing what they had grown on their private plots. Individual farmers were to compensate their failure to deliver grain with other products, in particular livestock or meat (fatback) and potatoes. The discovery of food reserves

---

35 *Kolektyvizatsiia i holod na Ukraïni, 1929–1933*, 549. Cf. "Resolution of the Politburo of the CC CP(B)U on measures to strengthen grain procurement" in *The Holodomor Reader*, 241.

36 *Holod 1932–1933 rokiv na Ukraïni: ochyma istorykiv, movoiu dokumentiv*, 254, 257.

from a collective farmer's private plot or an individual farmer's homestead could be made in various ways but, logically, the main one was a search. Hence, according to these documents, the calling cards of the Ukrainian Holodomor were fines in kind, that is, the confiscation of products grown and stored as reserves until the new harvest, as well as searches, in the course of which these products were subject to confiscation.

The resolution of the CC CP(B)U contained (this in the twentieth century!) a sheepish remark: mass searches of collective and individual farmers were not to be permitted. This matter was explained in detail in the instructions issued by the People's Commissariat of Justice of the Ukrainian SSR to prosecutors' offices on November 25. The commissariat instructed the prosecutors as follows:

> On the matter of recovering illegally distributed grain and confiscating stolen grain from particular collective and individual farmers, it is hereby explained:
>
> a) In this work, one must by all means rely on the best collective farmers—shock workers—and make every effort to achieve the desired effect without mass shakedowns and administrative measures, on the basis of self-examination, with regard to both the quantity of discovered and returned grain and the identification of actual wreckers in the collective-farm leadership, as well as loafers and freeloaders who have reserves of grain even though they have no workdays;
>
> b) Opportunities for the work of agents must be developed and utilized to the utmost in order to prevent, as much as possible, useless activity that yields no results.[37]

"Mass shakedowns," "useless activity"… These instructions are cited here for the sole purpose of showing that the republican authorities took the measures developed in the Kremlin for intensifying grain procurements in their literal meaning. Not in their worst nightmares could the leaders of the republic and local agencies have imagined that "measures to intensify grain procurements" might serve to cover up a campaign to confiscate all food reserves from the Ukrainian peasantry in the course of massive homestead searches. *All that remains is to identify the main consequence of the grain-procurement commission under Molotov's leadership in the Ukrainian SSR: the creation of a legislative basis for the punishment of grain-quota "debtors" by confiscating from them all foodstuffs produced on their private plots.*

In 1932, representatives of republican and local governments were not yet aware of what Stalin had in mind when he spoke of the "crushing blow." Since the times of Robert Conquest, however, we have known what Stalin meant by that expression. How, then, is the confiscation of food interpreted in post-Soviet Russian historiography?

In 2009 one of the most authoritative Russian specialists on the peasant question, Nikolai Ivnitsky, published a monograph on *The Famine of 1932–33 in the USSR*. His research on this tragedy is based on material from seven regions, including the Ukrainian SSR. Ivnitsky stresses that the "resolution of the Politburo of the CC CP(B)U dated November 18, 1932," which he analyzes in some detail, had "an exceptional impact on the collective farms and the peasantry through its

---

37   *Kolektyvizatsiia i holod na Ukraïni, 1929–1933*, 550.

measures."[38] Yet he does not develop this enigmatic statement, which nonetheless indicates the extent of his awareness. The in-kind meat and potato fines imposed on grain-quota debtors appear in his work only as a concept included in this resolution of the Politburo of the CC CP(B)U. Ivnitsky even assigns the authorship of the resolution, with its points about fines in kind, to the Politburo of the CC CP(B)U, adding only that the resolution was put together "with Molotov's participation." Two remarks must be made in this regard. First, what kind of authority could the head of the Soviet government have had when he arrived in Kharkiv with a mandate from Stalin as head of the extraordinary grain-procurement commission? Could he really have been authorized only to be present and observe? Second, in 2001 the Kyiv publishing house Heneza published, in the original Russian, the materials of Molotov's extraordinary commission in the Ukrainian SSR and Kaganovich's in the North Caucasus Krai. The book *Komandyry Velykoho holodu* (Commanders of the Great Famine) contains all the materials that preceded the appearance of the resolution adopted by the Politburo of the CC CP(B)U on November 18, 1932. They are analyzed in the book and show who the author of this document was.

Like the dekulakization campaign, Stalin's "crushing blow" could not have been delivered through the efforts of the Chekists alone. We are not dealing here with 3–5 percent of the rural population but with the Ukrainian peasantry as a whole. The local party and government apparatus had to be enlisted in the campaign of repression in Ukraine. Those who agreed to do the dirty work kept their jobs, and they and their families enjoyed the privilege of being supplied with foodstuffs that the communal state provided for its functionaries during the general famine. Those who sabotaged orders from the center through their own passivity were to be deprived of their positions, purged from the party, and subjected to repressive measures.

The Stalin-Molotov resolution of the CC CP(B)U "On Measures to Intensify Grain Procurement," dated November 18, 1932, speaks to this matter: "Since in a number of rural party organizations, especially during the period of grain procurements, whole groups of communists and individual leaders of party cells made common cause with kulakism, Petliurism, and so on, which in fact turns such communists and party cells into agents of the class enemy and is clear evidence of the total alienation of those cells and communists from the poor and middle collective-farm masses, the CC and CCC CP(B)U hereby approve the immediate purging of a number of rural party organizations that are clearly sabotaging the fulfillment of grain procurements."[39] Reference here was to the Snihurivka and Frunze districts of Odesa province and the Solone, Vasylivka, and Velyka Lepetykha districts of Dnipropetrovsk province. As was to be expected, the purge turned into a rout of party cadres. In the Velyka Lepetykha district, 80 of the 300 party members (27 percent) were expelled. In most villages of the district, leaders were expelled from their posts and from the party and then sent outside the republic. In particular, 10 of the 25 party-cell secretaries were subjected to repressive measures. But this devastating sweep produced no results, as was acknowledged in the CC CP(B)U resolution of December 20 "On the Course of

---

38 Nikolai A. Ivnitskii, *Golod 1932–1933 godov v SSSR* (Moscow: Sobranie, 2009), 157–58.
39 *Holod 1932–1933 rokiv na Ukraïni: ochyma istorykiv, movoiu dokumentiv*, 256.

the Purge in the Vasylivka, Solone, Frunzivka, Velyka Lepetykha, and Snihurivka District Party Organizations."⁴⁰

Terror by famine was initially applied to particular villages placed on the "blacklist" for their failure to settle up with the state in grain over a long period. At a meeting of the bureau of the North Caucasus Krai party committee on November 1, Kaganovich first announced his intention to place three to five villages (*stanitsy*) on the blacklist.⁴¹ On December 6, by resolution of the CC CP(B)U and the Radnarkom of the Ukrainian SSR, six villages in Ukraine were blacklisted.⁴² On December 8, Stanislav Kosior was already informing Stalin that the provincial party and executive committees had blacklisted as many as 400 collective farms.⁴³ If we look at the resolution describing blacklist status that was published in *Visti VUTsVK* on December 8, we see nothing out of the ordinary: cessation of cooperative and state trade, preterm loan collection, expulsion of "organizers of grain-procurement wrecking," and the like. All this was going on in other villages as well. What remained behind the scenes?

Inquisitive Italians took an interest in this, and on May 9, 1933 the Italian ambassador in Moscow, Bernardo Attolico, sent Rome the text of Consul Leone Sircana's report describing the state of agriculture in Ukraine "on the basis of newspaper reports and direct observation." Sircana described the situation as follows: "The placing of entire villages and collective farms on the so-called 'blacklist' entails severe penalties, such as the suspension of all deliveries of goods; the confiscation even of the insignificant stock of goods already available at the cooperatives; *an absolute ban on leaving the boundaries of one's village or farm; searches and seizures of produce*"⁴⁴ (emphasis added). So the blacklist penalties provided for "searches and seizures of produce." Barricaded in their villages and deprived of all foodstuffs, the peasants died of hunger.

In November the deputy head of the OGPU and special plenipotentiary of the GPU in the Ukrainian SSR, Vsevolod Balytsky, was sent to Kharkiv as part of a large group of Chekists. Stalin gave Balytsky some assignments that he soon announced in operational order no. 1 to the GPU of the Ukrainian SSR, dated December 5 (published for official use as a separate brochure). The order began with the assertion that Ukraine was experiencing the "organized sabotage of grain procurements and autumn sowing, organized mass theft on collective and state farms, terror against the staunchest and most steadfast communists and activists in the countryside,

---

40   Kul'chyts'kyi, *Tsina "velykoho perelomu,"* 282–83.

41   *Komandyry Velykoho holodu*, 254. First publication of primary source: RGASPI, fond 81, op. 3, d. 214, l. 1–11. Diary of Kaganovich's trip to the North Caucasus, November 1–8, 1932.

42   "Postanova Politbiuro TsK KP(b)U ta Radnarkomu USRR 'Pro zanesennia na "chornu doshku" sil, iaki zlisno sabotuiut' khlibozahotivli' vid 6 hrudnia 1932 r." in *Holod 1932–1933 rokiv na Ukraïni: ochyma istorykiv, movoiu dokumentiv*, 278–79. This resolution, signed by the head of the Ukrainian Radnarkom, Vlas Chubar, and the secretary of the CC CP(B)U, Stanislav Kosior, was published in the newspaper *Visti VUTsVK* (Kharkiv) on December 8, 1932.

43   "Lyst TsK KP(b)U Tsentral'nomu Komitetu VKP(b) pro stan khlibozahotivel' v USRR za pidpysamy S. Kosiora vid 8 hrudnia 1932 r." in *Holod 1932–1933 rokiv na Ukraïni: ochyma istorykiv, movoiu dokumentiv*, 282–88.

44   *Lysty z Kharkova: Holod v Ukraïni ta na Pivnichnomu Kavkazi*, 145, 147. These documents were first published in the original Italian by Professor Andrea Graziosi in Turin in 1991. Cf. "Report by the Novorossiisk royal vice consul, L. Sircana, 8 April 1933, 'Re: Developments in the agricultural season'" in *The Holodomor Reader*, 279.

the infiltration of dozens of Petliurite emissaries, and the distribution of Petliurite leaflets." Hence the conclusion about the "undoubted existence of an organized counterrevolutionary insurgent underground in Ukraine associated with foreign powers and foreign intelligence services, mainly with the Polish general staff."[45] The Chekists were given an advance description of whom they were to expose as belonging to counterrevolutionary organizations whose members were already arrested. Naturally, the Chekists received an assignment from Stalin to find grain concealed from the state inventory—evidence of counterrevolutionary activity.

While there was no problem in exposing individuals designated by the authorities as enemies of the people (in order no. 2 to the GPU of the Ukrainian SSR, dated February 13, Balytsky reported on the discovery of a counterrevolutionary underground in 200 districts),[46] fulfilling Stalin's mandate to discover pits of grain was not so simple. At a meeting of the Politburo of the CC CP(B)U on December 20, Balytsky reported that since the beginning of December, searches had turned up 7,000 pits and 100 "black granaries" concealing 700,000 poods of grain.[47] Two conclusions could be drawn from this information: a) peasants really were hiding remnants of the harvest from the state so as to not die of hunger; and b) the amount of grain uncovered was paltry, offering no hope of the "black granaries" fulfilling the grain-procurement plan.

There is every reason to assert that the procurement campaign of January 1933 in the Ukrainian countryside had nothing to do with grain quotas. Between December 20, 1932 and January 25, 1933, the use of sweeping home searches by Chekists, poor peasants (*nezamozhnyky*), and urban activists managed to turn up fewer than 8,000 pits, 521 "black granaries," and up to 1,400 other secret caches from which they confiscated one million poods of grain in all of Ukraine's rural localities. In order to bring the figure up to a million poods, they included grain obtained from repeat threshings of straw and chaff (so-called *ozadky*, or scraps) as well as grain confiscated from dealers. This overall figure is worth comparing with the grain-procurement plan approved by the Third All-Ukrainian Party Conference in July 1932 under pressure from their Kremlin guests, Molotov and Kaganovich—356 million poods from the peasant sector.[48]

Under the pretext of looking for grain concealed from the state by "peasant saboteurs," the Kremlin prepared a punitive campaign, the essence of which lay in the confiscation of all food from the Ukrainian countryside, which had long been seized by famine. This campaign was inhumane but constitutional. The constitution of the Ukrainian SSR adopted in March 1919 included article 28, which said: "The Ukrainian SSR recognizes work as the obligation of all citizens of the Republic and proclaims the slogan 'He who does not work, neither shall he eat.'" This article was copied from article 18 of the constitution of the Russian Soviet Federative Socialist

---

45 Shapoval and Zolotar'ov, *Vsevolod Balyts'kyi*, 189. Cf. "From operational order no. 2, GPU Ukrainian SSR, on the need to liquidate the insurgent underground before beginning sowing," in *The Holodomor Reader*, 256.

46 *Holod-henotsyd 1932–1933 rokiv v Ukraïni*, 297.

47 *Komandyry Velykoho holodu*, 316.

48 *Tretia konferentsiia KP(b)U, 6–9 lypnia 1932 r.: Stenohrafichnyi zvit* (Kharkiv, 1932), 17; Kul'chyts'kyi, *Holodomor 1932–1933 rr. iak henotsyd*, 245, 299.

Republic, which was adopted by the Fifth All-Russian Congress of Soviets in July 1918.[49]

The search for "enemies of the people," which turned out to be productive in almost half the districts of the Ukrainian SSR, was meant to paralyze the will of representatives of local party and government institutions. They watched the delivery of Stalin's "crushing blow" in total informational silence under cover of the winter grain-procurement campaign, already a habitual public fixture.

The "crushing blow" was a secret campaign, yet it spread across an enormous territory. Its secrecy was particular: the deadly famine could be mentioned only in a segment of the completely secret documentation of party and government agencies called "special files." No functionaries of any rank could speak the word "famine" aloud, which made discussion of the subject impossible. But owing to the "special files," with their special use and preservation status, they could carry out all the measures that the situation of epidemic starvation required of them.

The famine itself, however, could not be a secret, especially to the millions of peasants who were starving and dying of hunger. In that case, how were officials to speak of it on meeting with peasants? The people's commissar of agriculture, Yakov Yakovlev, gave an example in February 1933, when he spoke at a Moscow congress of shock workers (*udarniki*) from the collective farms. He accused Ukrainian collective farmers of failing to manage their sowing in 1932 and gather their harvest as they should have, causing "harm to the government and themselves" as a result. The "harm to the government" was the failure to fulfill the grain-procurement plan. Just what the "harm to themselves" looked like, Yakovlev did not specify, but he concluded his address with these words: "And from this, my Ukrainian collective-farm comrades, let us draw the conclusion: it is now time to settle accounts for the poor work of the past."[50]

So the commissar did not venture to repeat the abstract article of the constitution—"He who does not work, neither shall he eat"—in the concrete situation of epidemic famine. And he had even more reason to say nothing about what happens to a person who does not eat. Only one thing can be understood from his speech addressed to the Ukrainian collective farmers: you yourselves are guilty, as it were, and you yourselves will pay.

The regional congresses of shock workers from the collective farms organized by the CC AUCP(B) culminated with the all-Union congress at which Stalin spoke on February 19, 1933. He was not about to specify the nature of the harm that the collective farmers had brought upon themselves; rather, he emphasized that they would now start doing honest labor and become prosperous:

> Lenin, our great teacher, said, "He who does not work, neither shall he eat." What does this mean? Against whom are Lenin's words directed? Against the exploiters, against those who do not work themselves but compel others to work for them and get rich at the expense of others. And against whom else? Against those who loaf and want to live at the expense of others. Socialism demands not loafing but that all should work conscientiously; that they should

---

49   *Istoriia Radians'koï Konstytutsiï v dekretakh i postanovakh Radians'koho uriadu, 1917–1936* (Kyiv: Radians'ke budivnytstvo i pravo, 1937), 75, 118.

50   *Pravda* (Moscow), February 19, 1933.

work not for others, not for the rich and the exploiters, but for themselves, for the community. And if we work conscientiously, work for ourselves, for our collective farms, then we shall succeed in a matter of two or three years in raising all the collective farmers, both the former poor peasants and the former middle peasants, to the level of prosperous peasants, to the level of people enjoying an abundance of produce and leading a fully cultured life.[51]

The "takeaway" from this lengthy quotation is all too obvious: if you do not work on a collective farm, then you will die of hunger; if you do work, you will get rich. The example of people starving to death must have cowed all the rest. The essence of Stalin's "crushing blow" is completely in line with the expression first used by Robert Conquest: terror-famine.[52]

The interpretation of the famine given in Stalin's speech rippled through the country. At that time, most of the Red Army was made up of soldiers who served part-time, called up for a brief period without being relieved of their main jobs. Not long after the All-Union Congress of Shock Workers from the Collective Farms, a political worker from the Dnipro Region Division in the Ukrainian Military District lectured his audience: "Some of the part-timers are engaging in sabotage and do not want to work on the collective farms. That is why they are starving, but no one is to blame. The loafers can blame themselves; they should recall Lenin's slogan: 'He who does not work, neither shall he eat!' We know that the bourgeoisie, kulaks, and loafers do not work. So neither shall they eat!"[53]

In order to come up with a general picture of the famine throughout the republic, which was necessary for planning the sowing campaign, Stalin's governor in Ukraine, Pavel Postyshev, created an information group on sowing within the CC CP(B)U. Its reports not only paint a picture of the famine but also give the interpretation that Stalin and his henchmen expected of the local functionaries. In particular, in a report of February 28, Aronov, the head of the group, gave examples of starvation "accompanied by swelling, a number of deaths, and even cases of cannibalism." Seemingly for the sake of "objectivity," however, he stressed that "along with starvation caused by laziness [sic] and unwillingness to work on the collective farms, cases of starvation among conscientious collective farmers with a large number of workdays have been observed, although in significantly lesser number." This passage concluded the report: "It is interesting to note that in the Khrystynivka district, the collective farmers take a negative view of aid to starving families, as most of them barely worked and have very few workdays."[54]

A few days later, on March 3, after an inspection trip around the southern districts of the province, the secretary of the Dnipropetrovsk provincial party

---

51 I. Stalin, "Rech' na Pervom Vsesoiuznom s"ezde kolkhoznikov-udarnikov 19 fevralia 1933 g.," *Sochineniia* (Moscow: Gosudarstvennoe izdatel'stvo politicheskoi literatury, 1951), 13: 249. Cf. https://www.marxists.org/reference/archive/stalin/works/1933/02/19.htm.

52 Robert Conquest, *The Harvest of Sorrow: Soviet Collectivization and the Terror-Famine* (New York: Oxford University Press, 1986).

53 Liudmyla Hrynevych, "Refleksiï Chervonoï armiï na kolektyvizatsiiu i holod v Ukraïni (1932–1933)" in *Holod-henotsyd 1933 roku v Ukraïni: istoryko-politolohichnyi analiz sotsial'no-demohrafichnykh ta moral'no-psykholohichnykh naslidkiv. Mizhnarodna naukovo-teoretychna konferentsiia. Kyiv, 28 lystopada 1998 r. Materialy*, ed. Stanislav Kul'chyts'kyi et al. (Kyiv: Vydavnytstvo M. P. Kots', 2000), 204.

54 *Holod 1932–1933 rokiv na Ukraïni: ochyma istorykiv, movoiu dokumentiv*, 391, 394. First publication of primary source: TsDAHOU, fond 1, op. 1, spr. 2191, ark. 92.

committee, Mendel Khataevich, reported to Stalin: "There is a palpable sobering up after that orgy and intensification of the greed characteristic of owners and the petty bourgeoisie that most collective farmers experienced during the recent grain procurements. Among most of the collective farmers who so very recently pilfered and stole collective-farm grain, treated collective-farm property carelessly, and did not want to work honestly for collective-farm production, it is apparent that they are coming to appreciate more and more the need to work honestly and diligently for the collective farm."[55]

In a letter of March 12 to the Ukrainian general secretary, Stanislav Kosior, the people's commissar of agriculture of the Ukrainian SSR, Oleksandr Odyntsov, pedantically enumerates the number of deaths from hunger since the beginning of the year in the Uman, Shpola, and Bila Tserkva districts (Kochubeivka, 48 people; Ozyrne, 90; Mala Vilshanka, 86, and so on), discusses cannibals in naturalist fashion and in detail, and later comes to the conclusion expected of him: "Among the people there is a growing awareness that the way out of this situation is first and foremost to carry out the spring sowing. There is malice toward loafers and criminals on the part of the collective farmers who do their work faithfully. The collective farmer who works faithfully thinks, 'Let the loafers and criminals die of hunger.'"[56]

The motif of "educating by famine" is also clearly apparent in a letter of March 15 from the Ukrainian general secretary to Stalin: "Comrades who have been to the localities say that now there is hardly any talk in the Kyiv region to the effect that 'grain was taken,' and that people blame themselves for poor work, for not safeguarding grain and allowing it to be pilfered. In this regard, there is undoubtedly a certain about-face among the masses on the collective farms that manifests itself in their attitude toward those who did not work. But this is not by any means understood everywhere and by all collective farmers.... The fact that starvation has not yet knocked sense into the heads of a great many collective farmers is shown by the unsatisfactory preparations for sowing precisely in the most troublesome districts."[57]

In his correspondence with Kaganovich, as noted above, Stalin called the famine by its right name when describing the situation in Ukraine. But that applied to the first half of 1932, when famine was an unwanted consequence of requisitioning and was not being used as an instrument of murder. In late 1932–early 1933, when carrying out the deadly terror-famine, Stalin invariably came up with circumlocutions of the "crushing-blow" type. Only on May 20, 1933, at a meeting of leaders of the southern provinces in the CC AUCP(B) on the reaping and procurement campaign, did he allow himself to summarize quite frankly the effects of the "crushing blow" directed against the collective farmers. Yet here, quite deliberately, he emphasized

---

55 *Holod 1932–1933 rokiv na Ukraïni: ochyma istorykiv, movoiu dokumentiv*, 403. First publication of primary source: TsDAHOU, fond 1, op. 101, spr. 1283, ark. 108.

56 *Holodomor 1932–1933 rr. v Ukraïni: Zlochyn vlady — trahediia narodu*, 348. First publication of primary source: TsDAHOU, fond 1, op. 20, spr. 6274, ark. 177.

57 *Holod 1932–1933 rokiv na Ukraïni: ochyma istorykiv, movoiu dokumentiv*, 443. First publication of primary source: TsDAHOU, fond 1, op. 101, spr. 1243, ark. 172. Cf. "From a memorandum of the CC CP(B)U to the CC AUCP(B) on progress in preparing spring sowing, some reasons for the difficult food situation in a number of oblasts and raions of the republic, and measures to aid the starving" in *The Holodomor Reader*, 262.

not the collective farmers but the individual ones, who had practically ceased to exist in the collectivized countryside. The word "famine" did not appear in his speech, which was not for publication—the general secretary continued watching carefully to make certain that it would figure only in the "special files." But the word "death" did sound in a context related to the notion of famine. Stalin was not about to pass over in silence the effect of the famine that was obvious to all present—mortality. It is worth citing an extract of this speech, which is now available to all on the website of the Russian Federal Archives Agency in the "Documents of the Soviet Epoch" section:

> How has he [the individual farmer] been living? He calculated thus: 'Why should I break my bones working? The state farm fields are large, the collective-farm fields are large, I'll wait for the harvest and steal as much as I need from the state farms and collective farms.' That is how he's been living. He stole grain from the fields of the state and collective farms to feed himself. After we launched the repressions against criminals and thieves, after we arrested several hundred thousand people throughout the Union, he felt it, of course, and the individual farmer has found himself between two fires. He didn't sow, hoping that he'd be able to take something—steal—from the collective or state farms. Stealing is now very difficult and even dangerous. That's why he's left with no way out and dies. Don't you know how he's dying, or what? You know.[58]

And now, so do we. With a New Year's telegram from Stalin to the Ukrainian peasantry, murder by starvation began.

---

58   RGASPI, fond 558, op. 11, d. 1117, l. 19–21. Cf. sovdoc.rusarchives.ru: Lichnye fondy vidnykh deiatelei Sovetskoi ėpokhi / Fond 558. Stalin (nast. Dzhugashvili) Iosif Vissarionovich (1878–1953) / Opis' 11. Dokumenty I. V. Stalina i prislannye I. V. Stalinu / Delo 1117. Rechi, besedy Stalina I. V. za 1933 g. / Dokument 3. Dve rechi Stalina I. V. na soveshchanii pri TsK VKP(b).

6 | THE HOLODOMOR

Stalin's telegram of January 1, 1933, which initiated the Ukrainian Holodomor, was addressed to the leaders of the Ukrainian SSR in Kharkiv. In his first point, the general secretary demanded that all collective and individual farmers be notified through the village councils that they were voluntarily to deliver to the state their "previously stolen and hidden grain." The second and final point of the telegram concerned people who ignored this demand. It read: "As for the collective farmers, collective farms, and individual farmers who stubbornly continue to conceal grain stolen and hidden from the grain inventory, the harshest punitive measures provided by the resolution of the CEC and Sovnarkom of the USSR ("On Safeguarding the Property of State Enterprises, Collective Farms, and Cooperatives and Strengthening Public (Socialist) Property") of August 7, 1932, will be applied."[1]

The logical connection between the first and second points of the telegram prompted local authorities to organize searches of every peasant household on the whole territory of the Ukrainian SSR. After all, the threat of employing the Law of Spikelets against peasants who avoided delivering their "hidden grain" to the state could only be effectuated if it were determined that they had in fact resisted. Hence Stalin's telegram was not so much a threat as a signal to begin mass searches.

The legend about the "hidden grain" proved necessary not only to signal the need for these mass searches but also to provide plausible motivation for the actions of the tens of thousands of people who had to take part in them. It was no accident that at the time Stalin was sending his telegram, the New Year's edition of the newspaper *Pravda* published a report from the large village of Krynychky in the Dnipropetrovsk region. According to the journalist, there were fifty grain-procurement officials from the district and province in the village. On average, they were supposed to ensure the delivery of 1,000 quintals of grain daily but were managing to wring no more than 15 quintals out of the peasants. The report ended as follows: "We must keep looking, as there is a whole 'underground city of wheat.' Yet only rarely do the efforts of the best workers turn up one or two pits."

What were the objective consequences of Stalin's New Year's telegram? We have a more or less precise measurement of the extent of excess mortality and can therefore differentiate the all-Union famine of 1932 in Ukraine from the Ukrainian Holodomor of 1933. According to the latest calculations of experts at the Institute of Demography and Social Research, National Academy of Sciences of Ukraine—

---

1   *Holod 1932–1933 rokiv na Ukraïni: ochyma istorykiv, movoiu dokumentiv*, 308. First publication of archival source: TsDAHOU, fond 1, op. 101, spr. 1257, ark. 14–15a.

Omelian Rudnytsky, Nataliia Levchuk, Alla Savchuk, and Pavlo Shevchuk, under the leadership of Oleh Wolowyna (University of North Carolina)—excess mortality in 1933 was 3,335,000 people in the rural areas of the Ukrainian SSR and 194,000 in the cities. The corresponding statistics for 1932 were 207,000 in the villages and 43,000 in the cities.[2]

Death by starvation in 1932 was a consequence of the grain procurements. In extracting the *prodrazvërstka* from the 1931 harvest, Molotov "outdid himself" in a whole series of districts of the Ukrainian SSR, which led to mass mortality in the first half of 1932. In order to ensure the spring sowing and save the starving, the state provided food aid, which included the reduction of grain exports. At that time, no one was bent on the destruction of starving Ukrainian peasants. The fourteenfold difference between the famine of 1932 and the Holodomor of 1933 cannot be explained by grain procurements. In January 1933, under a total information blockade, all food supplies were confiscated from peasant households in the course of a campaign to uncover that nonexistent "underground city of wheat." On January 22, the information blockade was augmented with a physical one. Stalin himself wrote the directive of the CC AUCP(B) and Sovnarkom of the USSR to halt the mass exodus of peasants from Ukraine and the Kuban to other regions.[3]

The famine caused by grain procurements can be justified by whatever one wishes, even—and this is often done when genocide is being denied—by the need to establish a defense infrastructure in anticipation of the events of 1941. However, when the state confiscates not grain but any and all food, its intentions should be deemed murderous: there can be no other explanation. We are dealing here with mass murder—planned in advance and well organized—not only of those whom the Kremlin regarded as saboteurs but also of children and the elderly. The searches for and confiscation of foodstuffs were carried out by urban activists and local members of Committees of Poor Peasants under the direction of Chekists. The poor peasants were starving; they did not have to be inveigled to do what they did.

The fact that stores of food were confiscated by state agencies removes the grounds for opposition to calling the Holodomor a genocide. That is why objectors adamantly demand: "Show us the documents!" Yet documents on the confiscation of all food from peasants have not been found for the whole territory of Ukraine and the Kuban. The Kremlin rulers considered that such nightmarish intentions could not be set down on paper. Their assessment can be backed up with documents. In November 1932, the Starominsk AUCP(B) district committee in the North Caucasus Krai recommended repressions against the village of Novoe Selo: "Apply the harshest measures of influence and coercion, carrying out the confiscation of all foodstuffs."

---

2   Nataliia M. Levchuk, "Raionna dyferentsiatsiia vtrat naselennia Ukraïny unaslidok holodu v 1933 rotsi" in *Holod v Ukraïni u pershii polovyni XX stolittia: prychyny i naslidky*, 261; Omelian Rudnytskyi, "Urban-Rural Oblast Dynamics of 1932–34 Famine Losses in Ukraine," paper presented at the 18th Annual World Convention of the Association for the Study of Nationalities, Columbia University, New York, April 18–20, 2013.

3   *Tragediia sovetskoi derevni*, 3: 635. Archival source: RGASPI, fond 558, op. 11, d. 45, l. 109. The editor in chief of this volume, Ilia Zelenin, noted in the foreword: "The directive was written by Stalin himself (the holograph has been preserved) and initially signed only by him. After it was typed, the signature of Molotov as head of the Sovnarkom also appeared, clearly at the author's behest. This is one of the few documents (after the Law of August 7, 1932) that confirm Stalin's direct, hands-on participation in organizing the mass famine of 1932–33" (p. 32).

In a letter to the CC CP(B)U secretary Mendel Khataevich, Molotov hypocritically called this recommendation "un-Bolshevik" and prompted by "despair, for which we have no grounds, since the party is coming out against the practice of local authorities 'to take any grain wherever they want, ignoring the consequences, and so on.'"[4]

What was happening in the Ukrainian countryside has been described by witnesses to the Holodomor who were fortunate enough to survive. There are hundreds and thousands of documented and published testimonies asserting that the search brigades confiscated not only meat and potatoes, as provided by the legislation about in-kind fines, but all available foodstuffs. The online *Atlas of the Holodomor* created by researchers at Harvard University includes a map of the whereabouts of the witnesses who attested the confiscation of all food. The locations where the witnesses spent the Holodomor were plotted on a map, proving that food was being confiscated not only along the border with Romania and Poland but also in the districts of Polisia. Such a map constitutes a full-fledged document, not the subjective testimony of various individuals.

What was happening in the countryside in January 1933 is well demonstrated in the three-volume collection of survivor testimonies from people who told the US Commission on the Ukraine Famine of their experiences. Here are some of their stories.[5]

Anonymous witness, born in 1903, village of Osycha Balka, Zvenyhorodka district, Cherkasy region:[6]

> "One woman in our village, she was a very poor woman, an old maid, she had no field, just a garden, she had maybe a half-hectare garden, so she planted a little bit for herself, she sowed a little bit of rye, so she buried a bucket of rye and planted a cherry tree on top. They found it, someone had watched her or maybe they just found it, and they took the bucket of rye, they took everything in the house and sent her into exile in Kolyma."

Dmytro Korniienko, born in 1918, a hamlet in Ponornytsia district, Chernihiv region:[7]

> "Our mom was sentenced in early 1933 to 8 years in prison. They arrested her. My sister was born in 1927, and we were basically left within those walls, so our late grandma decided to look after us, since there wasn't anyone else. I

---

4   Viktor Kondrashin, *Golod 1932–1933 godov: tragediia rossiiskoi derevni* (Moscow: ROSSPĖN, 2008), 216. Kondrashin cites a document from RGASPI, fond 82, op. 2, d. 141, l. 74.

5   The US Congressional Commission, led by Staff Director James Mace, published a three-volume edition of testimony with the US Government Printing Office in Washington, DC in 1990, but in an extremely limited print run. At the initiative of the Institute of History, National Academy of Sciences of Ukraine, the three volumes were reprinted in Kyiv for the 75th anniversary of the Holodomor. See *Investigation of the Ukrainian Famine 1932–1933: Oral History Project of the Commission on the Ukraine Famine*, ed. James E. Mace and Leonid Heretz, 3 vols. (Washington: US GPO, 1990); *Velykyi holod v Ukraïni 1932–1933 rokiv*, 3 vols. (Kyiv: Kyievo-Mohylians'ka akademiia, 2008). The citations in the present volume refer not to the pages of the two editions, whose pagination is not identical, but to the volume and index number assigned to each witness.

6   Vol. 1, interview LH 19. This is the present-day village of Lysycha Balka, the site of the village council of Katerynopilsk district, Cherkasy oblast. The name of the village may well have been recorded incorrectly during the interview.

7   Vol. 1, interview LH 29.

remember one episode. The brigade came in—that's what they called the ones doing the grain procurement. Well, our late grandma brought us—maybe she borrowed it from her sons—half a cup of millet to cook us some porridge for dinner. It was lunchtime. And they found that glass with the millet. There were maybe five of them, mostly foreigners, I only noticed two of ours in that brigade. And the one when he found it, 'Aha, millet,' and he asked the others, 'Who's got the bag of millet so we can pour out this glass?' And they left us that cup empty. When they left our home, we had absolutely no food."

Fedir Kapusta, born in 1900, village of Horby, Kremenchuk county, Poltava region:[8]

"On January 21, or maybe November 21, brigades were organized in every village that had a village council, and these brigades went around to the collective and individual farmers and took everything until nothing was left. If they found a handful of millet, they took it; if they found a handful of pumpkins, they took them. And in the cellars where the cabbage, pickled beets, and potatoes were, they took every last bit. Why'd they take it? Those were their orders from the authorities who were doing this. And they got—the ones taking part in the grain procurements—they got 25 percent, so they tried to take as much as possible, you understand, because they got 25 percent. They also had no grain and were hungry."

Hryhorii Moroz, born in 1920, village of Mykolaivka, Buryn district, Sumy region:[9]

"They took whatever they could. These activists were a special kind—even the women among them, if there was something cooked in the oven, they'd knock it over. Like it was an accident. Knock it over so it spills out, and then:

'Well, what are you living on?'
'There's nothing.'
'Well, what are you living on?'
'Well, I'm living however I can.'
'How come you haven't croaked?'"

Teodora Soroka, Trypniak by marriage, born in 1924, homestead of Lozuvatka, Tsarychanka district, Dnipropetrovsk region:[10]

"The starvation started in the spring of '33. Sometime near the end of February. A terrible starvation started 'cause they were putting the squeeze on us; even if someone went to get something, then they'd take it all right away. Even if someone scrounged up a handful of millet, tossed in water, and boiled it in a pot, they'd smash that pot, throw it into the yard."

Oleksa Sonypul, born in 1915, Sosnytsia district, Chernihiv region; he would not name the village, as he still had family there.[11]

---

8   Vol. 1, interview LH 08.
9   Vol. 2, interview SW 09.
10   Vol. 3, interview SW 83.
11   Vol. 3, interview SW 88.

> "In '33 the brigades came 'round our village to wrest grain from us right before Christmas.[12] They took everything edible. That day they also found the potatoes we'd buried in Uncle's garden. And for that, on that day they took everything from our uncle, including the bundles Grandma had gathered for seed for the spring. The next day, the first day of Christmas, they came to us, they broke down the windows and doors and took them to the collective farm. Father didn't sleep at home that night, and Mother had already died. There were six of us then—our smallest sister was four. And Uncle took us to his house. The next day they came from the village council and said that we had 24 hours to get out of Uncle's house."

The three volumes of testimony published by James Mace's commission are filled to overflowing with stories like these from all regions of Ukraine. Similar testimonies have also been included in diaspora publications and, since 1989, in many books published in Ukraine.

Facts of this kind are also to be found in district newspapers (the censors felt that they could be published for edification: He who does not work, neither shall he eat) as well as in archives. In a collection of documents published by the Central State Archives of Public Organizations of Ukraine (compiled by Volodymyr Lozytsky, Olha Bazhan, Serhii Vlasenko, and Anatolii Kentii), we come across a horrific account in a report of January 19, 1933 from the People's Commissariat of Justice of the Ukrainian SSR addressed to Stanislav Kosior:[13]

> "Chernihiv province, Bakhmach district, village of Ivanhorod. During the confiscation of his grain, the middle peasant Bolokhovets hanged himself. He had completed the assignment for December 16 voluntarily. Since he had failed to complete further assignments, a brigade arrived at his home. Potatoes were found in niches beneath the stove, and the brigade attempted to take them. Then Bolokhovets and his family caused a commotion, ran out into the street and, having pulled the reins off the horses, he tried to hang himself, but the brigadier impeded him. Then Bolokhovets threw off his jacket, crawled into the barn, and hanged himself there. Taken from Bolokhovets: 116 kg of grain, 19 kg of potatoes, 4 kg of vetch, 1 kg of millet, 3 kg of beans, 10 kg of sunflowers, and 10 poppy heads."

The accounts presented here have been selected to illustrate the main point: under the guise of grain procurements, all food was taken from peasants for the sole purpose of forcing them to starve to death. Although there is no written documentation exposing this intention, and there could not possibly be any, the destructive operation initiated by Stalin's New Year's telegram spread all across Ukraine. Thus the Kremlin's intention to annihilate a certain portion of the Ukrainian population has a solid evidentiary basis in the accounts of hundreds and hundreds of people who managed to survive. We also have the objective results of Stalin's operation: the death by starvation of millions of people in the Ukrainian SSR and the Kuban.

---

12   Ukrainians celebrate Christmas according to the Julian calendar, which means that this would have happened in early January 1933. Christmas is generally celebrated for three days, with the main event, an evening meal, eaten on January 6, Christmas Eve. (Trans.)

13   *Holodomor 1932–1933 rokiv v Ukraini: Zlochyn vlady—trahediia narodu,* 301. First publication of archival source: TsDAHOU, fond 1, op. 20, spr. 6353, ark. 7.

By studying the recollections, it can be ascertained that many peasants still had potatoes and other food obtained from their personal plots. This helped them survive without the grain that was confiscated or never distributed by the collective farms. Hence it cannot be asserted that searches with the confiscation of all food extended to all peasant households. The Kremlin's control over carrying out its orders was not omnipresent. Moreover, Stalin's telegram called for searches not explicitly but obliquely. Perhaps some people made use of methods other than searches to find the peasants' "stolen and hidden grain." The state security agencies had an extensive network of informers in the countryside and made use of their services. In the recollections we also encounter tales of teachers (obviously informers) who were supposed to ask the children who among them had eaten grain before school.

It is important to note that after the Chekists' January operation in Ukraine, bazaar trade in foodstuffs practically came to a halt for the first half of 1933. All that remained was a chain of shops of the All-Union Association "Trade with Foreigners," or Torgsin, which were solicitously extended to all rural districts by the state.

The US Commission on the Ukraine Famine raised the subject of the Torgsin shops as a separate point when interviewing witnesses to the Holodomor. It truly deserves attention.

Here is the anonymous account of a former Cossack, born in 1920, from the Nezlobna village (*stanitsa*) in the Krasnodar region:[14]

> "When Father was serving the tsar as a Cossack he had gold crosses, silver clocks, golden clocks, some kind of award, that's what I know. I only heard that Father had been to the Turkish border. Under the tsar or after the revolution, I don't know. So she [Mother] took it all, all those crosses, golden clocks to the Torgsin. The state opened the Torgsin, where they sold first-rate rice, first-rate flour for baking, grain, or what have you, and some other kind of cereal. All of it for gold. Whoever had gold teeth or the like pulled them out, or golden wedding bands, they took them off and turned them in. Yes."

Yefrozynia Zoria, born in 1906 in the homestead of Kruhlyk near Hadiach:[15]

> "I got four cups for my earrings, removed them and handed over the earrings, and brought back four cups of wheat. That was it. The Torgsin was in Hadiach, Torgsin. So I went there. Those were my mother's earrings. They said, 'If you've got earrings, when you can get to Hadiach, take them and exchange them.' We lived on what I got for my earrings for a week—four souls on four little cups. Sometime in the spring, I pick something here, something there, different grasses, and that makes a little porridge. But it's not like it would fill you up. You have to divide everything as a mother—give yourself a bit less, and the kids you give enough to get them by, somehow. They won't get full, but they'll moisten their guts a bit. It was terrible, terrible!"

Anonymous female witness, born in 1906, who lived in a county center in Poltava province (town unnamed):[16]

---

14   Vol. 1, interview LH 04.
15   Vol. 1, interview LH 17.
16   Vol. 1, interview LH 27.

> "The Torgsin was how we survived. They opened the Torgsins. We gave up our rings, our earrings. I had a couple bracelets, a couple rings, and some other things. They tossed out the stones but weighed the gold and gave millet, gave bread. What else was there? You could get anything there. You could get meat there, but we didn't get any because we needed to have enough to buy grain. Thanks to that, we survived. Otherwise we wouldn't have survived, where could we have gotten anything?"

Anonymous witness, born in 1916, the village of Voronkiv, Boryspil district, Kyiv region:

> "And when people were taking gold, my mother took her earrings and got one and a half poods of flour. That's the kind of earrings she had—big and gold. Oh, and the people who took gold were photographed and then had their life stories examined, and then they were arrested and put in the jail on Lukianivka Street, and those people were mainly told: 'Give up your gold, where do you have it buried?' There were cases of torture when they'd fill cells full of these people, give them a salted herring to eat, and then not give them water. That's how they tortured people, so they'd suffocate and expire. That was in the Torgsins."[17]

It is clearly apparent that the system of Torgsin shops was developed in rural localities specifically to take advantage of the famine so as to increase the state's gold and hard-currency reserves. The state's self-interest only helped save people who had gold at home from death. But woe to those whom the Chekists believed to have large quantities of hard currency or gold. The three volumes of the US Congressional Commission's testimonies contain numerous accounts of the persecution of "underground millionaires."

The whole Torgsin operation was devoid of elements of charity. The International Commission of Inquiry into the 1932–1933 Famine in Ukraine found it imperative to note: "The fact that the shelves at Torgsin were bending under the weight of food when there was an enormous number of starvation victims testifies to the authorities' refusal to provide assistance to the starving."[18] But the crux of the problem was not at all that the authorities refused to help. The lawyers' conclusion wonderfully illustrates just how far they were from understanding this crux at a time when research on the Soviet famine was just beginning. Unfortunately, the global historiography of the famine in the USSR still does not differentiate the famine caused by requisitioning from the terror-famine carried out under the guise of Stalin's punitive operation that bore the code name "crushing blow."

Stalin's "crushing blow" consisted of two interrelated operations, one punitive, the other rescuing. The punitive operation lasted from January 1 to February 7, 1933 and was directed, as can be seen from its results, at preempting uprisings of starving villagers against the authorities. Transforming the famine into absolute starvation paralyzed the villagers' will to fight. That was the result sought by the Soviet organs of state security, and it was precisely the outcome observed by their Polish counterparts, who carefully followed the situation in Right-Bank Ukraine, home to many Poles. The chief of the Polish intelligence agency in Kyiv, Władysław Michniewicz, informed

---

17   Vol. 2, interview SW 17–SW 18.
18   Mezhdunarodnaia komissiia po rassledovaniiu goloda na Ukraine 1932–1933 godov. *Itogovyi otchet, 1990 g.* (Kyiv: Otdelenie redaktsionno-izdatel'skoi i reklamnoi deiatel'nosti UKrTsENDISI, 1992), 55.

the embassy on June 2, 1933 of the situation in the countryside around Kyiv: "Death from hunger is a constant occurrence. Cannibalism is the order of the day. There's nothing to report on the political mood; the only desire is for bread."[19]

The rescue operation took place to much fanfare, the echoes of which can still be heard today. In 2009 the Russian Archives published an expensive coffee-table book under the title *Golod v SSSR: Famine in the USSR, 1930–1934*.[20] It is a collection of 188 color photocopies of documents from six of the Russian Federation's central archives, including ones with extraordinarily limited access. Document no. 83 is laid out quite effectively in the publication: it is a page from the unbound file of the proceedings of the Politburo of the CC AUCP(B) dated February 8, 1933, with three points on the provision of food aid to the North Caucasus Krai party committee and the Dnipropetrovsk and Odesa provincial committees. Below the text is the red seal of the CC AUCP(B) and Joseph Stalin's signature in red ink.[21] The file was unbound and the document photographed with the truest possible reproduction of its colors to demonstrate how the Bolshevik leaders helped the starving regions.

How could there be any talk of genocide when the Soviet government had made every effort to save the starving? With this collection of full-color illustrations, the Russian Archives tried to make the argument for genocide appear absolutely unfounded. As for the survivors of the Holodomor, it remained incomprehensible to them, especially as discussions of it were illegal until December 1987. Nearly one-third of the witnesses who testified to James Mace's commission about what they had lived through did so anonymously. Half a century after the event and half a world away, with the protection of their American citizenship, they could not overcome the fear that the Stalin regime had instilled in them.

Depriving people of food was one form of Stalin's terror. We should accept the term "terror-famine" that Robert Conquest suggested in 1986. Like all other forms of state terror, it was meant to annihilate a limited segment of the population in order to make the behavior of the whole population predictable and acceptable to the authorities. Unlike other forms of terror, terror by famine was "blind." Its victims were not photographed en face and in profile; there were no investigations of their cases. Not infrequently the victims were grateful to the regime, which, *having confiscated everything edible, organized rescue food aid after a premeditated interval of a few weeks* through state and collective farms in order to safeguard the sowing campaign of 1933.

The will-paralyzing situation of absolute starvation was noted long ago by one of the most perspicacious scholars of the Soviet village, the late Ilia Zelenin. In 1994 he wrote: "It is not yet entirely clear whether the Holodomor of 1932–33 was an operation planned in advance and skillfully organized by Stalin or, on the contrary, the effect of his criminal anti-peasant policy. It is beyond doubt, however, that the 'terror-famine' caused a significant weakening and change in the character of peasant

---

19   *Hołodomor 1932-1933: Wielki Głód na Ukrainie*, 299. First publication of archival source: Centralne Archiwum Wojskowe w Warszawie. Oddział II SG, I.303.4.1928, podteczka 1933, dok. Nr 27, s. 89.

20   *Golod v SSSR: Famine in the USSR, 1930–1934*, comp. O. Antipova (Moscow: Federal'noe arkhivnoe agentstvo, 2009).

21   RGASPI, fond 17, op. 162 (Osobaia papka), d. 14, l. 59.

resistance, which could not have failed to enter into the calculations of Stalin and his entourage."[22]

The "crushing blow" was not limited to the confiscation of food. The agenda of Stalin's team also included a blockade, both physical and informational. In the first half of 1932, millions of Ukrainian peasants left their homes and made haste to Russia and Belarus to buy or trade for grain for their families. The Soviet government did not impede the "great migration," although its attitude toward that phenomenon was acutely negative. At that time the regime had no intention of annihilating peasants by means of famine, and they were allowed to return home with the provisions that saved their families. Moreover, the government bought grain abroad to provide food aid to a starving Ukraine.

A totally different picture could be observed in early 1933. The documentary collection *Tragediia sovetskoi derevni* (The Tragedy of the Soviet Village) contains three documents that provide a comprehensive overview of the measures taken by Stalin to put a stop to the flight from hunger. In his introduction, Ilia Zelenin, the editor in chief of the third volume of the collection, notes that the main document— the directive of the CC AUCP(B) and Sovnarkom of the USSR dated January 22, 1933—was handwritten by Stalin (the holograph has been preserved), and that the signature of the head of government, Viacheslav Molotov, appeared only in the typed version.[23]

If the directive is analyzed in conjunction with Stalin's New Year's address to the Ukrainian peasantry and his oral instructions on the confiscation of all foodstuffs, then it constitutes documentary proof that the ruler of the Kremlin intended to organize an absolute famine in the Ukrainian countryside. The introduction to this cipher, which argues the need for the proposed measures, is worth reproducing in full:

> The CC AUCP and Sovnarkom have received reports that a mass exodus of peasants "for bread" has begun from the Kuban and Ukraine to the Central Black Earth province, the Volga region, Moscow province, the Western province, and Belarus. The CC AUCP and Sovnarkom USSR have no doubt that this peasant exodus, like last year's migration from Ukraine, has been organized by enemies of Soviet rule, Socialist Revolutionaries and agents of Poland, with the aim of agitating "via peasants" in the northern regions of the USSR against collective farms and Soviet rule in general. Last year Ukraine's party, Soviet, and Chekist organs overlooked this counterrevolutionary plot of enemies of Soviet rule. Last year's mistake must not be allowed to be repeated this year.[24]

The directive started the blockade. The mass exodus of peasants from the North Caucasus to other regions was forbidden, as was migration to that territory from Ukraine. Similarly, the mass migration of peasants from Ukraine to other regions and migration to Ukraine from the North Caucasus were forbidden. All peasants who had managed to leave Ukraine and the North Caucasus in the interim were

---

22 Il'ia E. Zelenin, "'Revoliutsiia sverkhu': zavershenie i tragicheskie posledstviia," *Voprosy istorii* (Moscow), 1994, no. 10: 38.

23 *Tragediia sovetskoi derevni*, 3: 32.

24 Ibid., 3: 635. See RGASPI, fond 558, op. 11, d. 45, l. 109.

subject to being returned home (after the elimination of the "counterrevolutionary element" from their ranks).

On January 23 there appeared an identical document signed by Mendel Khataevich and Vlas Chubar,[25] and on January 25, a resolution of the bureau of the North Caucasus Krai committee of the AUCP(B), signed by Boris Sheboldaev, was issued.[26] The latter is quite detailed and therefore worth analyzing in detail to get a better picture of the nature of the blockade. First, village councils were forbidden to issue permits for trips out of the krai or into its ethnic enclaves, where there was no famine at all. Second, it was forbidden to issue tickets for train and water travel to anyone without village council identity papers. Third, checkpoints, operational mobile groups, and filtration points were put in place at the krai's rail exits. Fourth, Chekists, police, and local activists took control of land routes beyond the borders of settlements.

According to OGPU data provided by Nikolai Ivnitsky, over the 50 days after the directive was issued, 219,500 peasants were apprehended, including 38,000 in the Ukrainian SSR, 47,000 in the North Caucasus, 44,000 in the Central Black Earth province, 5,000 in the Western province, and 65,000 on trains. Of those apprehended, 186,500 were sent home with escorts, almost 3,000 were tried and sentenced, and all others were awaiting trial or under surveillance in filtration camps.[27]

When questioning witnesses, the US Congressional Commission that investigated the circumstances surrounding the organization of the Great Famine of 1932–33 in Ukraine paid special attention to details related to the physical blockade of the starving. A witness born in the Poltava region in 1910 who declined to divulge either his surname or the village he lived in told James Mace's committee:[28]

> "They took, you know, such pretty embroidered shirts, towels, skirts, kilims. They bartered. But, again, it was at the very beginning that people managed to get through, and then strict control was very firmly imposed. They would take everything from the train—bread and the rest—and send them home. Go home to Ukraine to your 'place of residence.' Back where you live. Which was perhaps the easiest. But lots of strong, healthy men, or what have you, were apprehended along the way and sent to concentration camps. As they say, wait: 'Loafers.'"

In areas bordering Russia, collective farmers tried to save themselves from starvation by crossing to Russian territory. The aforementioned Dmytro Korniienko, who lived in the Chernihiv region, was asked, "When did people start arriving from the south? You said that Ukrainians passed through your village." He answered,

---

25 "Postanovlenie Politbiuro TsK KP(b)U i SNK USSR po realizatsii direktivy TsK VKP(b) i SNK SSSR ot 22 ianvaria 1933 g." in *Tragediia sovetskoi derevni*, 3: 635–36. See RGASPI, fond 17, op. 42, d. 80, l. 9; see also *Holod 1932–1933 rokiv na Ukraïni: ochyma istorykiv, movoiu dokumentiv*. Primary source: TsDAHOU, fond 1, op. 16, spr. 9, ark. 115–16.

26 "Postanovlenie biuro Severo-Kavkazskogo kraikoma VKP(b) po realizatsii direktivy TsK VKP(b) i SNK SSSR ot 22 ianvaria 1933 g." in *Tragediia sovetskoi derevni*, 3: 636–38. Primary source: RGASPI, fond 17, op. 42, d. 72, l. 109–11.

27 Nikolai Ivnitskii, "Khlebozagotovki 1932–33 godov i golod 1933 goda" in *Holod-henotsyd 1933 roku v Ukraïni: istoryko-politolohichnyi analiz*, 114.

28 Vol. 1, interview LH 26.

> "Those migrants showed up in early '33. In the winter. Most of them showed up in the winter. And they were certainly hungry, exhausted, and looking for a piece of bread. They were all going from south to north. That's why so many of them were buried in our village. They weren't ours. There were, I repeat, maybe 20 of ours, maybe more, but the strangers were gathered every day and buried, gathered and buried."[29]

The starving were driven away from the railroads. If there was no hope of getting to Russia on foot, they would go to the nearest town and die there. Oleksii Keis, born in 1912, told Mace's committee this story:[30]

> "But the following episode occurred: my brother and I are walking around Yenakiieve, along Turtina Street—or was it Trutina, I've forgotten—when we see a woman lying near a fence. She's not so much lying as half sitting, half lying. Dead. We walked up to her, and there was a child with her. The woman was dead, but the child was alive. Less than a year old. Maybe one year, maybe a little less, maybe a little more. Hard to say, but the child was about a year old. It had pulled out its mother's breast and was sucking. But the mother was dead. My brother and I stopped and cried. We didn't feel sorry so much for the mother as for the child, who didn't know. It was sucking without understanding that there was nothing there. And along came the truck that gathered up corpses. They were always out because there were a whole lot of corpses lying around. And they scooped her up, two men jumped down, grabbed the woman by the legs and threw her on top, and the child too, where the dead were lying. They drove them off to the dump, to the cemetery just like that. That was something to see, I'm telling you. The woman and the child."

In the introduction to the third volume of the documentary collection *Tragediia sovetskoi derevni*, Ilia Zelenin devotes considerable attention to interpreting the directive of January 22, 1933. His conclusion is worth presenting in full:

> Thus there is some kind of chain of interrelated and interdependent actions taken by Stalin (either fully consciously or not) to organize the "great famine." In chronological order, they are: the law of August 7, 1932—the leader's brainchild; his speech of November 27, 1932 at the joint session of the Politburo of the CC and the Presidium of the CCC AUCP(B) (a theoretical justification of repressions against the peasantry as a whole and, simultaneously, a plan of action: "to respond with a crushing blow"); the resolution of December 27, 1932 on the passport system; and, finally, the ominous directive of January 22, 1933. The circle closed: the basic (subjective) preconditions for the peasantry-wide tragedy were put in place.[31]

Along with Viktor Danilov, Ilia Zelenin was the most authoritative expert on Soviet agrarian history. In his introduction he calls the directive of January 22, 1933 one of the few documents (after the law of August 7, 1932) that testify to Stalin's direct, hands-on participation (whether conscious or not, we shall not argue) in organizing mass starvation in 1932–33. Zelenin also offers his own explanation of the reasons, which should also be presented in his own words: "The question

---

29 Vol. 1, interview LH 29.
30 Vol. 1, interview SW 52.
31 *Tragediia sovetskoi derevni*, 3: 33.

nevertheless arises as to what goals motivated the general secretary—the desire to punish the peasants for their 'Italian' attempt [i.e., strike] to deprive the workers and the Red Army of grain, or to 'get grain' at all costs in order to carry out the program of industrialization and strengthen the country's defense. In my view, both the former and the latter were involved."[32]

What are the strengths and weaknesses of these two extracts from Ilia Zelenin's article? Their strength lies in the fact that the scholar established a chain of interrelated and interdependent actions taken by Stalin. Another strength lies in what Zelenin acknowledges: Stalin wanted to bring about a deadly famine among the peasants.

The question of why Stalin annihilated peasants (punishment for their 'Italian' behavior or a desire to 'get grain') is secondary. Zelenin's acknowledgment that the actions planned in advance by the Kremlin led to the annihilation of a certain portion of the peasantry is more significant. The UN Convention on the Prevention and Punishment of the Crime of Genocide is not concerned with motives for genocide. This international law defines its essence: "intent to destroy, in whole or in part, a national, ethnical, racial, or religious group, as such."[33]

In this definition of genocide we are not interested in the list of groups. Peasants are among the social groups unanticipated by the UN Convention, which is why Ilia Zelenin's position cannot be an argument in the matter of defining the famine of 1932–33 as a genocide. For our purposes it is important only that Zelenin recognized the Kremlin's intention to destroy people, which is one of the definitive signs of genocide according to the UN Convention.

Let us now consider the weak aspects of the extracts under analysis, adding to our consideration Danilov and Zelenin's joint article published in 2004 in the journal *Otechestvennaia istoriia* (History of the Homeland). This article was written after a discussion in Moscow of a book by Ukrainian scholars, *Holod 1932–1933 rokiv v Ukraïni: prychyny ta naslidky* (The Famine of 1932–1933 in Ukraine: Causes and Effects). The book was published by the Institute of Ukrainian History, National Academy of Sciences of Ukraine, for the seventieth anniversary of the Holodomor. Thirty authors contributed to the large-format volume of 888 pages, which includes an additional fascicle with 48 pages of illustrative matter.

The Institute of Ukrainian History arranged close cooperation with the Institute of World History at the Russian Academy of Sciences and, through it, with experts from other institutions in the Russian Federation under the framework of the Ukrainian-Russian Commission of Historians (the co-chairs being Academician of the NAS Ukraine Valerii Smolii and Academician of the NAS Russia Aleksandr Chubarian). Several copies of the Ukrainian historians' summary study of the famine of 1932–33 were sent to Moscow in advance, and on March 9, 2004 the Institute of World History held a discussion of it with the participation of many well-known Russian experts in agrarian history. The Ukrainian scholars' arguments,

---

32 Ibid., 3: 32.

33 Rafael' Lemkin: *Radians'kyi henotsyd v Ukraïni. Stattia 28 movamy* (Kyiv: Vydavnytstvo "Maisternia knyhy," 2009), 15 (in English), 25 (in Ukrainian). Cf. United Nations, General Assembly, *Convention on the Prevention and Punishment of the Crime of Genocide. Adopted by the General Assembly of the United Nations on 9 December 1948*, New York, 8 Dec. 1948 https://treaties.un.org/doc/publication/unts/volume percent2078/volume-78-i-1021-english.pdf, accessed January 5, 2017, p. 280.

which identified the Holodomor of 1933 as a genocide, did not, however, convince the Russian side. Without denying that Stalin had annihilated peasants, they could not agree that it was first and foremost Ukrainian peasants who were annihilated. In their joint article in *Otechestvennaia istoriia,* Viktor Danilov and Ilia Zelenin wrote: "If the famine of 1932–33 is to be characterized as an 'intentional genocide of the Ukrainian peasantry,' as certain historians of Ukraine have insisted, then we must bear in mind that this was a genocide of the Russian peasantry in equal measure."[34] The journal published the authors' names in a black frame of mourning. Not long after the meeting, our opponents passed away. This is a great loss to the field of Russian history, especially as promising Russian historians of the younger generation are in no hurry to take on the discussion of "difficult problems."

Let us return, however, to our analysis of Zelenin's arguments concerning a peasantry-wide tragedy, which he repeated word for word in the article that he co-wrote with Danilov. Undoubtedly, the law of August 7, 1932 and the promise to respond to sabotage with a "crushing blow" concerned the entire Soviet peasantry. The passport system is not worth examining in the context of the famine of 1932–33, but more on this below. Now we must think: against whom in particular was the "crushing blow" directed? Stalin's directive of January 22, 1933 provides the answer: against the Ukrainian SSR and the Kuban. On February 16, the directive was expanded to the Lower Volga region.[35]

Zelenin's chain of Stalin's operations does not include the most important link: Stalin's New Year's telegram to the Ukrainian peasants. This omission is not surprising, as the telegram was related to an operation for which there was no documentary evidence: the introduction of total searches of peasant households with the confiscation of all available food. The repressions carried out during the searches had a certain "legal" basis in the form of the law of August 7, 1932 and the resolutions on in-kind fines of meat and potatoes. Only, according to the testimony of people who managed to survive, the repressions went far beyond what existing punitive legislation allowed and turned into a campaign that deprived peasants of any kind of food, that is, created conditions incompatible with life.

Professor Stephan Merl of Bielefeld University in Germany rejected Conquest and Mace's conclusion about genocide, which they based on the testimonies of Ukrainian emigrants about the closing of the Ukraine-Russia border. He did not call the testimonies into question but asserted that the forced deportation of peasants to their own villages applied to all Soviet peasants and was brought about by the resolution of the Central Executive Committee and Sovnarkom USSR dated December 27, 1932 on the introduction of the passport system.[36]

Merl, like Conquest, may not have known about Stalin's directive of January 22, 1933 to close the Ukraine-Russia border. But he formulated his conclusion in 1995, whereas the contents of that directive, repeated in a letter of January 23, 1933

---

34 Viktor P. Danilov and Il'ia E. Zelenin, "Organizovannyi golod: K 70-letiiu obshchekrest'ianskoi tragedii," *Otechestvennaia istoriia* (Moscow), 2004, no. 5: 109.

35 "Direktiva TsK VKP(b) i SNK SSSR o predotvrashchenii massovogo vyezda golodaiushchikh krest'ian 22 ianvaria 1933 g." and "Postanovlenie Politbiuro TsK VKP(b) o rasprostranenii na Nizhniuiu Volgu direktivy TsK VKP(b) i SNK SSSR ot 22 ianvaria 1933 g." in *Tragediia sovetskoi derevni,* 3: 634–35, 644.

36 Shtefan Merl', "Golod 1932–1933 godov – genotsid ukraintsev dlia osushchestvleniia politiki rusifikatsii?" *Otechestvennaia istoriia* (Moscow), 1995, no. 1: 54, 56.

from the CC CP(B)U and Radnarkom Ukrainian SSR, had been made available to scholars in 1990 (it was published in *Holod 1932–1933 na Ukraïni: ochyma istorykiv, movoiu dokumentiv*). Yet the question arises: could the resolution on introducing the passport system, which was published earlier than the directive of January 22, 1933, have had an effect on the blockade of Ukraine?

The introduction of the system of internal passports with a residence permit (*propiska*) for those living in cities and new constructions was meant to create a legal basis for tethering the rural population to their homes. Ilia Zelenin indicated that the head of the committee for passportizing the population, Avel Yenukidze, formulated the main purpose of the internal passport as follows: "It is necessary to stave off the uncontrolled movement of enormous masses of the rural population around the country."[37] Yet the introduction of passports had no effect on the concrete situation that developed in the first months of 1933.

In the English version of his book on the peasant war in the USSR, Andrea Graziosi noted that passports provided a legal basis to deprive peasants of the possibility of saving themselves by fleeing the districts engulfed by hunger. When he reissued the book in Russian, Graziosi left those words in place but acknowledged his error in a footnote.[38] And indeed, issuing passports to the population could not have been accomplished in a few weeks or even months. The first resolutions on passports noted the categories of individuals who were to receive passports as well as those to whom they were forbidden to be issued. The state's intentions regarding the peasantry were not revealed until the adoption of the Sovnarkom resolution "On Issuing Passports to Citizens of the USSR on the Territory of the USSR" in April 1933. It stressed that rural residents were not to receive passports.[39]

The informational blockade of the Holodomor was absolute. The leaders of state security agencies who were directly committing Stalin's crime treated any "rumors of famine" as vicious anti-Soviet propaganda. The order of November 5, 1933 to the GPU of the Ukrainian SSR, "On the 16th Anniversary of October," signed by Karl Karlson, smacked of boundless cynicism: the "further victories on the front of the full-scale socialist offensive" were counterposed to the "capitalist world, seized by crisis, in which millions of peasants are doomed to death by hunger."[40]

The state security agencies were carefully monitoring to make sure that no one mentioned the tragedy that befell the Soviet people in 1933 in their everyday communication with others. For a diary entry about his son's death from exhaustion caused by hunger, Mykola Bokan, a resident of Baturyn, was arrested in 1937. The Chernihiv provincial court sent him to jail for eight years.[41]

37　*Tragediia sovetskoi derevni*, 3: 32. Primary source: RGASPI, fond 81, op. 3, d. 93, l. 24–25.

38　Andrea Gratsiozi (Graziosi), *Velikaia krest'ianskaia voina v SSSR: Bol'sheviki i krest'iane, 1917–1933* (Moscow: ROSSPĖN, 2001), 65, 94.

39　Tamara V. Vrons'ka, "Zaprovadzhennia pasportnoho rezhymu" in *Holod 1932–1933 v Ukraïni: prychyny ta naslidky*, 632. Primary source: "Postanovlenie SNK SSSR za № 861 'O vydache grazhdanam Soiuza SSR pasportov na territorii Soiuza SSR'" in *Sobranie zakonov i rasporiazhenii Raboche-krest'ianskogo Pravitel'stva SSSR, 1933*, no. 28.

40　*Rozsekrechena pam'iat'*, 58. Primary source: Branch State Archives of the Security Service of Ukraine, fond 9, op. 1, spr. 666, ark. 222.

41　*Nevidomi dokumenty z arkhiviv spetsial'nykh sluzhb*, vol. 7 (Warsaw and Kyiv, 2008), 1076, 1078; *Rozsekrechena pam'iat'*, 33.

A resident of the village of Khylkivka in the Pokrovska Bahachka district of the Poltava region, Mykola Reva, spent a few years working to make money in the Far East. When he returned home in April 1940, he saw that his family and other collective farmers were starving, after which he decided to complain to Stalin himself. In a letter to the chief he recounted the famine of 1933 in detail, believing that Stalin knew nothing about it. Reva ended his letter thus:

> "So I'm writing this letter to you, and I think that this letter won't be allowed to reach you, and I'll be sent to the polar bears like a common bandit for such 'counterrevolution.'"[42]

As though he had looked into a crystal ball, Reva got six years in prison. They could have given him more but probably took into consideration the fact that this collective farmer had not been spreading "counterrevolution" among the people but had addressed Stalin directly.

The retired teacher O. Radchenko, a pensioner who lived in the small town of Horodok in Kamianets-Podilskyi province, was arrested in August 1945 for the diary she had been keeping since 1926. At the trial in Proskuriv (present-day Khmelnytskyi), she boldly declared,

> "I dedicated my diary to my children so that they might read it 20 years later and see how the people had suffered and moaned, how terrible the famine was… Children won't believe that socialism was built by such cruel methods."

Her sentence: ten years in labor camps for slandering the Soviet government.[43]

It was not possible to write about the famine until December 1987. At that time, in a speech on the seventieth anniversary of the declaration of Soviet rule in Ukraine, the first secretary of the CC of the Communist Party of Ukraine, Volodymyr Shcherbytsky, mentioned the famine of 1933, ostensibly caused by a natural cataclysm—drought—as one of the difficulties in establishing a socialist order. The taboo on the famine of 1933 had outlasted the Twentieth Congress of the CPSU, which condemned Stalin's repressions, and even the Twenty-Second, which removed Stalin's embalmed corpse from the Lenin Mausoleum. This prohibition on mentioning the tragedy that was so firmly fixed in the memory of subsequent generations looked irrational in the mid-1980s. But the senior party leadership in the person of Politburo of the CC CPSU member Volodymyr Shcherbytsky ventured to violate the ban only when the US Commission on the Ukraine Famine began disseminating its first conclusions.

Scholars from Harvard University who conducted a survey of emigrants were particularly interested in the vitality of Stalin's prohibition on information about the famine. Here are a few answers from witnesses to the Holodomor.

Yefrozynia Zoria, born in 1906, survived the famine in the homestead of Hrebyshcha near Lubny.[44]

---

42   *Rozsekrechena pam'iat'*, 573, 576. Primary Source: Branch State Archives of the Security Service of Ukraine, spr. 75208 fp., ark. 122.
43   *Rozsekrechena pam'iat'*, 33–34.
44   Vol. 1, interview LH 17.

> "Question: What was the famine like? Immediately after the famine, did people talk about why it had happened? What did people think, who was to blame, why did it happen?
>
> Answer: My Lord! We couldn't say anything. And people were even afraid to really speak. They were afraid of one another. Because they didn't trust one another. Because as I'm telling you today, by tomorrow someone else will already know. I'm telling you, parents didn't tell their children anything. Only if you understand it yourself, if you understood anything at all, that was good. And if you didn't understand, your parents wouldn't tell you. Because parents were afraid to tell their own children, not just strangers."

Father Fedir Kovalenko, born in 1925, survived the famine in the village of Liutenka, Hadiach district, Poltava (then Kharkiv) province. In the fall of 1932 he started first grade. Out of 32 pupils, only 14 finished the year in June 1933; the rest died of hunger, and the families of several pupils were deported.[45]

> "Question: Did people wonder or talk about what was happening to them?
>
> Answer: It was impossible to talk about anything. Sons were even afraid to share their thoughts with their fathers, and fathers with their sons. We were even told at school that if we noticed our parents doing something against the Soviet government or saying something, or starting something, it was our duty to inform the school authorities."

Anonymous female witness, born in 1907 in the village of Pavlysh, now an urban-type settlement in the Onufriivka district, Kirovohrad (present-day Kropyvnytskyi) province. Almost half the people in her village died because everything was taken from them.[46]

> "Question: How did people speak among themselves about the famine? Or did they keep silent?
>
> Answer: Oh, it seems to me no. Or perhaps only among themselves in their families. But that's, well, so to speak, if you're riding along and you see this kind of horror. Well, everyone looks at it and keeps quiet. And I don't know how we perceived it all. Do we deserve this, must we endure this? I simply, you know, when there's a tragedy like that, you sort of get used to it, almost like it's normal. But it's not normal. When I rode by and I saw it, that's not normal. But to talk about it—no. We got used to it so that you were even afraid to talk to your husband in your house, because it seemed that even the walls had ears. Well, and it was very difficult to talk about it. Not among friends, nor really anywhere could you talk, people were so afraid. I think it's still like that, perhaps; I don't know what it's like now."

This narrator was *afraid* even during the questioning—dozens of years later and halfway around the world, protected by time, space, and American citizenship. It was by no means always the case that people who testified before the US Congressional Commission anonymously concealed their surnames because they still had relatives in the Soviet Union, as Aleksandr Babyonyshev (Sergei Maksudov) did. Many of

---

45 Vol. 1, interview LH 63.
46 Vol. 1, interview SW 56.

them simply had not overcome the inner fear instilled in them by Stalin's "crushing blow."

To summarize what has been said above, it may be asserted that Stalin's blow comprised three elements that made it, on the one hand, effective, and on the other, not immediately obvious because of the economic crisis, accompanied by rife starvation. The informational blockade of both the Holodomor, caused by the confiscation of any and all food, and the famine that resulted from the policy of "spurring," requires no documentary evidence. It is well known that the policy of maintaining silence about the Holodomor grew into a general denial of the famine of 1932–33 in the USSR. The physical blockade of the starving is supported by documentation on three regions of commercial agriculture: the Ukrainian SSR, the North Caucasus, and the Lower Volga. The main element of Stalin's blow has no documentary corroboration. The confiscation of food is established by statements from witnesses to the Holodomor and on the basis of the consequences of that operation: the manyfold increase in rural mortality as compared to mortality in other starving regions.

On the basis of testimonies of former Ukrainian citizens who emigrated, Robert Conquest stated in his documentary book on the Great Famine in the USSR that Stalin's terror had been directed against Ukrainians. Alec Nove responded to his fellow countryman's book in the next edition of his own book on the economic history of the USSR, indicating that Stalin's blow had been directed not against Ukrainians, many of whom were peasants, but rather against peasants, many of whom were Ukrainians.[47] Since then, scholars have been debating just whom Stalin was annihilating, Ukrainians or peasants. But is it even possible to pose the question in those terms? It is hard to imagine, after all, that the Soviet regime was constantly hunting people down just because they were born Ukrainian. It is likewise impossible to imagine that the authorities were annihilating people just because they were peasants. The famine of 1932–33 in Ukraine and Russia was the result of a confluence of concrete circumstances of time and place. Only a simultaneous study of the Kremlin's socioeconomic and nationality policies under the conditions of the early 1930s can allow us to understand the logic that guided Stalin's team.

As a rule, scholars focus either on the socioeconomic or the national and political aspects of the history of the 1930s. Yet it is impossible to separate the Kremlin's socioeconomic policy from its nationality policy. It can hardly be doubted that Ukraine was in the center of attention of Stalin's team, which was attempting to overcome the crisis of the early 1930s brought on by the communist onslaught. It is impossible to determine what Stalin feared more: losing Ukraine, as he admitted to Lazar Kaganovich in a letter of August 11, 1932,[48] or losing his own position. But it may be affirmed that these two grave threats were interrelated. That is why the "crushing blow" was directed first and foremost against Ukraine and the kindred Kuban.

It is possible that a repressive action of similar nature and scope was directed against other regions of the North Caucasus and Lower Volga (as a result of the entangled socioeconomic and national aspects of the Kremlin's policy). Here

---

47 Alec Nove, *An Economic History of the U.S.S.R.* (New York: Penguin, 1989), 170.
48 *Stalin i Kaganovich: Perepiska 1931–1936 gg.*, 274.

Russian scholars should say their piece. From this point of view, let us examine the most recent book of the Penza professor Viktor Kondrashin, *Golod 1932–1933 godov: tragediia rossiiskoi derevni* (The Famine of 1932–1933: The Tragedy of the Russian Village), published in 2008 by the ROSSPĖN press in a multivolume series of monographs on the "History of Stalinism." The scholar's evidence for the situation on the Lower Volga is especially interesting. We know that the Lower Volga was also ransacked by an extraordinary grain-procurement commission headed by Pavel Postyshev. As in Ukraine and the North Caucasus, the rural population of the region was blockaded in its places of residence.

The calling card of the terror-famine, assiduously concealed by the authorities, was the decline of the rural population, something that the all-Union censuses recorded. It is understood that the rural population was decreasing under the influence both of urbanization, the tempo of which had increased sharply, and of the campaign to "liquidate the kulaks as a class." But these factors affected all rural areas more or less identically, while it was in Ukraine that the all-Union famine grew into the Holodomor, and death by starvation in very significant numbers occurred in only a few regions.

Regional demographic catastrophes become apparent when we compare the changes in the rural population between the censuses of 1926 and 1937. Russia's leading specialist in the field of twentieth-century historical demographics, Valentina Zhiromskaia, has identified regions in which the decline of the rural population in 1937 was greatest as compared to the 1926 all-Union census taken as a base of 100. They are, in order:[49]

Saratov province	40.5
Kazakhstan	31.9
Volga German Republic	26.0
Ukraine	20.4
Stalingrad province	18.4
North Caucasus Krai	15.3

After the Holodomor, the Lower Volga region was divided into three administrative territorial units: Saratov and Stalingrad provinces and the Volga German Republic. Thus it would appear that the greatest relative rural losses were not in Ukraine but in the Lower Volga region.

Stalin's "crushing blow" comprised three elements: the confiscation of all food (the main element), the blockade of the population in their places of residence, and an informational blockade. What was the situation in the Lower Volga region as regards the main element? Viktor Kondrashin indicates that a punitive operation did take place, but he is quite cautious in writing about it:

---

49   Valentina B. Zhiromskaia, *Demograficheskaia istoriia Rossii v 1930-e gody: Vzgliad v neizvestnoe* (Moscow: Nauka, 2001), 67–68.

Under the grain deficit, farmers availed themselves of the possibilities of gardening in addition to gathering mushrooms and berries from nearby forests in the early morning. These gifts of nature did not eliminate the famine, but they did reduce its severity and stave off death by hunger. It would appear that they were not subject to state regulation and could be freely used according to their purpose. But in 1932–33 in the Volga region, the Don region, and the Kuban, just as in the country's other regions, it was different.

The other regions are not named, leading to the impression (this, in any case, is what the author hopes for) that it was the same everywhere. Just how "it was different" is explained in the following paragraph, albeit still quite cautiously: "In the course of the grain-procurement campaign of 1932, especially during the winter months, the grain-procurement authorities along with representatives of the village councils carried out special raids, sanctioned from above, of collective and individual farmers' cellars and basements." But Kondrashin leaves his readers in no doubt as to where he believes that "above" was located on the power vertical: "Of course, the party leadership did not sanction the confiscation of all stores of food from the collective and individual farmers' pantries and cellars, but the fact that they did not expediently stop it or employ the necessary measures to correct the iniquities relieves them of none of the responsibility for the deaths of thousands of peasants by starvation."[50]

There you have it: thousands of peasants. Kondrashin's table of regional data on the decline of the rural population between the two censuses appears elsewhere in the book and is not connected thematically with the confiscation of all non-grain foodstuffs or the implementation of a blockade in the region. Thus the author evades the conclusion about genocide that suggests itself when the elements of the punitive operation that is candidly described in the book are brought into the picture.

There is nothing novel about Kondrashin's transfer of responsibility for the all-Union famine and famine in the regions to the lower party and government agencies. Stalin was the first to transfer responsibility to them for his policy of total collectivization through the imposition of communes in his well-known article "Dizziness with Success" (March 1930). Yet—regardless of the particular situation—the system of authority in the Soviet Union was such that no level of government that was subject to a higher one had any independence in making decisions, all the way up to the Politburo of the CC AUCP(B). This maximum centralization of power, which was the natural outcome of building all organizational structures on the principle of "democratic centralism," turned the party, state, and society into voiceless executors of the will of the supreme leader. Responsibility for mass repressions and, first and foremost, for the killing of leading party and government activists, could be imputed to him, though only after his death. But if the famine of 1932–33 were to be characterized as a genocide, that would cast a dark shadow not on Stalin but on the entire political system as such. As successors to that system, political actors in today's Russia cannot allow themselves to find a genocide in their country's recent past. The famine in the Lower Volga region remains a "blank spot" to the present day.

---

50   Kondrashin, *Golod 1932–1933 godov*, 216, 218.

When Viktor Danilov and Ilia Zelenin denied Ukrainian historians' allegations of a deliberate genocide of the Ukrainian people, they were reacting to the statements of those politicians and scholars in Ukraine who identified the Kremlin with Moscow and Russia. But they were prepared to call the Ukrainian Holodomor a genocide if a genocide of the Russian peasantry were also recognized. These scholars' negative reaction to statements about genocide can be explained by their protest against the politicization of a scholarly problem—a politicization that was leading to the cooling of relations between the two peoples. But the negative reaction of official Russian circles to Ukrainian attempts to recognize the Holodomor as a genocide has a completely different explanation. They were unable to prevent the facts about the Holodomor—which pointed unerringly to a genocide—from coming out, especially as the revelation of those facts began not in Ukraine but across the ocean. But they made every effort to stop the global community, starting with the United Nations, from acting in solidarity with the law on the Holodomor-genocide adopted by the Ukrainian parliament. The Moscow diplomats' main counterargument was precisely what had troubled the Russian scholars—the politicization of the problem.

There is also an unconscious politicization of this painful subject that has nothing to do with politicians. It pertains to the term "Ukrainian holocaust," which has been detrimental to understanding the essence of this tragedy of the Ukrainian people. It first appeared as the title of a book on the famine of 1932–33 by Vasyl Hryshko.[51] In Ukraine, the term became firmly established after Yurii Mytsyk published a series of testimonies on the Holodomor.[52] The Holocaust is recognized by the world as a genocide, and some people who want the same for the Holodomor believe that using this evocative name will promote their cause. But those who say this must recognize two things. First, we do not have the moral right to employ the concept of a "Ukrainian holocaust" in its figurative sense. The Ukrainian Holocaust was the murder of 1.6 million Jews on the territory of Ukraine during the Second World War. Second, equating the Holodomor with the Holocaust is tantamount to claiming that Ukrainians in the Soviet Union were persecuted in the same way as Jews in Nazi Germany. In other words, the authorities killed or imprisoned them when and where they found them. Yet everyone understands the absurdity of such an assertion. Stalin's punitive operation must be regarded as terror by famine, not as an ethnic cleansing of the territory so that it could be settled by a different people.

James Mace was the first scholar to assert that Stalin's terror in Ukraine was directed not against people of a certain nationality or occupation but against the citizens of the Ukrainian state that was born during the collapse of the Russian Empire and survived its own demise to be reborn in the form of Soviet statehood. He formulated the thesis that famine was used to annihilate Ukrainians as members of a nation that had achieved statehood rather than as members of an ethnic community ("to destroy them as a political factor and as a social organism") at the first global conference on the famine of 1932–33, which took place in Montreal in 1983.[53]

---

51 Vasyl' I. Hryshko, *Ukraïns'kyi "Holokost," 1933* (New York and Toronto: DOBRUS and SUZhERO, 1978).
52 *Ukraïns'kyi holokost 1932–1933: svidchennia tykh, khto vyzhyv,* comp. Fr. Iurii Mytsyk, 10 vols. (Kyiv: Vydavnychyi dim "Kyievo-Mohylians'ka akademiia," 2003–13).
53 James E. Mace, "The Man-Made Famine of 1933 in Soviet Ukraine" in *Famine in Ukraine 1932–1933,* 12.

There is no doubt that depriving people of food was a brutal form of murder. It was used as a form of terrorism when the grain procurements were carried out in practice. The fate of the victims was supposed to intimidate the rural community as a whole in order to ease the state's confiscation of excessive quantities of grain. Just as the sad fate of the "kulaks" punished by the state (3–5 percent of the total rural population) forced all other peasants to join the collective farms, the fate of peasants who had all their food taken away forced the rest into fulfilling a grain-procurement plan that was beyond their strength.

The essence of all terror (when it concerns a state) or terrorism (when it concerns terror carried out by an individual or non-state organization—these concepts must be differentiated) is the same: a ruinous effect (up to physical annihilation) on a particular individual or on a certain minority of people with the goal of intimidating the majority into behaving in the desired way.[54] When we recognize that the seizure of food was directed at society in the aggregate in order to impose a desired course of action, we are confronted by something greater than terror by starvation. Something that has yet to be named. That is why we find ourselves constrained to use the expression "crushing blow," coined by the author of the terror. The mastermind and organizer of this historically unprecedented genocidal crime realized, as has been shown, that peasant sabotage of the government's plan to build communism throughout the Union could be combated only by recognizing rural producers' ownership rights to agricultural produce. Not only did he realize this, but he even initiated the resolution of the Sovnarkom USSR and CC AUCP(B) "On Mandatory Deliveries of Grain to the State by Collective Farms and Individual Farmers," dated January 19, 1933.[55] He also knew that the grain reserves remaining in the Ukrainian countryside as of early 1933 were insufficient to be of interest to the state. Nevertheless, disguising it as grain procurement, he delivered that "crushing blow," the outcome of which was the Holodomor. This means that the blow was motivated not by the policy of "spurring," which in agriculture took the form of unlimited requisitioning, but by something completely different.

Food difficulties that develop into famine are sufficient to arouse a people against their government. Anti-government uprisings are especially dangerous among workers, who are organized by virtue of the very process of production. But they can also be dangerous among peasants, as was shown by the events of early 1930, when Stalin found himself obliged to halt the forced collectivization of agriculture for six months. Pushed to the brink of despair, the peasants began acting against the government as a single whole without any kind of organization.

Starving for the second year in succession, Ukraine found itself on the verge of colossal social upheaval. Stalin knew this better than anyone, for it was he who had approved the grain-procurement plans and imposed a burden on Ukrainian peasants equivalent to the one borne by the peasants in all other regions of commercial agriculture combined. Without a doubt, he also knew that social upheaval would cost him his position as general secretary of the CC AUCP(B). But the experience of famine in the southern provinces of Ukraine in 1921 had taught him something else:

---

54 See *Politychnyi teror i teroryzm v Ukraïni XIX–XX st.: Istorychni narysy*, ed. Valerii Smolii (Kyiv: Naukova dumka, 2002).

55 *Pravda* (Moscow), January 20, 1933.

"kulak banditry" could be fought effectively by deliberately exacerbating starvation to its most critical point.

The peasants' potential to revolt was indeed determined by their degree of starvation. When they had a certain reserve of food in their pantries, the peasants were willing to protest. When they did not know what their families would eat the next day or the day after that, all thoughts were focused on finding food. In 1921 the insurgent movement lost the support of the peasantry even in the homeland of the anarchist Nestor Makhno, who was forced to end his struggle and emigrate. Once Soviet functionaries realized the dependence of the insurgent movement on the food situation, they began using force to extract the in-kind tax even from the starving southern provinces. An example of such extortion is an order from the Voznesensk county extraordinary provisions committee dated November 15, 1921. In the severely starving Voznesensk county of Odesa province, the committee gave the following orders to the local authorities:

> In every *volost* [subdivision of a county], take 15 to 25 people from the kulak and middle population hostage. Any village that refuses to sign a statement of its collective responsibility or, having signed and promised to fulfill the in-kind tax within a 48-hour period, fails to do so when that time expires, will be declared an enemy of Soviet rule. Half the hostages will be tried, including the use of capital punishment—execution—after which a new group will be taken. Any grain and fodder reserves not corresponding to the figures of tax in kind owing that are found on farms included in the collective responsibility will be confiscated.[56]

The crisis of the early 1930s was overcome not only by repressive measures but also by retreating from the former policy of "spurring." We must therefore examine this aspect of Kremlin policy as well.

Participants in the January (1933) joint plenum of the CC and CCC AUCP(B) reacted with "stormy, prolonged applause" to Stalin's announcement about the creation of political divisions of the MTS and state farms—extraordinary party and government agencies in the countryside.[57] The formation of these dictatorial, administrative, and punitive agencies began as early as November 1932 with the creation of a Politburo CC AUCP(B) commission comprised of Pavel Postyshev (chair), Yan Gamarnik, Yakov Yakovlev, Nikolai Yezhov, and A. M. Markevich. By the end of the year, the committee was supposed to select 1,000 chiefs and 2,000 deputy chiefs (for rank-and-file party work and for the OGPU) for the political divisions of the MTS in Ukraine, the North Caucasus, and the Lower Volga. Later on, the agricultural division of the CC AUCP(B), headed from December 1932 by Lazar Kaganovich, took on the function of providing the political divisions with cadres.[58] The political divisions did not report to local and republican organs of party and government.

---

56 *Holod 1921–1923 rokiv v Ukraïni: Zbirnyk dokumentiv i materialiv*, comp. Ol'ha M. Movchan et al. (Kyiv: Naukova dumka, 1993), 51. Primary source: State Archives of Odesa Oblast, fond R-2106, op. 3, spr. 656, ark. 38.

57 I. Stalin, "O rabote v derevne. Rech' 11 ianvaria 1933 r.," *Sochineniia* (Moscow: Gosudarstvennoe izdatel'stvo politicheskoi literatury, 1951), 13: 233.

58 Il'ia E. Zelenin, "Politotdely MTS – prodolzhenie politiki 'chrezvychaishchiny' (1933–1934 gg.)," *Otechestvennaia istoriia* (Moscow), 1992, no. 6: 43.

This turn of economic policy in the countryside was marked by the replacement of requisitioning with an in-kind tax and permission for collective and individual farmers to sell all produce over and above the firmly fixed rate owed to the state at free-market prices. The transition from a contract system with a limitless procurement plan to the mandatory delivery of a certain quantity of meat and milk on the basis of an in-kind tax had been completed earlier (April 23 and December 10, 1932). But meat and milk production played a secondary role in relations between town and country. Referring to the resolutions on meat and milk at a plenum of the CC and CCC, Molotov noted that they would also have to go over to the procurement of grain through an in-kind tax. Soon afterward, on January 19, the Sovnarkom USSR and CC AUCP(B) adopted a resolution "On the Mandatory Delivery of Grain to the State by Collective and Individual Farms."

Stanislav Kosior acted promptly to inform the Ukrainian party and government apparatus of the contents of the resolution of January 19. At the February (1933) plenum of the CC CP(B)U, he announced:

> The law on the mandatory delivery of grain to the state is a document of exceptional economic and political importance that must become a powerful weapon for successful sowing and all our work to strengthen the collective farms. The gist of the law is that instead of the previously existing system of contracted grain procurement, certain firm obligations for the delivery of grain to the state are being put in place. Every collective farm will now know in advance how much it is required to deliver and when. The better the collective farm carries out its sowing and the greater the harvest it gathers, the more grain it will have left over after fulfilling its obligations.[59]

The secretariat of the CC CP(B)U adopted various measures to make all peasants aware of the state's renunciation of requisitioning. In particular, a plan to publish the text of the resolution in the form of a brochure at several publishing houses was approved on January 26: Partvydav printed 200,000 copies and Ukraïns'kyi robitnyk 300,000. On January 27, Ukraïns'kyi robitnyk was ordered to publish 100,000 copies of the brochure in Russian, Sil'hospvydav 300,000 in both Ukrainian and Russian, and Natsmenvydav 80,000 copies in seven languages.[60] Republican, provincial, and district newspapers printed detailed explanations. On January 31, the newspaper *Kolhospne selo* (Collective-Farm Village) wrote:

> No later than March 15, 1933, district executive committees must present every collective farm with its obligations for delivering every sort of grain and set a deadline for completing them. The obligations will be based on the actual sowing of winter crops and the set plan for planting spring wheat. No supplementary plans or counterplans will be issued. Local authorities are forbidden to expect counterplans or impose obligations on collective farms to deliver grain in excess of per-hectare norms defined by legislation. Therefore, if a collective farm surpasses its quota of spring wheat and gets more than the planned yield, this will only increase its grain stores, of which it will fully dispose after fulfilling its firm quota and paying the MTS for its work.

---

59 Kul'chyts'kyi, *Tsina "velykoho perelomu,"* 362. Primary source: RGASPI, fond 17, op. 26, d. 66, l. 11.
60 Kul'chyts'kyi, *Tsina "velykoho perelomu,"* 362–63.

This explanation of all points in the resolution of January 19 had to be repeated frequently because the peasantry did not trust the state. A few local leaders also had difficulty imagining a collectivized countryside without requisitioning. At the June 1933 plenum of the CC CP(B)U, the following incident was recounted: "When Nikolenko, the head of the Kosior Collective Farm and a delegate to the First All-Union Congress of Leading Collective Farmers, organized a campaign for a good harvest and put forth a counterplan that increased both yield and wages for work (6.8 kg instead of 4.5 kg per workday), the leaders of the Lubny party organization found that the collective farm was showing signs of consumerism: 'By no means can the collective farmers be encouraged to strive for greater results per workday; this, it would seem, inspires consumerist attitudes on the collective farm. Besides the grain tax, there should obviously be some other channels by which to take grain from the collective farmers.'" The official of the Kharkiv provincial party committee who told this story informed members of the CC CP(B)U that the provincial committee had characterized similar statements by Trotsiuk, the secretary of the district committee, as anti-party activity and had made a special decision on the matter that was being discussed in the provincial party organization.[61]

The peculiar consensus between the state and the peasantry was ratified by the Model Statute of Agricultural Cooperatives approved at the All-Union Congress of Leading Collective Farmers in February 1935. The statute limited the size of private plots (to a quarter or half hectare, depending on local conditions). The motive for such a limitation was explained frankly in a speech at the congress by the head of the Kuibyshev Collective Farm in the Putyvl district of Chernihiv province, S. Oriekhov: "It's obvious, comrades, that the size of plots must be reduced. They have to be made such as not to deter collective farmers from going to work."[62]

After the Holodomor, Ukrainian peasants had to accept the rules of the game that Russian collective farmers, accustomed to communal agriculture, had accepted immediately. In order to stave off the threat of starvation that constantly hung over them after the establishment of collective farms, they obliged themselves to work hard and voluntarily in public agriculture. Having refused to work as slaves in the commune, they agreed to work as serfs in the cooperative.

The harvest of 1933 in Ukraine was accompanied by tremendous losses. The reason was not so much the collective farmers' unwillingness to work conscientiously, as in previous years, as their physical inability to do work. In many districts that had been hit particularly hard, there was a severe deficit of able bodies. This was overcome by creating mobile brigades of collective farmers from less affected districts, as well as by suspending conscription into the territorial units of the Red Army for a certain period. Red Army men, workers from large factories, and university students played a significant role in gathering the harvest. In recalling the shortcomings of the previous year's campaign, Kosior said in 1934 that according to the most conservative estimates, grain losses had reached a few hundred million poods, and only the good harvest "made up to some extent for all the blunders in gathering it."[63]

---

61 Ibid., 363–64. Primary source: TsDAHOU, fond 1, op. 1, spr. 413, ark. 9.
62 Mikhail A. Vyltsan, *Zavershaiushchii etap sozdaniia kolkhoznogo stroia, 1935–1937 gg.* (Moscow: Nauka, 1978), 28.
63 *Komunist* (Kyiv), June 17, 1934.

In previous years with decent harvests, losses had also been colossal. It is, in fact, impossible to determine the actual harvest of 1932. In 1933, the situation turned out very differently for the state owing to the transition from requisitioning to procurement. Between 1930 and 1932 the state had used grain procurements to take everything it could find, only to find less with every passing year. But by early November 1933 Ukraine had already fulfilled its grain-procurement quota for that year's harvest. The enormous losses did not affect the state's quota, since the mandatory deliveries were calculated on the basis of the unharvested crop. It was the Ukrainian peasantry, exhausted by famine, that suffered.

Although the collectivized peasantry won itself a measure of autonomy within the command economy, it was forced to relinquish an overly large portion of additional produce to the state. Similar weather conditions were observed in 1933 and 1936, and they can be compared. Before the harvest of 1933, there were 1.419 million poods of crop in the fields. With deliveries to the state amounting to 317 million poods, the ratio of commodity output to total output, or grain marketability, formally amounted to 22.3 percent. This was on the level of the late 1920s and approximately two-thirds of pre-revolution marketability. In 1933, however, as in previous years, there were enormous losses of the cultivated crop. To determine the actual level of grain marketability, these losses must be taken into account. If we suppose that a third of the harvest was lost (this amount is based on the estimates of party and government leaders and independent foreign experts at the time), then the proportion of grain relinquished to the state increases to 33.5 percent. This level of marketability is equivalent to the pre-revolutionary level. In 1936, the biological yield was 221 million quintals, or 1.381 million poods. The state requisitioned 545 million poods, more than in any previous year, including the requisitioning period of 1930–32. The proportion of procurements to the biological yield was 39.5 percent. In the silo, the harvest always amounts to less, so true marketability exceeded 40 percent. It is impossible to give a more precise figure without knowing the losses incurred between the field and the silo. Nevertheless, it is known that after the agricultural situation normalized, losses fell to a minimum, and real marketability was slightly more than 40 percent.[64] A comparison of 1933 with 1936 indicates that the state was able to turn all the savings realized by overcoming losses in agriculture to its advantage.

---

64 Kul'chyts'kyi, *Holodomor 1932–1933 rr. iak henotsyd*, 360–61.

Afterword

The enormity of the Holocaust is generally recognized. Humanity could not permit the existence of a regime that annihilated Jews because of the mere fact that they were Jewish. The Holodomor was also a crime of enormous proportions. The Ukrainian countryside was reduced to absolute starvation by a physical and informational blockade and the confiscation of all foodstuffs by the Soviet authorities. Over a few short months, the Holodomor caused millions of men, women, and children to die in the hellish torment of starvation. Yet the Soviet Union would continue to exist for more than fifty years.

Why has humanity recognized the Holocaust as a genocide while the Holodomor has not yet come under the UN Convention on the Prevention and Punishment of the Crime of Genocide, adopted on December 9, 1948? There is no longer any need to set up parliamentary commissions to investigate the facts of the mass mortality of starving Ukrainian peasants, separated from the present day by more than eighty years. The Odesa National Scholarly Library has registered 18,944 international publications on the Ukrainian Holodomor issued between 1932 and 2011.[1] We know the facts: all that remains is to establish the correct causal sequence.

There is an enormous amount of evidence that the Holodomor was the result of a thoroughly planned and well-disguised special operation undertaken by Soviet state security agencies. Unlike the Holocaust, which was a prolonged ethnic cleansing, the Holodomor was a terrorist operation intended to overcome an economic crisis that arose unexpectedly and threatened the Kremlin's builders of communism with the loss of their rule.

That scholars of the Holodomor misunderstand the nature of this operation is readily apparent from their inability to discern the qualitative difference between the all-Union famine of 1932–33 and the Holodomor of 1932–33, which claimed many times more victims in the countryside of several regions of the USSR. This thesis can be stated another way: it is believed that this most extensively researched phenomenon—the Holodomor in the Ukrainian SSR and the Kuban—was caused by the confiscation of grain. Some scholars go further, asserting that the state had to take the grain in order to get the desperately needed hard currency for the modernization of industry, without which the Soviet Union would not have been able to achieve victory in the Great Patriotic War with Hitler's Germany.

By invoking this "take the grain" argument, it is indeed possible to construct a picture of the past that justifies the Holodomor on the basis of insurmountable geopolitical circumstances. In an article published in 2003 that the Ukrainian community still has not forgotten, Valerii Soldatenko asked us: "What might have happened to the world, to civilization, if in the 1940s the Hitlerites had been

---

1   *Holodomor v Ukraïni 1932–1933 rr. Bibliohrafichnyi pokazhchyk,* vyp. 1 (Odesa and Lviv: Vydavnytstvo M. P. Kots', 2001), vyp. 2 (Odesa: Vydavnytstvo "Studiia 'Nehotsiant,'" 2008), vyp. 3 (Odesa: Odes'ka natsional'na naukova biblioteka im. O. M. Hor'koho; Instytut istoriï Ukraïny NAN Ukraïïny, 2004), (Electronic resource at the Institute of Ukrainian History portal), comp. Larysa M. Bur'ian and Inna E. Rykun, ed. Stanislav V. Kul'chyts'kyi.

confronted not by the powerful Soviet Union but by a country with much less potential than that which resulted from the huge economic and military-technical leap of the 1930s?" Relying on the "take the grain" thesis, he comes up with the following answer to his question: "To simplify the situation at that time, to reduce the explanation of the tragedy to the evil intent of the system alone, to the misanthropic essence of the ideology, to the maniacal ethnophobia of the party and state leadership is obviously to assess this historical moment less than correctly, thoroughly, or truthfully."[2]

The all-Union famine of 1932–33, just like the famine of the early 1920s that was masked by the catastrophic drought of 1921, was the consequence of a crisis that verged on economic collapse. The crisis was, in turn, the consequence of the Bolshevik leaders' attempts to realize communist doctrine to its fullest extent, that is: a) to bring about the total appropriation of the "commanding heights" of the economy by the state under the guise of nationalization; b) to collectivize agriculture; c) to replace trade both on the "commanding heights" and in relations between town and country with barter, that is, to abolish commodity-money relations and the free market. Vladimir Lenin got out of the crisis by canceling the prohibition on private enterprise, forgoing the collectivization of agriculture, and restoring free trade between town and country. After making the transition to the New Economic Policy, he declared that the previous policy of communist onslaught had been "war communism," or a set of extraordinary measures that had nothing to do with doctrine and were ostensibly generated by wartime conditions. Stalin's attempt to repeat a communist onslaught in 1929–32 was marked by substantial achievements in the modernization of industry and the violent implementation of the total collectivization of agriculture, although in cooperative form, which left the peasants with remnants of private ownership of the means of production in the form of private plots. But the state's attempts to replace free trade between town and country with barter failed. The state did not supply or, rather, had no intention of coming up with sufficient industrial production to make possible an equivalent exchange between town and country, and as a result contractual agreements between the state and the peasantry turned into requisitioning (*prodrazvërstka*) similar to Lenin's. The requisitioning of 1930–32 quite predictably brought the state to the brink of economic collapse. Peasants stopped working on the collective farms so as to focus on their private plots as a means of basic survival.

Unlike Lenin, who brought his communist onslaught to a halt, Stalin decided, when faced with an analogous situation, to save the collective-farm system and his own post of general secretary of the CC AUCP(B) in two ways: a) by moving Karl Marx's requirement that trade be replaced with barter from the first phase of communism (which figured in Marxist theory as socialism) to the second, purely utopian phase in which the distribution of material and cultural goods according to need would be established; and b) by organizing a terror-famine directed against the peasants, who were refusing to work on the collective farms for meaningless workdays. The crux of this terror was the confiscation of the produce that the peasants had grown on their private plots. This produce was practically their only

---

2 Valerii Soldatenko, "Holodnyi trydtsiat' tretii: sub'iektyvni dumky pro ob'iektyvni protsesy," *Dzerkalo tyzhnia* (Kyiv), no. 24, June 27, 2003.

source of nourishment, as the state was requisitioning what the collective farms produced.

The first method of avoiding economic collapse was a radical retreat from communist doctrine. As early as 1930, Stalin began retreating from postulates formulated by Marx. At that time, the Bolshevik leadership's renunciation of agricultural communes allowed it to eliminate the threat of a full-scale war with the peasantry. The cooperative, with its intrinsic element of private plots, hindered the transition from trade to barter, but this was the only form of collective farming that the state managed to bring about during the period of forced collectivization of agriculture. The peasantry's material interest in collective farming was promoted by the transition in January 1933 from unlimited requisitioning to tax obligations (bound by certain limitations) of the collective farms to the state. The collective farmers gained the opportunity to consume or sell collectively produced crops on the free market after fulfilling the predetermined obligations, as well as to dispose freely of the fruits of their individual labor on their private plots.

The retreat from the realization of communist doctrine to its fullest extent made possible the long-term functioning of the collective-farm system. But the situation that emerged in 1932 had to be dealt with immediately. Stalin regarded the peasants' unwillingness to work on collective farms in the primary grain-growing regions as sabotage. In the last months of 1932, hundreds of collective farms and villages in Ukraine and the North Caucasus were "blacklisted" as grain-quota debtors. In January 1933, that is, concurrently with the cardinal change in economic relations between town and country, both regions were blacklisted.

The punitive measures against the blacklisted villages, as published in the newspapers, barely differed from the measures applied earlier. In actual fact, however, blacklisting meant the requisitioning of all produce grown by peasants on their private plots and stored for the six months to come until the new harvest. Grain was the first item subject to confiscation, something that confuses students of the Holodomor. After all, there was practically no grain left in the countryside in the winter months of 1932–33, and not only because the state had confiscated all reserves. The economic crisis manifested itself first and foremost as the state's lack of sufficient grain reserves. The harvest of 1932 was not bad, just as in previous years. Yet by the third year of requisitioning the peasants had become convinced that, as in the previous two years, the state would confiscate the entire harvest; consequently, from the outset, they preferred to work their private plots rather than the collective-farm fields.

From the state's perspective, this was sabotage initiated by the actions of the state itself. Stalin understood that perfectly, rejecting unlimited requisitioning as he did in January 1933. Nonetheless, as he told the party and government nomenklatura, he was delivering a "crushing blow" to the peasantry. Camouflaged as winter grain procurement, the confiscation of food and physical blockade of the plundered peasantry created a situation of absolute starvation, with many millions of human victims. The death of so many by starvation forced the survivors to work diligently on the collective farms. The terror-famine can thus be identified as the essence of the "crushing blow."

The dates of the Ukrainian Holodomor are given as two years, and there is no reason to doubt this time frame. Although Stalin struck all Ukraine with his "crushing blow" in January 1933, the Holodomor must be dated to two years simply because hundreds of villages were added to the blacklist in the last months of 1932, with all the resulting consequences.

When we distinguish the all-Union famine of 1932–33 from the Ukrainian Holodomor of 1932–33, we must understand that the famine too, and not only the Holodomor, took place on the territory of Ukraine. The famine of the first half of 1932 in Ukraine was severe, more so than in other regions. There were also instances of cannibalism. But at that time the Soviet authorities strove to mitigate the starving people's suffering and therefore allowed peasants to travel to other regions in search of food. They also bought small quantities of grain abroad, as they lacked reserves of their own for the organization of food and seed aid. With the exception of blacklisted villages, the famine that flared up in Ukraine in the final months of 1932 as a result of the requisitioning of that year's harvest also did not differ initially from the all-Union famine. But starting in January 1933, that famine was superimposed on the Chekist special operation to confiscate produce grown on private plots. Thus the all-Union famine caused by a dearth of grain grew into the Holodomor.

Students of the Holodomor are confused by the scope of state aid to the starving. Whereas it was not large during the first half of 1932, it took on considerable proportions during the first half of 1933. Scholars often decline to call the Holodomor a genocide when they note the scale of the seed, fodder, and food aid provided to Ukraine and the North Caucasus in order to ensure the sowing campaign of spring 1933. But it should not be forgotten that the Holodomor was the consequence of terror by starvation. Terror of any kind is always meant to repress a minority in order to intimidate the majority into adopting the desired behavior. Stalin, it must be acknowledged, changed the external appearance of this terror formula without changing its essence. The idea was to deprive the whole population of all foodstuffs under the guise of grain procurements, which had already been conducted for a couple of years during the winter months, and then to begin giving food aid to the starving a few weeks later and publicize it in the mass media. Those who survived multiple weeks of starvation were trained to work on the collective and state farms by being fed at field camps. Those unable to work were left to die a slow death in their homes.

In the summer of 2008, the well-known French scholar and member of the Institut de France Alain Besançon traveled to Kyiv for the launch of the Ukrainian translation of his book, *The Misfortune of the Century: On Communism, Nazism, and the Uniqueness of the Holocaust*. In an interview with the newspaper *Dzerkalo tyzhnia* (Weekly Mirror), he said:

> "Twentieth-century world history knows three horrific genocides (in chronological order)—the Armenian, Ukrainian, and Jewish. But whereas the Armenian and Jewish genocides are well documented and known to the world, the situation with the Ukrainian one is completely different." The French academician explained the distinctness of the situation: "It must be admitted that the communists destroyed the evidence of their crimes much more diligently than the Nazis. They also had more time to do so. It is necessary to

inform [the world] consistently and insistently about the Ukrainian genocide, as the Jews and Armenians have already done."³

Can we agree with Besançon that we have not sufficiently informed our society and the world around us about the Holodomor of 1932–33? Perhaps we should take account of the fundamental difference between the Ukrainian and the Armenian and Jewish genocides: it is related not only to the nationality policy of the state that perpetrated genocide but also to the communist socioeconomic transformations of the Kremlin. It is no accident that an expert in the history of Russian communism such as Alain Besançon does not have to be convinced that the Holodomor was a genocide. Others still must be.

It turns out that an enormous number of publications is insufficient to convince anyone that the Holodomor really was a genocide of the Ukrainian people. In order to convince people, it is necessary to start with an analysis of socioeconomic transformations, as this book strives to do.

There is no reason to insist that Stalin's "crushing blow" was directed exclusively against the Ukrainian people. Such an assertion does not correspond to the facts, as is apparent even from an analysis of those of Stalin's texts in which that concept was born. In 2007, the Russian State Archives of Sociopolitical History (RGASPI) and the Hoover Institution on War, Revolution, and Peace published a transcript of the joint session of the Politburo CC and Presidium CCC AUCP(B) at which Stalin raised the question of the Smirnov group on November 27, 1932. At that time, influenced by the growing crisis, a few governmental figures of the RSFSR (Aleksandr Smirnov, Vladimir Tolmachev, and Nikolai Eismont) began to regard the general line of the CC AUCP(B) as it was being carried out by Stalin as a threat to the party and the country. It became evident that the general secretary's chair was starting to wobble beneath him. Denying personal responsibility for the failure of the grain procurements, which had heightened this group's attention, Stalin cited two reasons for the lack of success: a) the penetration of anti-Soviet elements into the collective and state farms for the purpose of organized wrecking and sabotage; and b) the wrong attitude of a significant number of rural communists toward collective and state farms. The general secretary called on Bolshevik leaders to stop idealizing collective and state farms and to employ "elements of force" in order to uproot "elements of sabotage and anti-Soviet phenomena." "It would be foolish," he continued, "if communists, proceeding from the premise that collective farms are a socialist form of agriculture, failed to respond to the blow struck by these individual collective farmers and collective farms with a crushing blow of their own."⁴ Slightly more than a month before this speech, a resolution of the Politburo CC AUCP(B) adopted on October 22 had created two extraordinary grain-procurement commissions whose activity brought about the Holodomor in Ukraine and the North Caucasus. A day after the speech, on November 28, an extraordinary grain-procurement commission was created in the Lower Volga Krai.

---

3 Oleksa Pidluts'kyi, "Alen Bezanson: Rosiia, tochnishe – Radians'ka derzhava, vidpovidal'na za Holodomor," *Dzerkalo tyzhnia* (Kyiv), July 4, 2008 <http://gazeta.dt.ua/SOCIETY/alen_bezanson_rosiya,_tochnishe__radyanska_derzhava,_vidpovidalna_za_golodomor.html>.

4 *Tragediia sovetskoi derevni*, 3: 559. Primary source: RGASPI, fond 17, op. 163, d. 1011, l. 13.

The joint publication of the Russian State Archives of Sociopolitical History and the Hoover Institution contains not only the transcript of this meeting, which was distributed to party and government activists throughout the USSR, but also the original text of a document that was kept in a secret archival collection. The document that was distributed does not specify where the "crushing blow" was to be directed. As the original text shows, Stalin was more candid with the Bolshevik leadership: he named the regions where the extraordinary grain-procurement commissions were starting work (the North Caucasus, Ukraine, the Lower Volga) as well as specific enemies—White Guardists and Petliurites.[5]

The essence of the matter, however, lies not so much in an analysis of Stalin's texts, however eloquent they may prove on careful reading, as in the formula of terror by famine, which the Bolshevik leadership developed and applied. As this book has shown, the formula consisted of three parts:
 - the confiscation of any and all food from the peasants;
 - the physical blockade of those who, owing to the actions of the Soviet regime, ended up in a situation of absolute starvation;
 - the mass media's total cover-up of the situation in the regions subjected to the "crushing blow."

Taken together, these parts clearly indicate the political leaders' intention to annihilate people—there is simply no other way to explain them. The most important of them, obviously, is the first. That is why we do not find any official documents in the archives with an order to organize the absolute starvation of the rural population. We can take it a step further: as already mentioned, when enterprising local leaders put forward such a proposal, the higher authorities condemned them. Nevertheless, there is Stalin's circular of January 1, 1933—also already mentioned—which indirectly created the situation that obliged local leaders to conduct blanket searches of peasant households, ostensibly to discover hidden grain. Under that pretext they carried out not only the confiscation of meat and potatoes, as provided in the legislation on in-kind fines, but of all other foodstuffs as well. Hundreds of publications on the Ukrainian Holodomor present the testimonies of witnesses who corroborate this fact. Their stories have now been collected in a large volume, *1933: "I choho vy shche zhyvi?,"* ed. Tetiana Boriak (Kyiv: Klio, 2016).

Witnesses to the Holodomor have also told of the blockade of the starving in their villages. There is perhaps no need to compile accounts to prove this, for there are official documents that confirm the blockade of Ukraine, the North Caucasus, and the Lower Volga. They are cited in this book.

Finally, the third element of the famine organized by Stalin requires no proof at all. Despite the fact that everyone in the Soviet Union knew about the hellish year of 1933, public mention of the famine was considered anti-Soviet propaganda. This raises another question: Why did the country's leaders not venture to speak of the famine of the early 1930s even after they had Stalin's corpse ejected from the Lenin Mausoleum? When he was dictating his memoirs in retirement, Nikita Khrushchev, who initiated that decision, limited himself to this remark: "How many people died then? I cannot now say. Information about it had leaked to the bourgeois

---

5 *Stenogrammy zasedanii Politbiuro TsK RKP(b)-VKP(b), 1923–1938 gg.*, ed. K. M. Anderson et al., 3 vols., vol. 3 *(1928–1938 gg.)* (Moscow: ROSSPĖN, 2007), 657–58.

press and, until the end of my tenure, articles would occasionally slip into it about collectivization and the cost of that collectivization in lives of Soviet people. But I'm saying this now; first of all, I knew nothing about it then, and, second of all, had I known anything, I would have found an explanation: sabotage, counterrevolution, kulak plots that had to be fought, and so on."[6]

While he was in power, it never even occurred to Khrushchev to lift Stalin's ban on speaking about the famine of the early 1930s. Even two decades later, Mikhail Gorbachev still did not venture to do so. Delivering a speech on the seventieth anniversary of the Bolshevik Revolution at a ceremonial meeting in the Kremlin Palace of Congresses on November 2, 1987, he limited himself to this passing remark: "Collectivization meant radical change to the whole substance of life on socialist principles for the bulk of the country's population. It created a social basis for the modernization of the agrarian sector and its shift to civilized management, made it possible to significantly raise the productivity of labor, and freed up a significant amount of manpower needed for other spheres of communist construction."[7] Let us not forget that the executive director of the US Congressional Commission on the Ukraine Famine, James Mace, had just then distributed the first reports on the investigation of Stalin's crime to the world at large.

Three weeks after Gorbachev's speech, the leader of the Communist Party of Ukraine, Volodymyr Shcherbytsky, gave a similar anniversary speech in Kyiv. For the FIRST TIME he acknowledged the famine of 1932–33, purportedly caused by a bad harvest. Since Ukraine had been at the epicenter of a famine that touched almost every family, he was no longer in a position to hold his tongue.

Why were the leaders of the Soviet Union unable to lift Stalin's ban for so long? After all, they had access to the Kremlin archives, including CC AUCP(B) documents that remained strictly classified until 1990, about the early-1930s famine that took on apocalyptic proportions in Ukraine, the North Caucasus, the Lower Volga, and Kazakhstan. The reason, in all likelihood, was that they knew this famine had only one legal definition—genocide. They did not dare to level an accusation of genocide against the political system that had propelled them to the heights of power.

In post-Soviet Russia, the topic of the early-1930s famine is not forbidden. Collections of essential documents and solidly researched monographs have been published. The work done by experts who have no desire to be reputed as falsifiers of history identifies all three components of the terror by famine that, taken together, point unerringly to genocide. But those components are not put together and therefore do not form a single whole.

Up to this point of my conclusions, the Ukrainian Holodomor has figured in conjunction with mass starvation in other regions. The reason is simple: I have been tracing the consequences of the socioeconomic policy that the Bolshevik leadership carried out from 1918 to 1932 (with a break in the years 1921–28). The political order that existed from November 1917 until the constitutional reform approved by the Nineteenth Congress of the CPSU (June–July 1988) and enacted by the Twelfth

---

6   Nikita S. Khrushchev, *Vremia. Liudi. Vlast'. Vospominaniia v 4-kh knigakh*, vol. 1 (Moscow: Informatsionno-izdatel'skaia kompaniia "Moskovskie novosti," 1999), 72.

7   M. S. Gorbachev, *Oktiabr' i perestroika: revoliutsiia prodolzhaetsia, 1917–1987* (Moscow: Izdatel'stvo politicheskoi literatury, 1987), 20.

Session of the Supreme Soviet of the USSR (November–December 1988) had nothing in common with Karl Marx's communist doctrine. Yet the leaders of the Bolshevik Party, which called itself communist, tried with incredible persistence to build communism, which they understood as a society deprived of private property. This persistence was by no means to be explained by a desire to ensure the distribution of material and cultural goods to members of society according to their needs. That slogan was the propagandistic wrapper for the "bright-future" communism that always remained just beyond the horizon. Depriving society of private property actually made people directly dependent on the communal state that Lenin built on the principles of "democratic centralism"—the complete subordination of lower levels of management to higher ones, all the way up to the Politburo of the Central Committee of the RCP(B)-AUCP(B)-CPSU. The building of communism made it possible to supplement the political dictatorship established by Lenin with an economic one.

Acting by means of terror and propaganda, the Bolshevik leaders brought both the working class and the peasantry under their control. The communal state managed to nationalize the "commanding heights" of the economy and subsequently modernize industry and transport, as well as to collectivize the peasantry, with the subsequent modernization of agriculture. Despite this, it proved unable to abolish commodity-money relations, as communist doctrine required. Attempts to implement a state-controlled barter system between town and country failed, thus demonstrating the utopianism of speculative ideas about communism. Twice this attempt was made, and twice it ended with an acute economic crisis and severe starvation of the population. As this book has shown, Bolshevik leaders got out of the crisis in different ways: Vladimir Lenin retreated to his New Economic Policy; Joseph Stalin postponed the task of doing away with trade indefinitely and salvaged the achievements of communist construction with the help of the most horrific form of mass terror—terror by famine.

It is worth repeating here the already quoted aphoristic observation of the English economist Alec Nove, who, after the publication of Robert Conquest's book on the Great Famine of 1932–33, disagreed with his claim about Stalin's blow having been directed against Ukrainians. Nove expressed his dissent thus: "[Stalin's motive] was surely to strike a 'devastating blow' at peasants in grain-surplus areas, many of whom were Ukrainian, rather than at Ukrainians, many of whom were peasants."[8] In telling the world about Stalin's "crushing blow," Conquest mostly used material provided to him by James Mace. Soon afterward, Mace published the final report of the US Commission on the Ukraine Famine, setting off a chain reaction of research in Ukraine itself. Nor was there a shortage of Russian investigations, but they were negative responses to the Ukrainian ones, inasmuch as they did not draw together the three components of Stalin's "crushing blow." The failure to identify the fundamental difference between the all-Union famine and famine in the various regions forced Alec Nove and his followers to treat assertions of the genocidal character of the Ukrainian Holodomor skeptically. That skepticism was only strengthened by the attempts of many Ukrainian scholars to present the Holodomor as an ethnic cleansing.

---

8   Alec Nove, *An Economic History of the USSR: 1917–1991* (New York: Penguin, 1992), 180.

The facts presented in this book allow us to rephrase Nove's aphorism as follows: "[Stalin's motive] was surely to strike a 'devastating blow' at Ukrainians in grain-surplus areas, many of whom were peasants, rather than at peasants, many of whom were Ukrainians." Indeed, Stalin had come to a mutual understanding with all Soviet peasants when he rescinded requisitions and halted attempts to replace trade with barter. Yet, in addition, he decided to deal with peasants in the state's most important grain-growing regions in a different way—terror by famine. It was no accident that Ukrainians ended up in the epicenter of that terror. Regional statistics on peasant uprisings against collectivization and requisitions attest to the particular activism of the Ukrainian peasantry. When prospects for active struggle with the authorities were exhausted, the peasants went over to passive resistance. The essence of this was their refusal to work in collectivized agriculture or, if refusal was impossible, the pretense of work. Passive resistance was dangerous in and of itself, since the state was receiving less and less grain from agriculture. Along with this, the state security agencies' ramified information network attested that the grain requisitioners' intention to fulfill the quota by total confiscation of the countryside's grain reserves was again creating preconditions for resistance to pass into an active phase. The Chekists considered social upheaval in Ukraine the most dangerous threat.

The acute economic crisis of the early 1930s called into question the existence of the collective-farm system and threatened to escalate into a political crisis. To stave off such a turn of events, Stalin resorted to a horrific preventative measure—terror by famine. Soviet Ukraine—the largest national republic, located on the border with Europe—and the Ukrainian people—a nation with a strong tradition of national-liberation struggle—found themselves in the epicenter of that terror. At the same time that terror by famine was being inflicted on the peasantry, a terror against the Ukrainian intelligentsia was unfolding under the slogan of the "struggle against bourgeois nationalism" as the greatest threat. In tandem with its onslaught in Ukraine, the Kremlin waged terror by famine against the Cossacks and peasants of the North Caucasus. It was aimed at quashing resistance to the imposition of the collective-farm system, but it also solved other problems for the Bolshevik leadership by defeating the aspiration of the people of the Kuban to be reunited with Ukraine. In a brief period, the previous achievements of Ukrainization in the districts of the North Caucasus, as well as in the districts of the Central Black Earth province adjacent to the Ukrainian SSR with majority Ukrainian populations, were destroyed. In the Ukrainian SSR itself, a struggle unfolded against so-called "Petliurite" Ukrainization, that is, against aspects of the Soviet regime's indigenization campaign that could pose a threat to the authorities themselves.

The Holodomor is the darkest page in the centuries-old history of the Ukrainian people. It extinguished Ukrainian patriots' hope of avenging the tragic failures of the liberation struggle of 1917–20. Its distant reverberations can be felt even today as the citizens of Ukraine stand up for their country's freedom and independence against the encroachments of Putin's Russia, where the worst features of Soviet communism have been reborn under the guise of tsarist ideology.

Glossary

Administrative divisions
In the Soviet Union, the county (Russ. *uezd*, Ukr. *povit*) and province (Russ. *guberniia*, Eng. gubernia) system of the tsarist period was replaced by the district (Russ. and Ukr. *raion*) and province (Russ. *okrug*, Ukr. *okruh*) system in 1924–25. In 1931–32, the term *oblast'* (both Russ. and Ukr.; Eng. oblast) replaced *okrug/okruh* to designate a province. The term *krai*, which designated large border regions in the tsarist period, was introduced in 1924 to denote six regions of the RSFSR inhabited by ethnic minorities (e.g., the North Caucasus Krai). English terms are generally used in this book, with the Ukrainian or Russian term given in parentheses on first mention in the text.

Agricultural cooperative (Russ. *artel'*)
See Collective farm.

Banderites
Followers of Stepan Bandera (1909–1959), leader of the Organization of Ukrainian Nationalists (Revolutionary faction), the foremost Ukrainian integral nationalist movement in Ukraine during World War II and, subsequently, in the emigration. Bandera was murdered by a Soviet assassin in Munich, where he lived as an émigré.

Black repartition (Russ. *chërnyi peredel*)
Slogan of proletarianized peasant masses who demanded that land and the means of production belonging to landowners' estates and wealthy peasants' farmsteads be transferred to them on grounds of equalization.

Blacklist (Ukr. *chorna doshka*, literally "blackboard")
A method of condemning the results of individual or collective labor. The name of the person or collective was listed on bills and postcards as well as in newspapers for the public to see. Stalin was the first to use the term "blacklist" in a speech at the Fourth Conference of the CP(B)U in March 1920 to morally condemn miners of the Donbas region who were evading conscription in the countryside (see *Chetverta konferentsiia Komunistychnoï partiï (bil'shovykiv) Ukraïny, 17–23 bereznia 1920 r. Stenohrama* [Kyiv: Vydavnychyi dim "Al'ternatyvy," 2003], 198). On November 4, 1932, Stalin's appointee as head of the extraordinary grain-procurement commission in the North Caucasus, Lazar Kaganovich, initiated a resolution of the North Caucasus Krai Committee of the AUCP(B) to blacklist collective farms that were "maliciously sabotaging" state grain procurements. The "blacklist" regime provided for a variety of repressive measures that were published in corresponding resolutions, including one adopted by the CC CP(B)U and the Radnarkom of the Ukrainian SSR on December 6, 1932 "On Adding Villages That Maliciously Sabotage Grain Procurements to the 'Blacklist.'" But the principal repressive measure—the confiscation of all foodstuffs from grain debtors and a ban on leaving their villages for travel—was not published. Harvard University's online *Atlas of the Holodomor* presents data gathered by Professor Heorhii Papakin on 1,200 collective farms, population centers, village councils, and districts added to blacklists at various levels: all-Ukrainian, provincial, or district. As of January 1933, the Ukrainian SSR as a whole was secretly blacklisted.

Literature:

Papakin, Heorhii. *"Chorna doshka": antyselians'ki represiï (1932–1933)*. Kyiv: Instytut istoriï Ukraïny NAN Ukraïny, 2013.

Collective farm (Russ. *kolkhoz*, a contraction of *kollektivnoe khoziaistvo*; Ukr. *kolhosp*)
An element of the Bolsheviks' communist socioeconomic transformations. There were three forms of collective farm that differed according to degree of alienation of rural means of production: the Association for Joint Cultivation of Land (*Tovarishchestvo po sovmestnoi obrabotke zemli*, TSOZ), the cooperative (*artel'*), and the commune. Although attempts were made by both Lenin (1919) and Stalin (1930), the Soviet government was unable to force peasants to join the communes, where all means of production

were collectivized. The TSOZ, which allowed peasants to retain independent control of production, was not acceptable to the authorities. A compromise was found in the agricultural cooperative, which allowed peasants to keep their private plots. Once the cooperatives became widespread, their status was equivalent to that of collective farms.

Collectivization of agriculture

The creation of collective farms in the countryside through voluntary or compulsory consolidation of peasant land, implements, and animals kept for labor and consumption. Collective farms (Ukr. *kolhosp*, Russ. *kolkhoz*) were divided into associations for joint cultivation of land (TSOZ), cooperatives (Russ. *artel'*), and communes, depending on the degree to which the means of production were amalgamated. Collectivization was considered complete if 68 to 70 percent of the farms in a given region had joined, encompassing 75 to 80 percent of the arable land.

Committees of Poor Peasants, known as *komnezamy* or KNS from Ukr. *komitet nezamozhnykh selian*

They existed only in the Ukrainian SSR from 1920 to 1933. Together with local state security agencies, they constituted a particular type of Soviet rule under the control of CP(B)U committees initially at the county (*povit*) level and, after the administrative and territorial reforms of 1923, at the district (*raion*) level. In July 1925 they were reformed from a state-level organization charged with administrative and economic functions into a purely public organization.

Literature:

Kul'chyts'kyi, Stanislav. *Komunizm v Ukraïni: pershe desiatyrichchia (1919–1928)*. Kyiv: Osnovy, 1996.

Radians'ke budivnytstvo na Ukraïni v roky hromadians'koï viiny (1919–1920): Zbirka dokumentiv i materialiv, ed. Mykhailo A. Rubach. Kyiv: Politvydav Ukraïny, 1957.

Zahors'kyi, Pavlo S., and Pylyp K. Stoian. *Narys istoriï komitetiv nezamozhnykh selian Ukraïny*. Kyiv: Politvydav Ukraïny, 1960.

Communal state, state of the commune

In 1917 Vladimir Lenin used this term twice when giving his party the task of creating a state capable of bringing about communist transformations. Later he used other terms: worker-peasant state, proletarian state, Soviet state, socialist state. The council or soviet (Russ. *sovet*, Ukr. *rada*) of worker, peasant, and Red Army deputies was the foundation of the communal state. These councils were organizationally distinct from the Communist Party, but their personnel consisted mainly of Bolsheviks. Thus the Bolshevik Party assumed two forms: that of a political party establishing a dictatorship and that of a Soviet governmental structure formed on the basis of elections controlled by party committees and exercising administrative functions.

Communist onslaught (*shturm*) of 1918–20

The Bolsheviks' first attempt to implement communist doctrine by expropriating all private property and making a transition from trade to barter with the elimination of commodity-money relations and the market.

Literature:

Carr, Edward Hallett. *The Bolshevik Revolution, 1917–1923*. 3 vols. London: Macmillan, 1950–53.

Kul'chyts'kyi, Stanislav. *Chervonyi vyklyk: Istoriia komunizmu v Ukraïni vid ioho narodzhennia do zahybeli*, vol. 1. Kyiv: Tempora, 2013.

Malia, Martin E. *The Soviet Tragedy: A History of Socialism in Russia, 1917–1991*. New York: Free Press, 1994.

Priestland, David. *The Red Flag: A History of Communism*. New York: Grove Press, 2009.

Famine of 1921–23

The Famine of 1921–23 was caused by droughts in 1921 and 1922, postwar economic devastation, the policy of grain procurements, and the excessive transport of grain outside the USSR (even for export by 1923). In 1921, 20 percent of the harvest was lost to drought, including 40 percent in the Donetsk gubernia, 63 percent in the Zaporizhia gubernia, and 64 percent in the Katerynoslav gubernia. To avoid interfering with the transport of grain from Ukraine to Russia, the Sovnarkom of the RSFSR did not acknowledge the existence of famine in the southern gubernias of the Ukrainian SSR until early 1922, when mass mortality began. The official recognition of the famine made it possible for the head of the Ukrainian SSR Radnarkom, Khrystyian Rakovsky, to appeal for aid to the American Relief Administration, which had been working in the Volga region since August 1921. The ARA gave starving southern Ukraine 180.9 million emergency rations, the Fridtjof Nansen charitable mission gave 12.2 million, and Workers' International Relief, created by the Comintern, gave 383,000. In the fall of 1922, the central government announced that the new harvest had ended the famine. In Ukraine, however, the famine lasted until mid-1923.

Literature:

Holod 1921–1923 rokiv v Ukraïni. Zbirnyk dokumentiv ta materialiv, comp. Ol'ha M. Movchan et al. Kyiv: Naukova dumka, 1993.

Kul'chyts'kyi, Stanislav, and Ol'ha M. Movchan. *Nevidomi storinky holodu 1921–1923 rr. v Ukraïni.* Kyiv: Instytut istoriï Ukraïny NAN Ukraïny, 1993.

GOELRO Plan

The GOELRO Plan (State Commission for the Electrification of Russia, Russ. *Gosudarstvennaia komissiia po elektrifikatsii Rossii*), projected in 1920 for 10–15 years, called for the renovation of old thermal power stations and the construction of 20 new ones in the regions, as well as of 10 hydroelectric stations with a capacity of 1.75 million kilowatts. Power plants with a 560,000-kW capacity, including thermal stations at Shterivka, Hryshyne, Lysychansk, Izium and others, as well as the 200,000-kW Dnipro Hydroelectric Station, with planned expansion in Oleksandrivsk (present-day Zaporizhia), were planned for the Southern region (Ukraine and southern Russia).

GOELRO was the first plan for industrializing the country. It foresaw electricity production increasing from 2 billion kWh in 1913 to 2.8 billion kWh (accomplished in 1931), coal output growing from 29.2 million metric tons to 62.3 million (accomplished in 1932), and steel production increasing from 4.3 million metric tons to 6.5 million (accomplished in 1933).

Literature:

Kul'chyts'kyi, Stanislav. *Ukraïna mizh dvoma viinamy (1921–1939 rr.).* Kyiv: Vydavnychyi dim "Al'ternatyvy," 1999.

Plan elektrifikatsii RSFSR. Moscow: Gospolitizdat, 1955.

Plan elektrifikatsii RSFSR. Doklad 8-mu s"ezdu Sovetov Gosudarstvennoi komissii po elektrifikatsii Rossii. Moscow: Gosudarstvennoe tekhnicheskoe izdatel'stvo, 1920.

Grain procurements

From 1921 to 1927, the state obtained grain for cities, the army, and a new export fund from peasants either as taxes in kind or by purchase on the free market. Displeased with state prices, peasants refused to sell their grain in 1927, and the country was gripped by a food crisis. In January 1928 the government overcame the crisis through extraordinary measures. Peasants were punished with sanctions when they failed to fulfill their grain quotas: confiscation of all available grain reserves, large fines, compulsory sale of property, imprisonment, or internal exile. Starting in 1929, a legal framework was created for the extraordinary measures, and they became ordinary. As in 1918–20, the state set quotas for grain procurement and allocated them among the regions, collective farms, and private farms, after which it began "hammering out" grain by force.

This method of procurement lasted until December 1932. The resistance of collectivized peasants and private farmers was passive but effective: they refused to sow grain and gather a harvest that would be taken from them without material compensation. In 1932–33, a famine broke out in the whole country (not to be confused with the Holodomor, caused only in certain regions by the seizure of all available food along with physical and informational blockade of the villages). Given the onset of famine, Stalin abandoned unlimited grain procurements, and in January 1933 a law was passed obliging collective and individual farmers to make mandatory grain deliveries to the state. The law indicated the transition to a tax-based system in relations between the state and the agricultural sector. All grain other than that delivered to the state in kind became the property of the producer and could be sold on the free market.

Great Terror of 1937–38

Name given by historians to the campaign of terror that firmly secured Stalin's dominant position in the system of Soviet rule. Stalin ended the economic collapse brought about by the communist onslaught of 1929–32 not only by economic (see **grain procurements**) and political (the 1936 Constitution of the USSR, the world's most democratic) means but also through a terror-famine that caused mass mortality in the most productive grain-growing regions and individual terror, which took on huge proportions in 1937–38.

Literature:

Conquest, Robert. *The Great Terror: A Reassessment*. New York: Oxford University Press, 1991.

Courtois, Stéphane, Nicolas Werth, Jean-Louis Panné, Andrzej Paczkowski, Karel Bartošek, and Jean-Louis Margolin. *The Black Book of Communism*, trans. Jonathan Murphy and Mark Kramer, ed. Mark Kramer. Cambridge, MA: Harvard University Press, 1999.

Politychnyi teror i teroryzm v Ukraïni, XIX–XX st.: Istorychni narysy, ed. Valerii A. Smolii. Kyiv: Naukova dumka, 2002.

Velykyi teror v Ukraïni: "Kurkul's'ka operatsiia" 1937–1938 rr., comp. Serhii Kokin and Mark Iunhe. 2 parts. Kyiv: Vydavnychyi dim "Kyievo-Mohylians'ka akademiia," 2010.

International Commission of Inquiry into the 1932–1933 Famine in Ukraine

The International Commission of Inquiry into the 1932–1933 Famine in Ukraine was initiated after the Toronto-based World Congress of Free Ukrainians appealed to attorneys and legal experts to contribute to an investigation into the Ukrainian Holodomor. An organizational meeting took place on February 12–14, 1988 in Toronto. Two hearings were held in 1988, the first in Brussels on May 23–27 and the second in New York from October 31 to November 4. The final meeting was held in London on November 15–18, 1989. Testimonies provided by the plaintiff were reviewed at the sessions, including materials from the **US Commission on the Ukraine Famine**, which investigated the Ukrainian famines of 1921–23 and 1932–33. The commission acknowledged the credibility of information supporting the existence of constituent elements of genocide in the events of 1932–33 in Ukraine. It noted that the famine and the policy that caused it were not limited to Ukraine, "even if territories with a majority Ukrainian population tragically prevailed."

A few members of the commission presented a separate opinion on fundamental issues. Professor Georges Levasseur of the University of Paris, a former member of the Commission on the Revision of the French Criminal Code, called the famine of 1932–33 a crime against humanity rather than genocide. Professor Ricardo Levene of the University of Buenos Aires, the president of the Supreme Court of Argentina, noted that the UN Convention on Genocide was adopted on December 9, 1948 and thus could not be applied to events that had occurred fifteen years previously. Professor

Jacob W. F. Sundberg of the University of Stockholm indicated that the USSR alone had the grounds and competence to examine the case of the famine of 1932–33 within the framework of the UN Convention on Genocide.

Literature:

International Commission of Inquiry into the 1932–33 Famine in Ukraine. "The Final Report (1990)." Manuscript (various paginations). Toronto: The Commission Documentation Office, 1990.

Kulak (literally, "fist"; Ukr. *kurkul'*)

In prerevolutionary usage, a wealthy peasant, a "bloodsucker"; figuratively, a greedy person, money-grubber, skinflint. In Soviet political practice, a kulak was a rural exploiter against whom middle peasant-owners and the proletarianized poor were supposed to join forces with state institutions. True kulaks, that is, peasants who exploited the labor of others in order to get rich, disappeared from the Ukrainian countryside after the **black repartition**. Yet the Soviet state continued to use this concept as a bogey in order to turn less-well off peasants against the better-to-do ones. If poor peasants or laborers opposed the authorities, they were subject to repressions as "kulak henchmen."

Mensheviks

A faction of the Russian Social Democratic Labor Party that was formed, like the Bolsheviks, after the schism at the Second Congress of the RSDLP in 1903. They played a leading role, along with the Socialist Revolutionaries, in the activity of workers' and soldiers' councils from the beginning of the Russian Revolution to the suppression of the Kornilov putsch. After November 1917, the Menshevik Party gradually crumbled under the pressure of Bolshevik repressions. The party was outlawed in 1923 and completely destroyed by the Chekists in 1925.

Literature:

Martov, Iulii O. *Mirovoi bol'shevizm*. Berlin, 1923.

Men'sheviki v 1917 g. 3 vols. Moscow: ROSSPĖN, 1994–97.

MTS (Machine and Tractor Stations)

State enterprises intended to serve the collective farms in organizational, technical, and agronomic capacities. They were established by a resolution of the Council of Labor and Defense on June 5, 1929. The technical equipment concentrated in the MTS (tractors, automobiles, complex agricultural equipment), as well as the services of agronomists, livestock specialists, and veterinarians were employed by the collective farms on the basis of business agreements. As a rule, payment for services was made in kind—a portion of the harvest. In 1958, all MTS equipment was sold to the collective farms, and they were reorganized as Machinery Service Stations (*remontno-tekhnicheskaia stantsiia*, RTS).

Literature:

Bondarenko, Viktor V. *Razvitie obshchestvennogo khoziaistva kolkhozov Ukrainy v gody dovoennykh piatiletok*. Kyiv: Izdatel'stvo AN USSR, 1957.

Istoriia ukraïns'koho selianstva: Narysy v 2-kh tomakh, ed. Volodymyr Lytvyn, vol. 1. Kyiv: Naukova dumka, 2006.

Rozvytok narodnoho hospodarstva Ukraïns'koï RSR (1917–1967 rr.), ed. Davyd F. Virnyk, vol. 1. Kyiv: Naukova dumka, 1967.

NEP (New Economic Policy)

The New Economic Policy (NEP) began in 1921, when *prodrazvërstka* was suspended and replaced with a fixed provisions tax, giving peasants the opportunity to sell their produce on the free market. The legalization of the market forced the Bolshevik leaders to allow entrepreneurial activity. Nationalized industry organized in trusts was converted to principles of cost accounting, which required the generation of revenue to fund production costs. The restoration of the credit and banking system, the introduction of a stable currency, and state promotion of cooperative and private enterprise led to the quick revival of productive forces.

Literature:

Kul'chyts'kyi, Stanislav. *Komunizm v Ukraïni: pershe desiatyrichchia (1919–1928).* Kyiv: Osnovy, 1996.

———. *Ukraïna mizh dvoma viinamy (1921–1939 rr.).* Kyiv: Vydavnychyi dim "Al'ternatyvy," 1999.

Petliurite

Follower of Symon Petliura (1879–1926), president of the Directory of the Ukrainian People's Republic (1918–20). Derogatory Soviet term for nationally conscious Ukrainians in general, as well as for real or imagined anti-Soviet elements in Ukraine.

Prodrazvërstka (Russ., requisitioning of agricultural produce)

A means of requisitioning grain and other foodstuffs used by the Soviet authorities in 1919–20 and 1930–32. The state would set the grain quota for agriculture depending on its needs, after which the quota was apportioned to the republics, regions, districts, collective farms, and peasant homesteads regardless of the availability of leftover grain on the farms. Failing to fulfill the quota brought on various repressive measures, up to liquidating the farms and exiling the debtors to the farthest regions of the country.

Red partisan

A person who fought on the side of the Soviet authorities during the Ukrainian liberation struggle (1918–20). This phrase became an official concept; with supporting documents, it could be entered on all official forms and helped in career promotion.

Russian Constitutional Democratic Party

Popularly known as Cadets (*Kadety*), founded in Moscow in October 1905. The official name was changed in April 1906 to the Party of the People's Freedom. Their only leader was the well-known Russian historian Pavel Miliukov. The party played an important role in the Provisional Government. After the Bolsheviks seized power, they declared the Cadets the "party of enemies of the people." Party members went underground, and a number of them emigrated after the defeat of the White movement.

Russian Revolution, 1917–18

The events that sparked the Russian Revolution began with a demonstration on International Women's Day, March 8, 1917, that passed along Nevsky Prospekt in Petrograd with demands for work and bread. Demonstrations and strikes in the imperial capital grew into a revolution. The Petrograd Soviet of Workers' Deputies and the Provisional Committee of the State Duma were formed on March 12 (February 27 O.S.). On March 14 (March 1 O.S.), the Petrograd Soviet of Workers' and Soldiers' Deputies held its first meeting and declared that it was taking power into its own hands. Tsar Nicholas II signed an act of abdication on March 15 (2 O.S.). With the consent of the Petrograd Soviet, power passed to a government created by the Provisional Committee of the State Duma.

On November 7 (October 25), the Bolshevik Party carried out a coup d'état under the banner of Soviet slogans. A Council of People's Commissars (Sovnarkom) headed by Vladimir Lenin came to power and undertook to realize the principal demand of the Russian Revolution—elections to the Constituent Assembly. The elections were held in the prescribed period, and the **Socialist Revolutionaries** won an unconditional victory. A session of the Constituent Assembly opened on the evening of January 18 (5 O.S.) 1918, lasting until the morning of the 19th. The chief of security for the premises of the Constituent Assembly, the sailor Anatolii Zhelezniakov, informed the deputies that the guard was tired, and that it was time to go home. The Russian Revolution was finally extinguished on this subdued quotidian note.

In global historiography, the Russian Revolution is customarily divided into two distinct revolutions—those of February and October. In the Marxist-Leninist lexicon, the February Revolution was deemed bourgeois-democratic and that of October proletarian or socialist. In reality, the Russian Revolution encompassed the whole country, and people from almost all walks of life took part in it. During the fall of the autocracy, the failed Kornilov putsch, and Lenin's successful coup, the councils of soldiers' and workers' deputies played a key role in the revolutionary events. The soldiers' deputies acted as spokesmen for the peasants' will.

Literature:

Kul'chyts'kyi, Stanislav. *Rosiis'ka revoliutsiia 1917 roku: novyi pohliad*. Kyiv: Nash chas, 2008.

Seksot

An abbreviation of the Russian words *sekretnyi sotrudnik*, or "secret collaborator." Seksots were recruited by state security agencies from all strata of society, mainly by force—threats and blackmail. They were required to inform Chekists about people's attitudes in the collectives where they worked.

Self-Taxation of the Rural Population

The collection of funds by residents of rural population centers to satisfy their cultural and economic needs. It was regulated by corresponding government resolutions. See, e.g.:

Resolution of the CEC USSR "On the Self-Taxation of the Population for the Satisfaction of Local Public Needs," August 29, 1924 (*Sbornik zakonov SSSR*, 1924, no. 6: 69).

Resolution of the CEC RSFSR "On the Termination of Collection of Illegal Taxes and Forms of Self-Taxation Prohibited by Law," January 18, 1926 (*Sbornik uzakonenii RSFSR*, 1926, no. 11: 81).

Resolution of the All-Russian CEC and Sovnarkom USSR "On the Self-Taxation of the Population," August 24, 1927 (*Sbornik zakonov SSSR*, 1927, no. 51: 509).

The mechanism of self-taxation was used when the state began assigning grain-procurement plans to republics, regions, and districts. As the final link in this chain, peasants were obligated to decide at general meetings how to present the mandatory grain-procurement plan assigned to the village to each household.

Senior officials

Members of the nomenklatura who occupied leadership positions in the administrative apparatus. They were subject to confirmation by party committees at various levels and responsible for particular areas or spheres of government activity.

Socialist Revolutionaries (SRs)

Organized as a party in early 1906, made use of terrorism in the political struggle. They were the most popular political party in Russia, with more than a million members in the summer of 1917. The party shared power with the Mensheviks in the Russian Provisional Government. In November 1917 it split into two organizationally independent parties—the Left and Right SRs. The Left SRs entered into an alliance with the Bolsheviks that lasted until the summer of 1918. After the Bolsheviks came to power, the Right SRs went into the underground and finally ceased to exist in 1925.

Literature:

Gusev, Kirill V. *Partiia Ėserov: ot melkoburzhuaznogo revoliutsionarizma k kontrrevoliutsii*. Moscow: Mysl', 1975.

Meshcheriakov, V. N. *Partiia sotsialistov-revoliutsionerov*. Moscow, 1922.

Sletov, Stepan N. *K istorii vozniknoveniia partii sotsialistov-revoliutsionerov*. Petrograd, 1917.

State farm (Russ. *sovkhoz*, a contraction of *sovetskoe khoziaistvo*, "Soviet farm"; Ukr. *radhosp*, from *radians'ke hospodarstvo*)

This term was used to refer to estates that were expropriated from landowners and transferred to state control. Later it meant agricultural enterprises established by state investment or **collective farms** reorganized as state enterprises.

Torgsin **(abbreviated from Russ.** ***Torgovlia s inostrantsami,*** **"trade with foreigners")**
This was a chain of stores established in the summer of 1930 to provide goods to foreigners visiting the USSR or foreign experts who worked in the USSR and received a portion of their salaries in hard currency. Beginning in late 1931, Torgsin and its branch stores expanded to the district level and became accessible to Soviet citizens who had hard currency, prerevolutionary gold coins, and golden or valuable wares. In years of hunger, people took their savings to the Torgsin in order to buy bread and other provisions.

Literature:

Osokina, Elena A. *Zoloto dlia industrializatsii: TORGSIN*. Moscow: ROSSPĖN, 2009.

"Triumphal march of Soviet power"

These words, which became a cliché in Soviet historiography, were used by Vladimir Lenin to characterize the expansion of Soviet rule from the imperial capital to the entire periphery. The process was quite prolonged, extending from the overthrow of the Provisional Government on October 25 (November 7 N.S.), 1917 to March 1918, when the Soviet Treaty of Brest-Litovsk with the Central Powers—Germany, Austria-Hungary, Bulgaria, and the Ottoman Empire—was signed and ratified. The establishment of Soviet rule across the whole territory of Russia and withdrawal from the war allowed the Bolshevik leaders to initiate the radical socioeconomic transformations required by communist doctrine. In April 1918, Lenin published the article "Ocherednye zadachi sovetskoi vlasti" (The Immediate Tasks of Soviet Power) in *Pravda*, launching the **communist onslaught**.

US Commission on the Ukraine Famine

At the request of the Ukrainian diaspora, in November 1983 a bill was introduced in the US Congress House of Representatives to create a commission to investigate the Great Famine in Ukraine, whose existence Soviet leaders adamantly denied. When it turned out that that a majority of Congressional representatives were not willing to pay for a commission charged with researching events that had occurred fifty years earlier on the other side of the globe, the Ukrainian diaspora organized a campaign under the slogan "Grassroots," sending tens of thousands of individual and collective petitions to members of Congress and President Ronald Reagan. In October 1984 a commission consisting of two senators, four representatives, three officials of the executive branch, and six members of the Ukrainian community was established. James Mace, an associate of the Harvard Ukrainian Research Institute, became its director. The commission began disseminating the results of its investigation throughout the world in 1987, forcing the head of the Communist Party of Ukraine, Volodymyr Shcherbytsky, to officially acknowledge the existence of the famine of 1932–33 in December 1987. This opened the way for Soviet scholars to research the forbidden topic. In April 1988 James Mace prepared a final report on the commission's academic and investigative work, which was published immediately. On June 5, 1988, the report reached the General Department of the Central Committee of the Communist Party of Ukraine. In 2008 the Institute of Ukrainian History, National Academy of Sciences of Ukraine prepared the report for reissue along with the three-volume collection of eyewitness testimonies about the Holodomor, and both were published by the Kyiv-Mohyla Academy Publishing House.

Literature:

Kul'chitskii, Stanislav. *Pochemu ON NAS unichtozhal? Stalin i ukrainskii Golodomor*. Biblioteka hazety "Den'." Kyiv: Izdatel'stvo ZAO "Ukrainskaia press-gruppa," 2007. Published in Romanian in 2008 and in Armenian in 2010.

Kul'chyts'kyi, Stanislav. *Holod 1932–1933 rr. v Ukraïni iak henotsyd: movoiu dokumentiv, ochyma svidkiv*. Kyiv: Nash chas, 2008.

Mace, James E. "Diial'nist' Komisiï Konhresu SShA z vyvchennia holodu v Ukraïni" in *Holod 1932–1933 rokiv v Ukraïni: prychyny ta naslidky*. Kyiv: Naukova dumka, 2003.

_____. and Leonid Heretz, ed., *Investigation of the Ukrainian Famine 1932–1933: Oral History Project of the Commission on the Ukraine Famine*, 3 vols. Washington, DC: US GPO, 1990.

Report to Congress. Commission on the Ukraine Famine. Printed for the use of the Commission on the Ukraine Famine. Washington, DC: US GPO, 1988.

Velykyi holod v Ukraïni 1932–1933 rokiv, 3 vols. Kyiv: Kyievo-Mohylians'ka akademiia, 2008.

War communism

Term used by Vladimir Lenin to describe the **communist onslaught** of 1918–20, which ended in economic collapse and starvation. It was meant to camouflage the failed efforts to realize communist doctrine. The Bolshevik leader insisted that the Soviet authorities' measures aimed at building communism had nothing in common with the doctrine of communism and had been precipitated by wartime conditions. In the years 1918–20 the Bolsheviks did not conceal that they were building communism; the term "war communism" did not appear until 1921, after the transition to the New Economic Policy.

Literature:

Kul'chyts'kyi, Stanislav. *Komunizm v Ukraïni: pershe desiatyrichchia (1919–1928)*. Kyiv: Osnovy, 1996.

Westernization

the process whereby less-developed countries borrow technological advancements, production techniques, cultural values and so on from Western countries. In both prerevolutionary Russia and the Soviet Union, it was used to modernize the economy with the goal of catching up to the West in industry, first and foremost in arms production.

Literature:

Huntington, Samuel P. *The Clash of Civilizations and the Remaking of World Order*. New York: Simon and Schuster, 1996.

McNeill, William H. *The Rise of the West: A History of the Human Community*. Chicago: Chicago University Press, 1963, enlarged ed. 1992.

Toynbee, Arnold J. *A Study of History*. Abridgement of Volumes I–VI by D. C. Somervell. New York: Oxford University Press, 1974.

Workday (*trudoden'*)

Unit for evaluating and calculating the quantity and quality of labor on collective farms from 1930 to 1966 (when guaranteed wages for work were introduced). The very phrase "guaranteed wages for work" indicates that the calculation of labor in workdays offered no guarantee that collective farmers would be compensated materially for their labor on farms in the state sector. At the end of the year, the profit accruing to the collective farm after fulfilling obligations to the state and making payments in kind to the MTS for its services was divided among the collective farmers in proportion to their earned workdays. Not infrequently, however, the collective farms had nothing left over after fulfilling their obligations, and the farmers were then offered advances, usually in kind.

Literature:

Bondarenko, Viktor V. *Razvitie obshchestvennogo khoziaistva kolkhozov Ukrainy v gody dovoennykh piatiletok*. Kyiv: Izdatel'stvo AN USSR, 1957.

Istoriia ukraïns'koho selianstva, ed. Valerii Smolii, vol. 1. Kyiv: Naukova dumka, 2006.

Abbreviations and Acronyms

Agitprop	agitation and propaganda department (in party committees at all levels)
AUCP(B)	All-Union Communist Party (Bolsheviks) (Russ. *Vsesoiuznaia Kommunisticheskaia partiia (bol'shevikov), VKP(b)*)
CC	Central Commitee (Russ. *Tsentral'nyi komitet*)
CCC	Central Control Commission (Russ. *Tsentral'naia kontrol'naia komissiia*)
CEC	Central Executive Committee (Russ. *Tsentral'nyi ispolnitel'nyi komitet*)
Cheka	All-Russian Extraordinary Commission for Combating Counterrevolution and Sabotage (Russ. *Vserossiiskaia chrezvychainaia komissiia po bor'be s kontrrevoliutsiei i sabotazhem*). Officials of the Cheka were known as Chekists (*chekisty*).
CP(B)U	Communist Party (Bolsheviks) of Ukraine (Ukr. *Komunistychna partiia (bil'shovykiv) Ukraïny*)
CPSU	Communist Party of the Soviet Union (Russ. *Kommunisticheskaia partiia Sovetskogo Soiuza*)
DOBRUS	Democratic Association of Ukrainians Formerly Repressed by the Soviets (Ukr. *Demokratychne ob'iednannia buvshykh represovanykh ukraïntsiv sovietamy*)
FZO	factory apprenticeship school (Russ. *Shkola fabrichno-zavodskogo obucheniia*)
GOELRO	State Commission for Electrification of Russia (Russ. *Gosudarstvennaia komissiia po elektrifikatsii Rossii*)
Gosplan	State Planning Commission (Russ. *Gosudarstvennaia planovaia komissiia SSSR*)
GPU	State Political Directorate (Russ. *Gosudarstvennoe politicheskoe upravlenie;* Ukr. acronym: DPU)
KGB	Committee for State Security (Russ. *Komitet gosudarstvennoi bezopasnosti;* Ukr. acronym: KDB)
KNS	Komnezam, or Committee of Poor Peasants (Ukr. *Komitet nezamozhnykh selian*)
Kolkhoztsentr	Collective Farm Center, All-Union Association of Agricultural Collectives (Russ. *Vsesoiuznyi soiuz sel'skokhoziaistvennykh kollektivov;* Ukr. *Kolhosptsentr*)
MGB	Ministry of State Security (Russ. *Ministerstvo gosudarstvennoi bezopasnosti*)
Miskpartkom	urban party committee (Ukr. *mis'kyi partiinyi komitet*)

MOPR	International Red Aid (Russ. *Mezhdunarodnaia organizatsiia pomoshchi bortsam revoliutsii*)
MTS	Machine and Tractor Station (Russ. *Mashinno-traktornaia stantsiia*)
MVD	Ministry of Internal Affairs (Russ. *Ministerstvo vnutrennikh del*)
NAN Ukraïny	National Academy of Sciences of Ukraine (Ukr. *Natsional'na akademiia nauk Ukraïny*)
Narkomiust	People's Commissariat of Justice of the USSR, also People's Commissar of Justice (Russ. *Narodnyi komissariat iustitsii SSSR*)
Narkomzem USSR	People's Commissariat of Agriculture of the USSR (Russ. *Narodnyi komissariat zemledeliia SSSR*)
Narsud	People's Court (Russ. *Narodnyi sud*)
NKVD USSR	People's Commissariat of Internal Affairs (Russ. *Narodnyi komissariat vnutrennikh del SSSR*)
OGPU	Joint State Political Directorate (Russ. *Ob"edinënnoe gosudarstvennoe politicheskoe upravlenie*; Ukr. acronym: ODPU)
OrgDepart	Organizational department (in party committees at all levels)
Rabkrin	RKI or Workers' and Peasants' Inspectorate (People's Commissariat merged with the CCC AUCP(B)) (Russ. *Raboche-krest'ianskaia inspektsiia*)
Radnarkom	Council of People's Commissars of the Ukrainian SSR (Ukr. *Rada narodnykh komisariv USRR*)
RCP(B)	Russian Communist Party (Bolsheviks) (Russ. *Rossiiskaia Kommunisticheskaia partiia (bol'shevikov)*)
RSFSR	Russian Soviet Federative Socialist Republic (Russ. *Rossiiskaia Sovetskaia Federativnaia Sotsialisticheskaia Respublika*)
Russian Archives	*Rosarkhiv*, Federal Archive Agency of the Russian Federation (Russ. *Federal'noe arkhivnoe agentstvo Rossiiskoi Federatsii*)
Sovnarkom RSFSR	Council of People's Commissars of the RSFSR (Russ. *Sovet narodnykh komissarov RSFSR*)
Sovnarkom USSR	Council of People's Commissars of the USSR (Russ. *Sovet narodnykh komissarov SSSR*)
SUZhERO	Ukrainian Association of Victims of Russian Communist Terror (Ukr. *Soiuz ukraïntsiv-zhertv rosiis'ko-komunistychnoho teroru*)

UGB-NKVD	Directorate of State Security at the NKVD (Russ. *Upravlenie gosudarstvennoi bezopasnosti NKVD*)
Ukrainian SSR	Ukrainian Socialist Soviet Republic (*Ukraïns'ka Sotsialistychna Radians'ka Respublika, USRR*). After the adoption of the Soviet constitution of 1936, the official name was changed to "Ukrainian Soviet Socialist Republic" (*Ukraïns'ka Radians'ka Sotsialistychna Respublika, URSR*)
Ukrkolhosptsentr	Ukrainian Collective Farm Center, Union of Agricultural Collectives of the Ukrainian SSR (Ukr. *Soiuz sil'skohospodars'kykh kolektyviv USRR*)
USSR	Union of Soviet Socialist Republics (Russ. *Soiuz Sovetskikh Sotsialisticheskikh Respublik*)
VTsIK	All-Russian Central Executive Committee (Russ. *Vserossiiskii tsentral'nyi ispolnitel'nyi komitet*)
VUTsVK	All-Ukrainian Central Executive Committee (Ukr. *Vseukraïn'skyi tsentral'nyi vykonavchyi komitet*)
Zagotzerno	All-Union Zagotzerno Association, from *zagotovka zerna*, "procurement of grain": All-Union Association for the Procurement of Cereals, Legumes, Groats, Oilseeds, and Forage Crops (Russ. *Vsesoiuznoe ob"edinenie po zagotovke zernovykh, bobovykh, krupianykh, maslichnykh i furazhnykh kul'tur*)

Bibliography

1. ARCHIVES

RGASPI – Rossiiskii gosudarstvennyi arkhiv sotsial'no-politicheskoi istorii (Russian State Archives of Sociopolitical History)

TsDAHOU – Tsentral'nyi derzhavnyi arkhiv hromads'kykh ob'iednan' Ukraïny (Central State Archives of Public Organizations of Ukraine)

TsDAVO Ukraïny – Tsentral'nyi derzhavnyi arkhiv vyshchykh orhaniv vlady i upravlinnia Ukraïny (Central State Archives of Supreme Organs of Government and Administration of Ukraine)

2. WRITINGS, SPEECHES, AND DECREES OF COMMUNIST LEADERS

A) VLADIMIR LENIN

"Doklad o prave otzyva na zasedanii VTsIK 21 noiabria (4 dekabria) 1917 g." *Polnoe sobranie sochinenii*, 35: 109–11. Moscow: Izdatel'stvo politicheskoi literatury, 1974. Cf. https://www.marxists.org/archive/lenin/works/1917/nov/21.htm.

"Doklad o taktike RKP na III kongresse Kommunisticheskogo internatsionala 5 iiulia 1921 g." *Polnoe sobranie sochinenii*, 44: 34–54. Moscow: Izdatel'stvo politicheskoi literatury, 1974. Cf. https://www.marxists.org/archive/lenin/works/1921/jun/12.htm.

"Doklad ob ocherednykh zadachakh Sovetskoi vlasti na zasedanii VTsIK 29 aprelia 1918 g." *Polnoe sobranie sochinenii*, 36: 241–67. Moscow: Izdatel'stvo politicheskoi literatury, 1974. Cf. https://www.marxists.org/archive/lenin/works/1918/apr/29.htm.

"Doklad Vserossiiskogo Tsentral'nogo Ispolnitel'nogo Komiteta i Soveta Narodnykh Komissarov o vneshnei i vnutrennei politike na VIII Vserossiiskom s"ezde Sovetov 22 dekabria 1920 g." *Polnoe sobranie sochinenii*, 42: 128–61. Moscow: Izdatel'stvo politicheskoi literatury, 1974. Cf. https://www.marxists.org/archive/lenin/works/1920/8thcong/ch02.htm.

"Nashi zadachi i Sovet rabochikh deputatov." *Polnoe sobranie sochinenii*, 12: 59–70. Moscow: Izdatel'stvo politicheskoi literatury, 1972. Cf. https://www.marxists.org/archive/lenin/works/1905/nov/04b.htm.

"O kooperatsii." *Polnoe sobranie sochinenii*, 45: 369–77. Moscow: Izdatel'stvo politicheskoi literatury, 1975. Cf. https://www.marxists.org/archive/lenin/works/1923/jan/06.htm.

"O prodovol'stvennom naloge (znachenie novoi ėkonomicheskoi politiki i ee usloviia)." *Polnoe sobranie sochinenii*, 43: 205–45. Moscow: Izdatel'stvo politicheskoi literatury, 1974. Cf. https://www.marxists.org/archive/lenin/works/1921/apr/21.htm.

"O zadachakh proletariata v dannoi revoliutsii." *Polnoe sobranie sochinenii*, 31: 113–18. Moscow: Izdatel'stvo politicheskoi literatury, 1974.

"Ocherednye zadachi Sovetskoi vlasti." *Polnoe sobranie sochinenii*, 36: 165–208. Moscow: Izdatel'stvo politicheskoi literatury, 1974.

"Rech' na Pervom Vserossiiskom s"ezde sovetov narodnogo khoziaistva 26 maia 1918 g." *Polnoe sobranie sochinenii*, 36: 377–86. Moscow: Izdatel'stvo politicheskoi literatury, 1974. Cf. https://www.marxists.org/archive/lenin/works/1918/may/26b.htm.

"Rech' pri obsuzhdenii zakonoproekta SNK 'O merakh ukrepleniia i razvitiia krest'ianskogo sel'skogo khoziaistva' na fraktsii RKP(b) VIII s"ezda Sovetov 24 dekabria 1920 g." *Polnoe sobranie sochinenii*, 42: 178–84. Moscow: Izdatel'stvo politicheskoi literatury, 1974. Cf. https://www.marxists.org/archive/lenin/works/1920/8thcong/ch03.htm.

"Rezoliutsiia TsK RKP(b) 'O Sovetskoi vlasti na Ukraine.'" *Polnoe sobranie sochinenii*, 39: 334–37. Moscow: Izdatel'stvo politicheskoi literatury, 1974. Cf. https://www.marxists.org/archive/lenin/works/1919/nov/x01.htm.

b) JOSEPH STALIN

"Beseda s inostrannymi rabochimi delegatsiiami 5 noiabria 1927 g." *Sochineniia*, 10: 206–38. Moscow: Gosudarstvennoe izdatel'stvo politicheskoi literatury, 1949. Cf. https://www.marxists.org/reference/archive/stalin/works/1927/11/05.htm.

Ėkonomicheskie problemy sotsializma v SSSR. Moscow: Gospolitizdat, 1952. Cf. https://www.marxists.org/reference/archive/stalin/works/1951/economic-problems/ch14.htm.

"God velikogo pereloma. K XII godovshchine Oktiabria." *Sochineniia*, 12: 118–35. Moscow: Gosudarstvennoe izdatel'stvo politicheskoi literatury, 1949.

"Golovokruzhenie ot uspekhov. K voprosam kolkhoznogo dvizheniia." *Pravda*, no. 60, March 2, 1930. Cf. https://www.marxists.org/reference/archive/stalin/works/1930/03/02.htm.

"Itogi pervoi piatiletki. Doklad 7 ianvaria 1933 g. na ob"edinennom plenume TsK i TsKK VKP(b)." *Sochineniia*, 13: 161–215. Moscow: Gosudarstvennoe izdatel'stvo politicheskoi literatury, 1951. Cf. https://www.marxists.org/reference/archive/stalin/works/1933/01/07.htm.

"K voprosam agrarnoi politiki v SSSR. Rech' na konferentsii agrarnikov-marksistov 27 dekabria 1929 g." *Sochineniia*, 12: 166. Moscow: Gosudarstvennoe izdatel'stvo politicheskoi literatury, 1949.

"Konspektnaia zapis' dvukh tostov Stalina I. V. na prieme v Kremle 2 maia 1933 g., sdelannaia R. Khmel'nitskim." RGASPI, fond 558, op. 11, d. 1117, l. 10.

"Letter from Stalin to Kaganovich and Molotov on organizing the 1932 grain-procurement campaign." In *The Holodomor Reader*, ed. and comp. Bohdan Klid and Alexander J. Motyl, 233. Edmonton and Toronto: CIUS Press, 2012.

"Na khlebnom fronte." *Sochineniia*, 11: 81–97. Moscow: Gosudarstvennoe izdatel'stvo politicheskoi literatury, 1949. Cf. https://www.marxists.org/reference/archive/stalin/works/1928/may/28.htm.

"O khlebozagotovkakh i perspektivakh razvitiia sel'skogo khoziaistva. Iz vystuplenii v raznykh raionakh Sibiri v ianvare 1928 g. (Kratkaia zapis')." *Sochineniia*, 11: 1–9. Moscow: Gosudarstvennoe izdatel'stvo politicheskoi literatury, 1949. Cf. https://www.marxists.org/reference/archive/stalin/works/1928/01/x01.htm.

"O pravom uklone v VKP(b)." *Sochineniia*, 12: 1–107. Moscow: Gosudarstvennoe izdatel'stvo politicheskoi literatury, 1949. Cf. https://www.marxists.org/reference/archive/stalin/works/1929/04/22.htm.

"O rabote v derevne. Rech' 11 ianvaria 1933 r." *Sochineniia*, 13: 216–33. Moscow: Gosudarstvennoe izdatel'stvo politicheskoi literatury, 1951.

"Politicheskii otchet Tsentral'nogo komiteta XV s"ezdu VKP(b)." In *Piatnadtsatyi s"ezd VKP(b). Dekabr' 1927 goda. Stenograficheskii otchet*, 2 vols., 1: 63-65. Moscow: Gosudarstvennoe izdatel'stvo politicheskoi literatury, 1961.

"Politicheskii otchet Tsentral'nogo komiteta XVI s"ezdu VKP(b) 27 iiunia 1930 g." *Sochineniia*, 12: 235–373. Moscow: Gosudarstvennoe izdatel'stvo politicheskoi literatury, 1949. Cf. https://www.marxists.org/reference/archive/stalin/works/1930/aug/27.htm.

"Rech' na Pervom Vsesoiuznom s"ezde kolkhoznikov-udarnikov 19 fevralia 1933 g." *Sochineniia*, 13: 236–56. Moscow: Gosudarstvennoe izdatel'stvo politicheskoi literatury, 1951. Cf. https://www.marxists.org/reference/archive/stalin/works/1933/02/19.htm.

c) OTHER COMMUNIST LEADERS

Bukharin, Nikolai I. "Teoriia proletarskoi diktatury." In his *Izbrannye proizvedeniia*, 1–23. Moscow: Politizdat, 1988.

Gorbachev, Mikhail S. *Oktiabr' i perestroika: revoliutsiia prodolzhaetsia, 1917–1987*. Moscow: Izdatel'stvo politicheskoi literatury, 1987.

Khrushchev, Nikita S. *Vremia. Liudi. Vlast'. Vospominaniia v 4-kh knigakh*, vol. 1. Moscow: Informatsionno-izdatel'skaia kompaniia "Moskovskie novosti," 1999.

Bibliography ■ 163

Marx, Karl. *Capital: A Critique of Political Economy*, 3 vols. New York: International Publishers, 1967.

Marx, Karl, and Friedrich Engels. "Manifesto of the Communist Party." In Karl Marx, *The Revolutions of 1848*, ed. David Fernbach. Harmondsworth: Penguin, 1973.

3. PUBLISHED DOCUMENTS AND DOCUMENTARY COLLECTIONS

A) PUBLISHED DOCUMENTS

— **All-Union Communist Party (Bolsheviks)**

"Direktiva TsK VKP(b) i SNK SSSR o predotvrashchenii massovogo vyezda golodaiushchikh krest'ian 22 ianvaria 1933 g." and "Postanovlenie Politbiuro TsK VKP(b) o rasprostranenii na Nizhniuiu Volgu direktivy TsK VKP(b) i SNK SSSR ot 22 ianvaria 1933 g." In *Tragediia sovetskoi derevni*, comp. V. P. Danilov et al., 5 vols., vol. 3 (*konets 1930–1933*), 634–35, 644. Moscow: ROSSPĖN, 2001.

"Direktiva TsK VKP(b) partorganizatsiiam o khlebozagotovkakh, 5 ianvaria 1928 g." In *Tragediia sovetskoi derevni. Kollektivizatsiia i raskulachivanie. Dokumenty i materialy*, comp. V. P. Danilov et al., 5 vols., vol. 1 (*mai 1927–noiabr' 1929*), 136–37. Moscow: ROSSPĖN, 1999.

"From a memorandum of the CC CP(B)U to the CC AUCP(B) on progress in preparing spring sowing, some reasons for the difficult food situation in a number of oblasts and raions of the republic, and measures to aid the starving." In *The Holodomor Reader*, ed. and comp. Bohdan Klid and Alexander J. Motyl, 262. Edmonton and Toronto: CIUS Press, 2012.

"Materialy komissii politbiuro TsK VKP(b) pod predsedatel'stvom V. M. Molotova po vyrabotke mer v otnoshenii kulachestva, 15–30 ianvaria 1930 g." In *Tragediia sovetskoi derevni, Kollektivizatsiia i raskulachivanie. Dokumenty i materialy*, comp. V. P. Danilov et al., 5 vols., vol. 2 (*noiabr' 1929–dekabr' 1930*), 116–31. Moscow: ROSSPĖN, 2000.

"Materialy noiabr'skogo plenuma TsK VKP(b), 12, 14–15 noiabria 1929 g." In *Tragediia sovetskoi derevni. Kollektivizatsiia i raskulachivanie. Dokumenty i materialy*, comp. V. P. Danilov et al., 5 vols., vol. 1 (*mai 1927–noiabr' 1929*), 746–64. Moscow: ROSSPĖN, 1999.

"O direktivakh po sostavleniiu piatiletnego plana narodnogo khoziaistva. II. Problema piatiletnego plana i khoziaistvennaia politika partii." In *Piatnadtsatyi s"ezd VKP(b). Dekabr' 1927 goda. Stenograficheskii otchet*, 2 vols., 2: 1444–51. Moscow: Gosudarstvennoe izdatel'stvo politicheskoi literatury, 1961–62.

"O proekte programmy." In *Vos'moi s"ezd RKP(b). Mart 1919 goda. Protokoly*, 385. Moscow: Gosudarstvennoe izdatel'stvo politicheskoi literatury, 1959. Cf. https://www.marxists.org/history/etol/newspape/isr/vol22/no04/rcpb.html.

"Postanova TsK VKP(b) ta RNK SRSR pro khlibozahotivli na Ukraïni, Pivnichnomu Kavkazi ta u Zakhidnii oblasti." In *Holod 1932–1933 rokiv na Ukraïni: ochyma istorykiv, movoiu dokumentiv*, ed. Ruslan Ia. Pyrih, 291–94. Kyiv: Politvydav Ukraïny, 1990.

"Postanovlenie biuro Severo-Kavkazskogo kraikoma VKP(b) po realizatsii direktivy TsK VKP(b) i SNK SSSR ot 22 ianvaria 1933 g." In *Tragediia sovetskoi derevni*, comp. V. P. Danilov et al., 5 vols., vol. 3 (*konets 1930–1933*), 636–38. Moscow: ROSSPĖN, 2001.

"Postanovlenie SNK SSSR za № 861 'O vydache grazhdanam Soiuza SSR pasportov na territorii Soiuza SSR.'" In *Sobranie zakonov i rasporiazhenii Raboche-krest'ianskogo Pravitel'stva SSSR*, 1933, no. 28.

"Programma Rossiiskoi kommunisticheskoi partii (bol'shevikov)." In *Vos'moi s"ezd RKP(b). Mart 1919 goda. Protokoly*, 390-411. Moscow: Gosudarstvennoe izdatel'stvo politicheskoi literatury, 1959.

"Report by the Novorossiisk royal vice consul, L. Sircana, 8 April 1933, 'Re: Developments in the agricultural season.'" In *The Holodomor Reader*, ed. and comp. Bohdan Klid and Alexander J. Motyl, 279. Edmonton and Toronto: CIUS Press, 2012.

"Resolution of the Politburo of the CC CP(B)U on measures to strengthen grain procurement." In *The Holodomor Reader*, ed. and comp. Bohdan Klid and Alexander J. Motyl, 241. Edmonton and Toronto: CIUS Press, 2012.

"Resolution 'On Safekeeping Property of State Enterprises, Collective Farms, and Cooperatives and Strengthening Public (Socialist) Property.'" In *The Holodomor Reader*, ed. and comp. Bohdan Klid and Alexander J. Motyl, 239. Edmonton and Toronto: CIUS Press, 2012.

XVI s"ezd VKP(b). Stenograficheskii otchet. Moscow and Leningrad: Gosizdat, 1930.

XVII konferentsiia VKP(b): Stenograficheskii otchet. Moscow: Partizdat, 1932.

— **Communist Party (Bolsheviks) of Ukraine**

"From operational order no. 2, GPU Ukrainian SSR, on the need to liquidate the insurgent underground before beginning sowing." In *The Holodomor Reader*, ed. and comp. Bohdan Klid and Alexander J. Motyl, 256. Edmonton and Toronto: CIUS Press, 2012.

"Konstytutsiia Ukraïns'koï Sotsialistychnoï Radians'koï Respubliky." In *Istoriia Radians'koï Konstytutsiï v dekretakh i postanovakh Radians'koho uriadu, 1917–1936*, 114. Kyiv: Vydavnytstvo TsVK URSR "Radians'ke budivnytstvo i pravo," 1937.

"Lyst TsK KP(b)U Tsentral'nomu Komitetu VKP(b) pro stan khlibozahotivel' v USRR za pidpysamy S. Kosiora vid 8 hrudnia 1932 r." In *Holod 1932–1933 rokiv na Ukraïni: ochyma istorykiv, movoiu dokumentiv*, ed. Ruslan Ia. Pyrih, 282–88. Kyiv: Politvydav Ukraïny, 1990.

"Postanova Politbiuro TsK KP(b)U ta Radnarkomu USRR 'Pro zanesennia na "chornu doshku" sil, iaki zlisno sabotuiut' khlibozahotivli' vid 6 hrudnia 1932 r." In *Holod 1932–1933 rokiv na Ukraïni: ochyma istorykiv, movoiu dokumentiv*, ed. Ruslan Ia. Pyrih, 278–79. Kyiv: Politvydav Ukraïny, 1990.

"Postanova TsVK i RNK SRSR 'Pro likvidatsiiu okruh' vid 23 lypnia 1930 r." *Visti VUTsVK* (Kharkiv), August 5, 1930.

"Postanovlenie Politbiuro TsK KP(b)U i SNK USSR po realizatsii direktivy TsK VKP(b) i SNK SSSR ot 22 ianvaria 1933 g." In *Tragediia sovetskoi derevni*, comp. V. P. Danilov et al., 5 vols., vol. 3 (*konets 1930–1933*), 635–36. Moscow: ROSSPĖN, 2001.

Tretia konferentsiia KP(b)U, 6–9 lypnia 1932 r.: Stenohrafichnyi zvit. Kharkiv, 1932.

Tretii z'ïzd Komunistychnoï partiï (bil'shovykiv) Ukraïny, 1–6 bereznia 1919 roku. Kyiv: Parlaments'ke vydavnytstvo, 2002.

b) **Soviet documentary collections**

Dekrety sovetskoi vlasti. 13 vols. Moscow: Gosudarstvennoe izdatelstvo politicheskoi literatury, 1957–99.

Direktivy KPSS i Sovetskogo pravitel'stva po khoziaistvennym vosprosam, 4 vols. Moscow: Politizdat, 1957–58.

Istoriia Radians'koï Konstytutsiï v dekretakh i postanovakh Radians'koho uriadu, 1917–1936. Kyiv: Vydavnytstvo TsVK URSR "Radians'ke budivnytstvo i pravo," 1937.

Kommunisticheskaia partiia Sovetskogo Soiuza v rezoliutsiiakh i resheniiakh s"ezdov, konferentsii i plenumov TsK, 8th ed., 14 vols. Moscow: Izdatel'stvo politicheskoi literatury, 1970–82.

Kommunisticheskaia partiia Sovetskogo Soiuza v rezoliutsiiakh i resheniiakh s"ezdov, konferentsii i plenumov TsK, 9th ed., 16 vols. Moscow: Politizdat, 1983–90.

Komunistychna partiia Ukraïny v rezoliutsiiakh i rishenniakh z'ïzdiv, konferentsii i plenumiv TsK. 2 vols. Kyiv: Politvydav Ukraïny, 1976–77.

Sbornik uzakonenii RSFSR (Moscow), 1929, no. 60.

Sbornik zakonov SSSR (Moscow), 1930, no. 24; 1932, no. 31.

Sobranie zakonov i rasporiazhenii Raboche-krest'ianskogo Pravitel'stva SSSR, 1933, no. 28.

Zbirnyk uzakonen' USRR, 1919, no. 36, art. 430.

Zbirnyk zakoniv USRR (Kharkiv), 1929, no. 18, art. 153.

c) **Post-Soviet documentary collections**

Golod v SSSR: Famine in the USSR, 1930–1934. Comp. O. Antipova. Moscow: Federal'noe arkhivnoe agentstvo, 2009.

Holod 1921–1923 rokiv v Ukraïni: Zbirnyk dokumentiv i materialiv. Comp.
Ol'ha M. Movchan et al. Kyiv: Naukova dumka, 1993.
Holod 1932–1933 rokiv na Ukraïni: ochyma istorykiv, movoiu dokumentiv. Ed.
Ruslan Ia. Pyrih et al. Kyiv: Politvydav Ukraïny, 1990.
Holodomor 1932–1933 rr. v Ukraïni: Dokumenty i materialy. Comp. Ruslan Ia. Pyrih. Kyiv: Vydavnychyi dim "Kyievo-Mohylians'ka akademiia," 2007.
Holodomor 1932–1933 rr. v Ukraïni: Zlochyn vlady — trahediia narodu. Dokumenty i materialy. Comp. Volodymyr S. Lozyts'kyi. Kyiv: Heneza, 2008.
Hołodomor 1932–1933: Wielki Głód na Ukrainie w dokumentach polskiej dyplomacji i wywiadu. Comp. Jan Jacek Bruski. Warsaw: Polski Instytut Spraw Międzynarodowych, 2008.
Kolektyvizatsiia i holod na Ukraïni, 1929–1933: Zbirnyk dokumentiv i materialiv. Comp. Hanna M. Mykhailychenko and Ievheniia P. Shatalina; ed. Stanislav Kul'chyts'kyi. Kyiv: Naukova dumka, 1992.
Kollektivizatsiia sel'skogo khoziaistva: Vazhneishie postanovleniia Kommunisticheskoi partii i Sovetskogo pravitel'stva, 1927–1935. Ed. Polina Sharova; comp. L. F. Kuz'mina. Moscow: Politizdat, 1987.
Komandyry Velykoho holodu: Poïzdky V. Molotova i L. Kahanovycha v Ukraïnu ta na Pivnichnyi Kavkaz, 1932–1934 rr. Ed. Valerii Vasyl'iev and Iurii Shapoval. Kyiv: Heneza, 2000.
Lysty z Kharkova: Holod v Ukraïni ta na Pivnichnomu Kavkazi v povidomlenniakh italiis'kykh dyplomativ. 1932–1933 roky. Comp. Andrea Hratsiozi (Graziosi). Kharkiv: Folio, 2007.
Nevidomi dokumenty z arkhiviv spetsial'nykh sluzhb, vol. 7. Warsaw and Kyiv, 2008.
Rozsekrechena pam'iat': Holodomor 1932–1933 rokiv v Ukraïni v dokumentakh HPU-NKVD. Comp. Viktor Borysenko, Kyiv: Vydavnychyi dim "Stylos," 2007.
Stalin i Kaganovich: Perepiska 1931–1936 gg. Comp. Oleg V. Khlevniuk. Moscow: ROSSPĖN, 2001.
Stenogrammy zasedanii Politbiuro TsK RKP(b)-VKP(b), 1923–1938 gg. Ed. K. M. Anderson et al. 3 vols. Moscow: ROSSPĖN, 2007.
Tragediia sovetskoi derevni: kollektivizatsiia i raskulachivanie: dokumenty i materialy v 5 tomakh, 1927–1939. Comp. Viktor P. Danilov, Roberta Thompson Manning, and Lynne Viola. Moscow: ROSSPĖN, 1999–2004.

4. **PERIODICALS**

Izvestiia VTsIK (Moscow), May 10, 1918; November 24, 1918; 23 February 1919.
Komunist (Kyiv), June 17, 1934.
Partaktyvist (Kharkiv), 1932, no. 9.
Pravda (Moscow), February 6, 1930; January 20, 1933; February 19, 1933; April 1, 1937.
Visti VUTsVK (Kharkiv), December 8, 1932.

5. **SECONDARY LITERATURE**

After the Holodomor: The Enduring Impact of the Great Famine on Ukraine. Ed. Andrea Graziosi, Lubomyr A. Hajda, and Halyna Hryn. Cambridge, MA: Harvard Ukrainian Research Institute, 2013.
Babko, Iurii, and Mykola Bortnychuk. *Tretia Vseukraïns'ka konferentsiia KP(b)U.* Kyiv: Politvydav Ukraïny, 1968.
Conquest, Robert. *The Harvest of Sorrow: Soviet Collectivization and the Terror-Famine.* New York: Oxford University Press, 1986.
Danilov, Viktor P., and Il'ia E. Zelenin. "Organizovannyi golod: K 70-letiiu obshchekrest'ianskoi tragedii." *Otechestvennaia istoriia* (Moscow), 2004, no. 5: 97–110.
Davies, Robert W., and Stephen G. Wheatcroft. *The Years of Hunger: Soviet Agriculture, 1931–1933.* New York, NY: Palgrave Macmillan, 2004.
Famine in Ukraine, 1932–1933. Ed. Roman Serbyn and Bohdan Krawchenko. Edmonton: Canadian Institute of Ukrainian Studies, 1986.

Famine-Genocide in Ukraine 1932–33: Western Archives, Testimonies and New Research. Ed. Wsevolod Isajiw. Toronto: Ukrainian Canadian Research and Documentation Centre, 2003.

Golod 1930-kh godov v Ukraine i Kazakhstane: voprosy istoriografii i podkhody k issledovaniiu problemy (k 80-letiiu tragedii). Sbornik materialov vystuplenii, dokladov i soobshchenii uchastnikov mezhdunarodnoi nauchno-metodicheskoi konferentsii 3 dekabria 2013 goda. Ed. E. B. Sydykov. Astana: Evraziiskii natsional'nyi universitet im. L. N. Gumileva, 2014.

Gratsiozi (Graziosi), Andrea. *Velikaia krest'ianskaia voina v SSSR: Bol'sheviki i krest'iane, 1917–1933.* Moscow: ROSSPĖN, 2001.

Holocaust-Genozid in der Ukraine 1932–1933: Sammelband der wissenschaftlichen Beiträge. Ed. D. Blochyn. Munich and Poltava: ASMI, 2009.

Holod 1932–1933 rokiv v Ukraïni: prychyny ta naslidky. Ed. Volodymyr Lytvyn. Kyiv: Naukova dumka, 2003.

Holod v Ukraïni u pershii polovyni XX stolittia: prychyny i naslidky (1921–1923, 1932–1933, 1946–1947). Materialy mizhnarodnoï naukovoï konferentsiï, Kyïv, 20–21 lystopada 2013 r. Ed. Myroslava Antonovych et al. Kyiv: Instytut demohrafiï ta sotsial'nykh doslidzhen' im. M. V. Ptukhy NAN Ukraïny, Instytut istoriï Ukraïny NAN Ukraïny, 2013.

Holod-henotsyd 1933 roku v Ukraïni: istoryko-politolohichnyi analiz sotsial'no-demohrafichnykh ta moral'no-psykholohichnykh naslidkiv. Mizhnarodna naukovo-teoretychna konferentsiia. Kyiv, 28 lystopada 1998 r. Materialy. Ed. Stanislav Kul'chyts'kyi et al. Kyiv: Vydavnytstvo M. P. Kots', 2000.

Holod-henotsyd 1932–1933 rokiv v Ukraïni: The Famine-Genocide of 1932–1933 in Ukraine. Ed. Iurii Shapoval. Kingston, Ontario: Kashtan Press, 2005.

Holodomor and Gorta Mór: Histories, Memories and Representations of Famine in Ukraine and Ireland. Ed. Christian Noack, Lindsay Janssen, and Vincent Comerford. London and New York: Anthem Press, 2012.

The Holodomor Reader: A Sourcebook on the Famine of 1932–1933 in Ukraine. Comp. and ed. Bohdan Klid and Alexander J. Motyl. Edmonton and Toronto: CIUS Press, 2012.

Holodomor: Reflections on the Great Famine of 1932–1933 in Soviet Ukraine. Ed. Lubomyr Luciuk. Kingston, Ontario: Kashtan Press, 2008.

Holodomor v Ukraïni 1932–1933 rr. Bibliohrafichnyi pokazhchyk, vyp. 1. Comp. Larysa M. Bur'ian and Inna E. Rykun; ed. Stanislav V. Kul'chyts'kyi. Odesa and Lviv: Vydavnytstvo M. P. Kots', 2001.

Holodomor v Ukraïni 1932–1933 rr. Bibliohrafichnyi pokazhchyk, vyp. 2. Comp. Larysa M. Bur'ian and Inna E. Rykun; ed. Stanislav V. Kul'chyts'kyi. Odesa: Vydavnytstvo "Studiia 'Nehotsiant,'" 2008.

Holodomor v Ukraïni 1932–1933 rr. Bibliohrafichnyi pokazhchyk, vyp. 3. Comp. Larysa M. Bur'ian and Inna E. Rykun; ed. Stanislav V. Kul'chyts'kyi. Odesa: Odes'ka natsional'na naukova biblioteka im. O. M. Hor'koho; Instytut istoriï Ukraïny NAN Ukraïny, 2004. Electronic resource at the Institute of Ukrainian History portal, history.org.ua/uk.

Hrynevych, Liudmyla. "Refleksiï Chervonoï armiï na kolektyvizatsiiu i holod v Ukraïni (1932–1933)." In *Holod-henotsyd 1933 roku v Ukraïni: istoryko-politolohichnyi analiz sotsial'no-demohrafichnykh ta moral'no-psykholohichnykh naslidkiv. Mizhnarodna naukovo-teoretychna konferentsiia. Kyiv, 28 lystopada 1998 r. Materialy*, ed. Stanislav Kul'chyts'kyi et al., 191–204. Kyiv: Vydavnytstvo M. P. Kots', 2000.

———. "Sotsial'ni pochuttia ta politychni nastroï chervonoarmiitsiv v roky holodomoru." In *Holod 1932–1933 rokiv v Ukraïni: prychyny ta naslidky*, ed. Volodymyr Lytvyn, 638–49. Kyiv: Naukova dumka, 2003.

———. "Vyiavlennia natsional'noï identychnosti ukraïns'koho selianstva v roky kolektyvizatsiï." In *Holod 1932–1933 rokiv v Ukraïni: prychyny ta naslidky*, ed. Volodymyr Lytvyn, 416–29. Kyiv: Naukova dumka, 2003.

Hryshko, Vasyl' I. *Ukraïns'kyi "Holokost," 1933.* New York and Toronto: DOBRUS and SUZhERO, 1978.

Iakovlev, Aleksandr N. *Reabilitatsiia: Politicheskie protsessy 30–50-kh godov.* Moscow: Izdatel'stvo Politicheskoi literatury, 1991.
Investigation of the Ukrainian Famine 1932–1933: Oral History Project of the Commission on the Ukraine Famine. Ed. James E. Mace and Leonid Heretz. 3 vols. Washington: US GPO, 1990.
Istoriia kolektyvizatsiï sil's'koho hospodarstva Ukraïns'koï RSR, 1917–1937 rr. Ed. Ivan Hanzha et al. 3 vols. Kyiv: Naukova dumka, 1962–71.
Ivnitskii, Nikolai A. "Golod 1932–1933 godov: kto vinovat?" In *Sud'by rossiiskogo krest'ianstva*, ed. Iurii N. Afanas'ev, 333–63. Moscow: Rossiiskii gosudarstvennyi gumanitarnyi universitet, 1996.
———. *Golod 1932–1933 godov v SSSR.* Moscow: Sobranie, 2009.
———. "Khlebozagotovki 1932–33 godov i golod 1933 goda." In *Holod-henotsyd 1933 roku v Ukraïni: istoryko-politolohichnyi analiz sotsial'no-demohrafichnykh ta moral'no-psykholohichnykh naslidkiv. Mizhnarodna naukovo-teoretychna konferentsiia. Kyiv, 28 lystopada 1998 r. Materialy*, ed. Stanislav Kul'chyts'kyi et al., 84–123. Kyiv: Vydavnytstvo M. P. Kots', 2000.
———. "Kollektivizatsiia i raskulachivanie (nachalo 30-kh godov). Po materialam Politbiuro TsK VKP(b) i OGPU." In *Sud'by rossiiskogo krest'ianstva*, ed. Iurii N. Afanas'ev, 249–97. Moscow: Rossiiskii gosudarstvennyi gumanitarnyi universitet, 1996.
Kondrashin, Viktor. *Golod 1932–1933 godov: tragediia rossiiskoi derevni.* Moscow: ROSSPĖN, 2008.
Kostiuk, Hryhorii. *Stalinizm v Ukraïni (heneza i naslidky).* Kyiv: Smoloskyp, 1995.
Kul'chitskii (Kul'chyts'kyi), Stanislav V. "Sozdanie sovetskogo stroia." In *Istoriia Ukrainy: Nauchno-populiarnye ocherki*, ed. Valerii Smolii, 599–631. Moscow: OLMA-Media-Grupp, 2008.
Kul'chyts'kyi, Stanislav V. *Holodomor 1932–1933 rr. iak henotsyd: trudnoshchi usvidomlennia.* Kyiv: Nash chas, 2007.
———. "Kontseptsiia 'kooperatyvnoho sotsializmu.'" *Ukraïns'kyi istorychnyi zhurnal* (Kyiv), 1995, no. 2: 3–17.
———. "Narodzhennia radians'koho ladu (1917–1938)." In *Ukraïna i Rosiia v istorychnii retrospektyvi*, vol. 2, *Radians'kyi proekt dlia Ukraïny*, ed. Vladyslav Hrynevych, Viktor Danylenko, and Stanislav Kul'chyts'kyi, 7–122. Kyiv: Naukova dumka, 2004.
———. "Restavratsiia Ukraïns'koï SRR." In *Narysy istoriï Ukraïns'koï revoliutsiï 1917–1921 rokiv*, 2 vols., 2: 315–81. Kyiv: Naukova dumka, 2011–12.
———. "Sutsil'na kolektyvizatsiia ukraïns'koho sela." In *Holod 1932–1933 rokiv v Ukraïni: prychyny ta naslidky*, ed. Volodymyr Lytvyn, section 4: 324–402 (five articles). Kyiv: Naukova dumka, 2003.
———. *Tsina "velykoho perelomu."* Kyiv: Vydavnytstvo "Ukraïna," 1991.
Levchuk, Nataliia M. "Raionna dyferentsiatsiia vtrat naselennia Ukraïny unaslidok holodu v 1933 rotsi." In *Holod v Ukraïni u pershii polovyni XX stolittia: prychyny i naslidky (1921–1923, 1932–1933, 1946–1947). Materialy mizhnarodnoï naukovoï konferentsiï, Kyïv, 20–21 lystopada 2013 r*, ed. Myroslava Antonovych et al., 257–64. Kyiv: Instytut demohrafiï ta sotsial'nykh doslidzhen' im. M. V. Ptukhy NAN Ukraïny, Instytut istoriï Ukraïny NAN Ukraïny, 2013.
Mace, James E. "The Famine of 1933: A Survey of the Sources." In *Famine in Ukraine, 1932–1933*, ed. Roman Serbyn and Bohdan Krawchenko, 45–65. Edmonton: Canadian Institute of Ukrainian Studies, 1986.
———. "The Man-Made Famine of 1933 in Soviet Ukraine." In *Famine in Ukraine, 1932–1933*, ed. Roman Serbyn and Bohdan Krawchenko, 1–14. Edmonton: Canadian Institute of Ukrainian Studies, 1986.
Martin, Terry. "The 1932–1933 Ukrainian Terror: New Documentation on Surveillance and the Thought Process of Stalin." In *Famine-Genocide in Ukraine 1932–33: Western Archives, Testimonies and New Research*, ed. Wsevolod Isajiw, 97–114. Toronto: Ukrainian Canadian Research and Documentation Centre, 2003.

Merl', Shtefan (Stephan Merl). "Golod 1932–1933 godov – genotsid ukraintsev dlia osushchestvleniia politiki rusifikatsii?" *Otechestvennaia istoriia* (Moscow), 1995, no. 1: 49–61.

Mezhdunarodnaia komissiia po rassledovaniiu goloda na Ukraine 1932–1933 godov. *Itogovyi otchet, 1990 god.* Kyiv: Otdelenie redaktsionno-izdatel'skoi i reklamnoi deiatel'nosti UKrTsENDISI, 1992.

La morte della terra: La grande "carestia" in Ucraina nel 1932–33. Atti del Convegno, Vicenza, 16–18 ottobre 2003. Ed. Gabriele De Rosa and Francesca Lomastro. Rome: Viella, 2004.

Nove, Alec. *An Economic History of the U.S.S.R.* New York: Penguin, 1989.

Nove, Alec. *An Economic History of the USSR: 1917–1991.* New York: Penguin, 1992.

"O dele t.n. 'Soiuza marksistov-lenintsev,'" *Izvestiia TsK KPSS* (Moscow), 1989, no. 6.

Ocherki istorii kollektivizatsii sel'skogo khoziaistva v soiuznykh respublikakh: sbornik statei. Ed. Viktor P. Danilov. Moscow: Gospolitizdat, 1963.

"Part IV: Peasantry as a Class." In *Peasants and Peasant Societies: Selected Readings,* 2d ed. Ed. Teodor Shanin, 329–77. Oxford: Basil Blackwell, 1987.

Pidluts'kyi, Oleksa. "Alen Bezanson: Rosiia, tochnishe – Radians'ka derzhava, vidpovidal'na za Holodomor." *Dzerkalo tyzhnia* (Kyiv), July 4, 2008. Cf. http://gazeta.dt.ua/SOCIETY/alen_bezanson_rosiya,_tochnishe__radyanska_derzhava,_vidpovidalna_za_golodomor.html.

Politychnyi teror i teroryzm v Ukraïni XIX–XX st.: Istorychni narysy. Ed. Valerii Smolii. Kyiv: Naukova dumka, 2002.

Popov, Gavriil Kh. "Programma, kotoroi rukovodstvovalsia Stalin." In his *Teoriia i praktika sotsializma v XX veke,* 15–29. Moscow: ROSSPĖN, 2006.

Rafael' Lemkin: Radians'kyi henotsyd v Ukraïni. Stattia 28 movamy. Kyiv: Vydavnytstvo "Maisternia knyhy," 2009.

Rudnytskyi, Omelian. "Urban-Rural Oblast Dynamics of 1932–34 Famine Losses in Ukraine." Paper presented at the 18th Annual World Convention of the Association for the Study of Nationalities, Columbia University, New York, April 18–20, 2013.

Shapoval, Iurii, and Vadym Zolotar'ov. *Vsevolod Balyts'kyi: osoba, chas, otochennia.* Kyiv: "Stilos," 2002.

Slyn'ko, Ivan I. *Sotsialistychna perebudova i tekhnichna rekonstruktsiia sil's'koho hospodarstva Ukraïny.* Kyiv: AN URSR, 1961.

Soldatenko, Valerii. "Holodnyi trydtsiat' tretii: sub'iektyvni dumky pro ob'iektyvni protsesy." *Dzerkalo tyzhnia* (Kyiv), no. 24, June 27, 2003.

Strilever, I., S. Khazanov, and L. Iampol'skii. *Khlebooborot i standarty.* Moscow, 1935.

Ukraïns'kyi holokost 1932–1933: svidchennia tykh, khto vyzhyv. Comp. Fr. Iurii Mytsyk. 10 vols. Kyiv: Vydavnychyi dim "Kyievo-Mohylians'ka akademiia," 2003–13.

Velykyi holod v Ukraïni 1932–1933 rokiv. Ed. James E. Mace, Leonid Heretz, and Stanislav V. Kul'chyts'kyi. 3 vols. Kyiv: Kyievo-Mohylians'ka akademiia, 2008.

Vert, Nikolia (Nicolas Werth). *Terror i besporiadok: Stalinizm kak sistema.* Moscow: ROSSPĖN, 2010.

Viola, Lynne. *Peasant Rebels under Stalin: Collectivization and the Culture of Peasant Resistance.* New York: Oxford University Press, 1996.

Voznesenskii, Nikolai A. *Khozraschet i planirovanie na sovremennom etape.* Detskoe selo, 1931.

Vrons'ka, Tamara V. "Zaprovadzhennia pasportnoho rezhymu." In *Holod 1932–1933 rokiv v Ukraïni: prychyny ta naslidky,* ed. Volodymyr Lytvyn, 630–37. Kyiv: Naukova dumka, 2003.

Vyltsan, Mikhail A. *Zavershaiushchii etap sozdaniia kolkhoznogo stroia, 1935–1937 gg.* Moscow: Nauka, 1978.

Zelenin, Il'ia E. "Politotdely MTS – prodolzhenie politiki 'chrezvychaishchiny' (1933–1934 gg.)." *Otechestvennaia istoriia* (Moscow), 1992, no. 6: 42–61.

―――. "'Revoliutsiia sverkhu': zavershenie i tragicheskie posledstviia." *Voprosy istorii* (Moscow), 1994, no. 10: 28–42.

Zhiromskaia, Valentina B. *Demograficheskaia istoriia Rossii v 1930-e gody: Vzgliad v neizvestnoe.* Moscow: Nauka, 2001.

Author's Selected Works

1) *Uchast' robitnykiv Ukraïny u stvorenni fondu sotsialistychnoï industrializatsiï*. Kyiv: Naukova dumka, 1975.
2) *Vnutrennie resursy sotsialisticheskoi industrializatsii SSSR*. Kyiv: Naukova dumka, 1979.
3) With Panteleimon P. Hudzenko and Ievheniia P. Shatalina. *Trudovi pochyny robitnychoho klasu, 1921–1937 (Na materialakh Ukraïns'koï RSR)*. Kyiv: Naukova dumka, 1980.
4) With Mykola Kotliar. *Kiev drevnii i sovremennyi*. Kyiv: Politizdat Ukrainy, 1982.
5) "Do otsinky stanovyshcha v sil's'komu hospodarstvi URSR v 1931–1933 rr." *Ukraïns'kyi istorychnyi zhurnal* (Kyiv), 1988, no. 3: 15–27.
6) *Demohrafichni naslidky holodu 1933 r. na Ukraïni*. Kyiv: Instytut istoriï AN URSR, 1989.
7) *1933: trahediia holodu*. Kyiv: Tovarystvo "Znannia" URSR, 1989.
8) "Trahichna statystyka holodu" in *Holod 1932–1933 rokiv na Ukraïni: ochyma istorykiv, movoiu dokumentiv*. Ed. Ruslan Ia. Pyrih, 66–84. Kyiv: Politvydav Ukraïny, 1990.
9) With Valerii Volkovyns'kyi. *Khrystyian Rakovs'kyi: Politychnyi portret*. Kyiv: Politvydav Ukraïny, 1990.
10) With Viktor Danylenko and Heorhii Kas'ianov. *Stalinizm na Ukraïni: 20–30-ti roky*. Kyiv and Edmonton: Vydavnytstvo "Lybid'," 1991.
11) *Tsina "velykoho perelomu."* Kyiv: Vydavnytstvo "Ukraïna," 1991.
12) With Ol'ha M. Movchan. *Nevidomi storinky holodu 1921–1923 rr. v Ukraïni*. Kyiv: Instytut istoriï Ukraïny AN Ukraïny, 1993.
13) *Komunizm v Ukraïni: pershe desiatyrichchia (1919–1928)*. Kyiv: Osnovy, 1996.
14) *Ukraïna mizh dvoma viinamy (1921–1939 rr.)*. Kyiv: Vydavnychyi dim "Al'ternatyvy," 1999.
15) With Iurii Pavlenko, Svitlana Ruda, and Iurii Khramov. *Istoriia Natsional'noï akademiï nauk Ukraïny, 1918–1998*. Kyiv: Feniks, 2000.
16) With Iurii Aleksieiev and Anatolii Sliusarenko. *Ukraïna na zlami istorychnykh epokh (Derzhavotvorchyi protses 1985–1999 rr.)*. Kyiv: Eks.Ob., 2000.
17) "Peredmova naukovoho redaktora" in *Holodomor v Ukraïni 1932–1933 rr.: Bibliohrafichnyi pokazhchyk*, 25–66. Odesa and Lviv: Vydavnytstvo M. P. Kots', 2001.
18) With Hennadii Iefimenko. *Demohrafichni naslidky holodomoru 1933 r. v Ukraïni: Vsesoiuznyi perepys 1937 r. v Ukraïni. Dokumenty i materialy*. Kyiv: Instytut istoriï Ukraïny NAN Ukraïny, 2003.
19) *Problema OUN-UPA: Zvit robochoï hrupy istorykiv pry Uriadovii komisiï z vyvchennia diial'nosti OUN i UPA. Osnovni tezy z problemy OUN-UPA (istorychnyi vysnovok)*. Kyiv: Instytut istoriï Ukraïny, 2004.
20) With Vladyslav Hrynevych, Viktor Danylenko, and Oleksandr Ie. Lysenko. *Ukraïna i Rosiia v istorychnii retrospektyvi*, vol. 2, *Radians'kyi proekt dlia Ukraïny*. Kyiv: Naukova dumka, 2004.
21) With Borys Parakhons'kyi. *Ukraïna i Rosiia v istorychnii retrospektyvi*, vol. 3, *Novitnii ukraïns'kyi derzhavotvorchyi proekt*. Kyiv: Naukova dumka, 2004.
22) *Ukraïna i Rosiia: perevahy i nebezpeky "osoblyvykh vidnosyn": Rozdumy istoryka*. Kyiv: Instytut istoriï Ukraïny NAN Ukraïny, 2004.
23) With Valerii Soldatenko. *Volodymyr Vynnychenko: Osobystist' i doba*. Kyiv: Al'ternatyvy, 2005.
24) *Pomarancheva revoliutsiia*. Kyiv: Heneza, 2005.
25) *Holod-henotsyd 1932–1933 rr. v Ukraïni: Materialy do navchal'noho kursu*. Kyiv: Instytut istoriï Ukraïny NAN Ukraïny, 2006.
26) *Holodomor 1932–1933 rr. v Ukraïni iak henotsyd: trudnoshchi usvidomlennia*. Kyiv: Nash chas, 2007.
27) *Pochemu ON NAS unichtozhal? Stalin i ukrainskii Golodomor*. Kyiv: Izdatel'stvo ZAO "Ukrainskaia press-gruppa," 2007.
28) *Holod 1932–1933 rr. v Ukraïni iak henotsyd: movoiu dokumentiv, ochyma svidkiv*. Kyiv: Nash chas, 2008.
29) *Dzheims Meis*. Kyiv: TOV "Atlant," 2008.

30) "Peredmova naukovoho redaktora perekladu chotyrytomnoho vydannia" in *Velykyi holod v Ukraïni 1932–1933 rokiv. Svidchennia ochevydtsiv dlia Komisiï konhresu SShA*, vol. 1, 10–81. Kyiv: Vydavnytstvo Kyievo-Mohylians'koï akademiï, 2008.
31) "Peredmova naukovoho redaktora" in *Holodomor v Ukraïni 1932–1933 rr.: Bibliohrafichnyi pokazhchyk*, vyp. 2, 15–49. Odesa: Astroprynt, 2008.
32) *Rosiis'ka revoliutsiia 1917 roku: novyi pohliad*. Kyiv: Nash chas, 2008.
33) "Iak tse bulo" in *Natsional'na knyha pam'iati zhertv Holodomoru 1932–1933 rokiv v Ukraïni*, 11–44. Kyiv: Instytut natsional'noï pam'iati, 2008.
34) "Ukrainskii Golodomor kak genotsid" in *Sovremennaia rossiisko-ukrainskaia istoriografiia goloda 1932–1933 gg. v SSSR*, 107–94. Moscow: ROSSPĖN, 2011.
35) *Stalins'kyi "sokrushitel'nyi udar" 1932–1933*. Kyiv: Tempora, 2013.
36) *Ukraïns'kyi Holodomor v konteksti polityky Kremlia pochatku 1930-kh rr*. Kyiv: Instytut istoriï Ukraïny NAN Ukraïny, 2013.
37) *Chervonyi vyklyk: Istoriia komunizmu v Ukraïni vid ioho narodzhennia do zahybeli*, 3 vols. Kyiv: Tempora, 2013.
38) "Peredmova naukovoho redaktora" in *Holodomor v Ukraïni 1932–1933 rr.: Bibliohrafichnyi pokazhchyk*, vyp. 3, 15–53. Odesa: Odes'ka natsional'na naukova biblioteka im. M. Hor'koho, 2014.
39) *Nation-Building in the Independent Ukraine*. Kyiv and New York: Ukrainian American Association of University Professors, 2003.
40) "Il tema della carestia nella vita politica e sociale dell'Ucraina alla fine degli anni Ottanta" in *La morte della terra: La grande "carestia" in Ucraina nel 1932–33*, 431–449. Rome: Viella, 2004.
41) "Defining the Holodomor as Genocide" in *Reflections on the Great Famine of 1932–1933 in Soviet Ukraine*, ed. Lubomyr Luciuk, 129–39. Kingston, Ontario: Kashtan Press, 2008.
42) "Holodomor in Ukraine 1932–1933: An Interpretation of Facts" in *Holodomor and Gorta Mór: Histories, Memories and Representation of Famine in Ukraine and Ireland*, ed. Christian Noack, Lindsay Janssen, and Vincent Comerford, 19–35. London and New York: Anthem Press, 2012.
43) "Why Did Stalin Exterminate the Ukrainians?" in *The Holodomor Reader: A Sourcebook on the Famine of 1932–1933 in Ukraine*, comp. and ed. Bohdan Klid and Alexander Motyl, 26–35. Edmonton and Toronto: Canadian Institute of Ukrainian Studies Press, 2012.
44) "The Holodomor and Its Consequences in the Ukrainian Countryside" in *After the Holodomor: The Enduring Impact of the Great Famine on Ukraine*, ed. Andrea Graziosi, Lubomyr Hajda, and Halyna Hryn, 1–15. Cambridge, MA: Harvard Ukrainian Research Institute, 2013.
45) "The Holodomor of 1932–33: How and Why?" *East-West: Journal of Ukrainian Studies* 2, no. 1 (2015): 93–116.

About the Author

Stanislav Kulchytsky was born in Odesa in 1937. He studied at the Department of History at the I. I. Mechnikov State University in Odesa, graduating in 1959. He has worked as a fellow in the Odesa Oblast State Archives (1958–60), as a senior fellow at the Institute of Economics, Academy of Sciences of the Ukrainian SSR (1960–72), and a senior fellow (1972–77), deputy director of scholarly work (1977–79, 1990–2009), and chair of the Department of Ukrainian History of the 1920s and 1930s (1977–2015) at the Institute of Ukrainian History, National Academy of Sciences of Ukraine. Since the fall of 2015, he has been the Institute's head senior fellow.

SCHOLARLY DEGREES AND TITLES:
Candidate of Sciences, Economics (1963), PhD, History (1976), professor (1988), Person of Merit in Ukrainian Science and Technology (1996).

ACADEMIC SUPERVISION:
academic adviser of 29 Candidates of Sciences, academic consultant of 26 PhDs.

SCHOLARLY PUBLICATIONS:
as of early 2016, more than 2,000 publications on Ukrainian history of the nineteenth to twenty-first centuries (monographs, chapters in multi-author collections, textbooks and curricular materials for secondary and high school, informational publications, articles, interviews, etc.).

ACADEMIC AWARDS:
Ukrainian State Award (2001) for the book *Ukraïna mizh dvoma viinamy (1921–1939 rr.)* (Ukraine between the Wars, 1921–1939). Honorable mention in the journal *Przegląd Wschodni* (2008) in the category of "Foreign Publications" for the monograph *Holodomor 1932–1933 rr. v Ukraïni iak henotsyd: trudnoshchi usvidomlennia* (*The Holodomor of 1932–1933 in Ukraine as Genocide: Difficulties of Realization*), translated into Polish and published in Wrocław (2008).
Omelan and Tatiana Antonovych Foundation Award (2011) for contributions to world knowledge about the Holodomor in Ukraine.
Grand prix, XVI All-Ukrainian Book of the Year Ratings (2014) for *Chervonyi vyklyk: Istoriia komunizmu v Ukraïni vid ioho narodzhennia do zahybeli*, 3 vols. (The Red Challenge: The History of Communism in Ukraine from Birth to Demise).

PUBLIC SERVICE:
Deputy academic secretary, Department of History, Philosophy, and Law, National Academy of Sciences of Ukraine (1983–88, 1998–2009).
Member, Expert Council in History, Supreme Certification Commission of the USSR (1988–91).
Head, Expert Council in History, Supreme Certification Commission of Ukraine (2000–2004).
Head, Archivists' Union of Ukraine (1991–2000).
Co-chair, Ukrainian-Polish expert commission on improving the content of school textbooks in history and geography (1993–2017).
Head, working group to develop proposals for a historical assessment to be submitted to the Governmental Commission on Studying the Problem of the OUN-UPA (1998–2006).
Member, State Interdepartmental Commission on Honoring the Memory of Victims of War and Political Repression attached to the Cabinet of Ministers of Ukraine (2007–17).
Head, Nova Doba All-Ukrainian Educators' Association (2009–17).

Index

Alma-Ata, 34
Aronov, 112
Artemivsk district, 58
Attolico, Bernardo, 52, 109

Babanka district, 49
Babychev, 96
Babyonyshev, Aleksandr (Maksudov, Sergei), 130
Bakhmach district, 119
Baltic states, xxi, 11
Balytsky, Vsevolod, 103–5, 109–10
Baturyn, 128
Bazhan, Olha, 119
Belarus, xxi, 11, 123
Berlin, xxi
Besançon, Alain, 143–44
Besarab, Oleksii Vasyliovych, 99
Bila Tserkva: district, 113; province (*okruh*), 90; region, 49
Birkin, 96
Bohdanivka, 96
Bohuslav district, 49
Bokan, Mykola, 128
Bolokhovets, 119
Boriak, Tetiana, 145
Boryspil district, 121
Brest-Litovsk treaty (1918), 13
Brezhnev, Leonid, xi
Brusyliv district, 91
Bukharin, Nikolai, 20, 23, 52, 89, 92
Buky district, 49
Buryn district, 118

Canada, 50, 96
Central Asia, 103
Central Black Earth province, 35–36, 47–48, 50, 95, 123–24, 148
Cherenkov, A., 94
Cherkasy: oblast, 117n6; region, 117
Chernihiv, 128; province, viii, 97, 100, 119, 138; region, 92, 117–18, 124
Chicherin, Georgii, 94
China, 50
Chubar, Vlas, 55, 99, 104–6, 109n42, 124
Chubarian, Aleksandr, 126
Conquest, Robert, xiin3, xvn16, xvin22, 107, 112, 122, 127, 131, 147
Crimea, xi

Danilov, Viktor, 125–27, 134
Davies, Robert W., 47, 100n25
Davydenko, 47

Den' (Kyiv), xvi
Denikin, Anton, 15–16
Denysenko, 96
Dnipro region, 112
Dnipropetrovsk, 91, 112–13, 122; province, viii, 49, 96, 100, 108; region, 115, 118
Dolyna, 91; district, 49
Don region, 133
Donbas, 15
Donetsk: oblast, 46; province, viii, 100
Dubovyk, 97
Dzerkalo tyzhnia (Kyiv), xvi, 143
Dzhugashvili, Joseph. *See* Stalin, Joseph

Eismont, Nikolai, 144
Engels, Friedrich, xxii, xxiv, 2, 7, 55
England, xxv
Europe, xxi, 3, 15–16, 94, 148; East-Central, 11; Eastern, 3; Western, 3

Förster, Otfrid, 22
Frunze district, 108
Frunzivka district, 109

Gamarnik, Yan, 136
Georgia, xxi
Germany, 1, 13, 37, 127, 134, 140
Getie, Fedor, 22
Gorbachev, Mikhail, xi, xix, 30, 146
Graziosi, Andrea, 109n44, 128

Hadiach, 120, 130
Haisyn district, 45
Hare, Cyril, xxv
Himka, John-Paul, xviin22
Hitler, Adolf, 1, 4, 37, 140
Hlobyne district, 49
Horby, 118
Horodok, 129
Hrebyshcha homestead, 129
Hrynevych, Andrii, 46–47
Hrynevych, Liudmyla, 36
Hryshko, Vasyl, 134
Hungary, 15

Iampol'skii, L., 100n25
Ilovaisk, 94
Innitzer, Theodor, 61, 64
Irkutsk, 96
Ivanhorod, 119
Ivanivka, 97
Ivnitsky, Nikolai, 107–8, 124
Izvestiia VTsIK (Moscow), 91

Index

Kaganovich, Lazar, xiv, xivn13, xxv, 48–49, 51, 54, 57, 59, 97, 104–5, 108–10, 113, 131, 136
Kalinin, Mikhail, 34
Kalmanovich, Moisei, 97, 99
Kamenev, Lev, 23, 90, 92–93
Kamianets-Podilskyi province, 129
Kapusta, Fedir, 118
Karlson, Karl, 128
Karszo-Siedlewski, Jan, 52
Kasianov, Heorhii, xvi–xviin22
Katerynopilsk district, 117n6
Kazakhstan, xxi–xxii, 35, 47, 132, 146
Keis, Oleksii, 125
Kentii, Anatolii, 119
Kharkiv, 29, 34, 43, 52, 61, 71, 90, 92, 95, 103–5, 108–9, 115, 138; province, viii, 49, 97, 99–100, 130
Khataevich, Mendel, 98, 104, 113, 117, 124
Khazanov, S., 100n25
Khmelnytskyi. *See* Proskuriv
Khrushchev, Nikita, xi, 145–46
Khrystynivka district, 112
Khylkivka, 129
Kirovohrad. *See* Zinovievsk
Klid, Bohdan, xi
Kobeliatsky, 93
Kocherov, 93
Kochubeivka, 113
Kolhospne selo (Kyiv), 137
Kolyma, 117
Kondrashin, Viktor, 117n4, 132–33
Koptiieve, 97
Korniienko, Dmytro, 117, 124
Korosten, 94
Kosior, Stanislav, 28–29, 41, 49–50, 56–58, 90–92, 96, 104–6, 109, 109n42, 113, 119, 137–38
Kovalenko, Fedir, 130
Krasnodar region, 120
Krasnoperekopsk, 89
Krasnopillia, 99
Kremenchuk, 94; county, 118
Kropyvnytskyi. *See* Zinovievsk
Kruhlyk homestead, 120
Krynychky, 115
Kuban, xix, xxiii, 116, 119, 123, 127, 131, 133, 140, 148; province, 104; region, 49, 95
Kuibyshev, Valerian, 52, 138
Kulchytsky, Stanislav, xi–xviii
Kyiv, xi, xiv, xxi, 18, 92, 108, 117n5, 121–22, 143, 145–46; province, viii, 49, 90, 97, 100; region, 49, 92, 113, 121

Lenin, Vladimir, xix, xxiii–xxiv, 1, 3–6, 9, 10n11, 11, 13–24, 27, 30–31, 39, 51–52, 55–56, 111–12, 129, 141, 145, 147
Leningrad, 10
Leninske, 96
Levchuk, Nataliia, 116
Literaturna Ukraïna (Kyiv), xiv, xivn11
Liubchenko, Panas, 29, 34
Liutenka, 130
Lozuvatka homestead, 118
Lozytsky, Volodymyr, 119
Lubny, 129, 138
Lykhachiv, 92
Lysycha Balka. *See* Osycha Balka

Mace, James, xiin3, xiii, xiiin9, xiv, xivn10–11, xvin22, 117n5, 119, 122, 124–25, 127, 134, 146–47
Makhno, Nestor, 136
Mala Vilshanka, 113
Mariupol, 93
Markevich, A.M., 136
Martin, Terry, xviin22, 36
Marx, Karl, xxii, xxiv, 2, 7, 13, 55, 141–42, 147
Melitopol, 94
Merl, Stephan, 127
Meshcheriakov, Vladimir, 15
Michniewicz, Władysław, 121
Mikoyan, Anastas, 34
Moldavian Autonomous Soviet Socialist Republic (Moldavian ASSR), viii, 9, 46, 50, 100
Moldova, xxi
Molotov (Skriabin), Viacheslav, xiv, xivn13, xviii, xxv, 33–34, 41, 43–46, 54–55, 91, 97–99, 103–5, 107–8, 110, 116, 116n3, 117, 123, 137
Montreal, 134
Moroz, Hryhorii, 118
Moscow, xiv, xix, 10, 15, 24, 36n43, 41, 52, 59, 89–92, 103, 109, 111, 126, 134; province, 35, 123
Mykheienko, Dmytro, 43–44, 46
Mykolaiv, 58
Mykolaivka, 118
Myroshnychenko, Ye., 93
Mytsyk, Yurii, 134

Netiaha, H., 94
News from Ukraine (Kyiv), xiiin8
Nezlobna (*stanitsa*), 120
Nikolenko, 94, 138
Nikopol, 93, 99
North America, xix

North Caucasus, xivn13, xxiii–xxiv, 9, 11, 36, 43, 48–49, 94–95, 123–24, 131–32, 136, 141–46, 148
North Caucasus Krai, 47, 52, 97, 103–4, 108–9, 116, 122, 124, 132
North Korea, xxi
Nosivka, 92
Nova Praha district, 49
Nove, Alec, 131, 147–48
Nove Zhyttia, 58
Novoe Selo, 116
Novoheorhiïvsk district, 97
Novoukrainka, 99; district, 96
Nyzhni Sirohozy, 96
Nyzhniodniprovsk, 93
Nyzkousov, 97

Odesa, xi, xx, 52, 122, 140; province, viii, 58, 96, 99–100, 108, 136
Odyntsov, Oleksandr, 113
Olyshivka district, 97
Onufriivka district, 130
Orativ district, 49
Oriekhov, S., 138
Osycha Balka (Lysycha Balka), 117
Otechestvennaia istoriia (Moscow), 126–27
Otsup, Petr, 33
Ozyrne, 113

Pavlohrad district, 96
Pavlysh, 130
Pearce, Samara, 61
Penza, 132
Perederii, 96
Persia, 50
Petliura, Symon, 18
Petrograd, 3, 5
Petrovsky, Hryhorii, 21, 29, 34–35, 43, 45–46, 55
Piatykhatka, 92
Pidiablonsky, S., 93
Piłsudski, Józef, 18
Plyskiv district, 49
Pokrovska Bahachka district, 129
Poland, 48, 117, 123
Polisia region, 34, 117
Polohy, 93
Poltava province, 120, 130; region, 118, 124, 129
Ponornytsia district, 117
Popov, Gavriil, 30, 30n27
Postnov, 97
Postyshev, Pavel, xivn13, xxv, 98, 104–5, 112, 132, 136
Pravda (Moscow), 3, 24, 35, 55, 58, 115
Proskuriv (Khmelnytskyi), 129

Putin, Vladimir, xxi, 148
Putylovets, 96
Putyvl district, 138
Pyrih, Ruslan, xiv
Pyrohov, 93

Radchenko, O., 129
Radomyslsky, Grigorii. *See* Zinoviev, Grigorii
Reva, Mykola, 129
Riazan, 34
Riutin, Martemian, 89, 90, 92–94
Rokytne district, 49
Romania, 117
Romanov dynasty, 3
Rome, 109
Rostov-on-Don, 104
Rudnytsky, Omelian, 116
Rudzutaks, Janis, 56
Russia: central, 9; post-Soviet, xi, xxi, 126, 132–33, 146, 148; Soviet, xxv, 3–4, 9–10, 15, 18, 123–25, 127, 131, 134. *See also* Union of Soviet Socialist Republics
Russian Empire (Russia), 3, 8, 134
Russian Federation, xxi, 11, 122, 126
Russian Soviet Federative Socialist Republic (Russian SFSR, RSFSR), 17, 26, 97, 110–11; southeastern, 103; Western Province: 11, 95, 123–24. *See also* Union of Soviet Socialist Republics
Rykov, Aleksei, 23, 34, 89, 92

Samsonov, Samson, xxv
Saratov: province, 132; region, xivn13
Sarkisov, Sarkis, 97
Savchuk, Alla, 116
Shanin, Teodor, 45
Shapoval, Yurii, 105
Shatalina, Ie. P., xvin21
Shavynsky, I., 94
Shcherbytsky, Volodymyr, xiii, 129, 146
Sheboldaev, Boris, 52, 124
Shelest, Petro, xiiin5
Sheptytsky, Andrei, 61
Shevchuk, Pavlo, 116
Shlepakov, Arnold, xix
Shlikhter, Oleksandr, 57
Shovkoplias, S., 96
Shpola district, 113
Siberia, 25, 35, 42; Western, 95
Sircana, Leone, 109
Skriabin, Viacheslav. *See* Molotov, Viacheslav
Skrypnyk, Mykola, 57, 104
Slovechne district, 97
Smirnov, Aleksandr, 90, 97, 144
Smolii, Valerii, 126
Snihurivka district, 108–9

Soldatenko, Valerii, 140
Solodov, 92
Solone district, 108–9
Sonypul, Oleksa, 118
Soroka (Trypniak), Teodora, 118
Sosnytsia district, 118
Soviet Union. *See* Union of Soviet Socialist Republics
St. Petersburg, 5
Stalin (Dzhugashvili), Joseph, xi, xiv, xivn13, xv, xviin22, xviii, xix, xxiii–xxv, 1, 6, 8–9, 11, 23–27, 29–42, 44–45, 47–59, 89–93, 95–100, 102–116, 116n3, 119–23, 125–29, 131–36, 141–48
Stalingrad province, 132
Starominsk, 116
Stetsky, Aleksei, 52
Strilever, I., 100n25
Stroganov, Vasilii, 99
Svishchev-Paol, M., 20
Sumy region, 118
Syrtsov, Sergei, 34

Tarasiuk, Ivan, 91
Tetiiv district, 49
Tkachenko, H., 49, 91
Tolmachev, Vladimir, 144
Tomsky, Mikhail, 23, 89, 92
Transcaucasus, 50
Trotsiuk, 138
Trotsky, Leon, 15, 23, 93
Trypniak, Teodora. *See* Soroka, Teodora
Tsarychanka district, 118
Turin, 109n44
Tyshkivka, 45

Ukrainian Military District, 91, 112
Ukrainian People's Republic, 36, 48
Ukraïns'kyi istorychnyi zhurnal (Kyiv), xiin2
Ulianova, Maria, 22
Uman district, 49, 113; *okruh*, 90; region, 45, 49
Union of Soviet Socialist Republics (Soviet Union, USSR), xi–xii, xvi, xviin22, xviii, xix–xxi, xxiv–xxv, 1–2, 6, 9–11, 13, 26–27, 32–34, 36, 39–41, 44, 46, 48, 50, 54–55, 57–59, 61, 90, 95, 97–99, 104, 107, 115–16, 121–23, 127–28, 130–31, 133–35, 137, 140–41, 145–47; European USSR, 47–48, 51; Far East: xix, 129. *See also* Russia

Vasyliev, Valerii, 105
Vasylivka district, 108–9
Velyka Bilozerka district, 96
Velyka Lepetykha district, 108–9

Vienna, 61
Vinnytsia province, viii, 49, 90, 100
Viola, Lynne, 36
Visti VUTsVK (Kharkiv), 58, 105, 109, 109n42
Visti z Ukraïny (Kyiv), xiiin8
Viuny, 96
Vlasenko, Serhii, 119
Volga German Republic, 132
Volga Krai: Lower, 144
Volga region: 43, 98, 123, 133; Lower xxiii, 48, 127, 131–33, 145
Volga River: Lower, xxiv, 36, 47, 95, 131–32, 136, 145–46; Middle, 47–48, 78, 95
Voronezh, 34
Voronkiv, 121
Voroshilov, Kliment, 34
Vovkodav, I., 93
Voznesensk county, 136
Voznesensky, Nikolai, 40

Washington, DC, 117n5
Werth, Nicolas, 94
Wheatcroft, Stephen G., 47, 100n25
Wienerberger, Alexander, 61, 63–88
Wolowyna, Oleh, 116

Yakovlev (Epshtein), Yakov, 32–34, 40–41, 46, 111, 136
Yanukovych, Viktor, xi
Yaremenko, 92
Yasynovata, 93
Yeltsin, Boris, xxi
Yenakiieve, 125
Yenukidze, Avel, 128
Yermak, 96
Yevdokimov, Yefim, 103–5
Yezhov, Nikolai, 136
Yukhnovsky, M. N., 27
Yurkin, Tikhon, 34, 40–41

Zatonsky, Volodymyr, 43, 99
Zelenin, Ilia, 116n3, 122–23, 125–28, 134
Zhiromskaia, Valentina, 132
Zinoviev (Radomyslsky), Grigorii, 23, 90, 92–93
Zinovievsk (Kirovohrad, Kropyvnytskyi), 43–44; district, 46–47, 50
Znamianka, 93, 99; district, 47
Zoria, Yefrozynia, 120, 129
Zvenyhorodka district, 117